8/21/19
$27.95

EVERYBODY'S DOIN' IT

ALSO BY DALE COCKRELL

Demons of Disorder:
Early Blackface Minstrels and Their World

The Ingalls Wilder Family Songbook (editor)

Excelsior: Journals of the Hutchinson Family Singers, 1842–1846 (editor)

EVERYBODY'S DOIN' IT

Sex, Music, and Dance in New York, 1840-1917

DALE COCKRELL

W. W. NORTON & COMPANY

Independent Publishers Since 1923

New York ✣ London

For information about permission to reproduce selections from this book,
write to Permissions, W. W. Norton & Company, Inc.,
500 Fifth Avenue, New York, NY 10110

For information about special discounts for bulk purchases,
please contact W. W. Norton Special Sales at
specialsales@wwnorton.com or 800-233-4830

Manufacturing by Sheridan
Book design by Dana Sloan
Production manager: Anna Oler

Library of Congress Cataloging-in-Publication Data

Names: Cockrell, Dale, author.
Title: Everybody's doin' it : sex, music, and dance in New York, 1840–1917
    / Dale Cockrell.
Description: First edition. | New York : W. W. Norton & Company,
    [2019] | Includes bibliographical references and index.
Identifiers: LCCN 2019000965 | ISBN 9780393608946 (hardcover)
Subjects: LCSH: Popular music—New York (State)—New York—To
    1901—History and criticism. | Popular music—New York (State)—
    New York—1901–1910—History and criticism. | Popular music—New
    York (State)—New York—1911–1920—History and criticism. | Popu-
    lar music—Social aspects—New York (State)—New York—History.
Classification: LCC ML3477.8.N48 C63 2019 |
    DDC 781.6409747/109034—dc23
LC record available at https://lccn.loc.gov/2019000965

W. W. Norton & Company, Inc., 500 Fifth Avenue, New York, N.Y. 10110
www.wwnorton.com

W. W. Norton & Company Ltd., 15 Carlisle Street, London W1D 3BS

1 2 3 4 5 6 7 8 9 0

Dedicated to the untold thousands of women upon whose anonymous bodies an American music was built. We must never forget.

CONTENTS

PREFACE

*But I must have said this before, since I say it now. I have to
speak in a certain way, with warmth perhaps, all is possible,
first of the creature I am not, as if I were he, and then, as if I
were he, of the creature I am.*

—SAMUEL BECKETT

*E*VERYBODY'S *DOIN'* *IT* began, as has so much in my scholarly
life, while I was enfolded in the majestic silence of the American
Antiquarian Society's Reading Room. The National Endowment for
the Humanities had awarded me a research fellowship in the mid-1990s
to complete work on what became *Demons of Disorder: Early Blackface
Minstrels and Their World*, and I was joyously working my way through
the rich resources of the AAS. During my intellectual journey there
I first started to glimpse with some modest clarity the relationship
between Jacksonian-Era people who inhabited New York's working-
class neighborhoods and those who practiced the music of early blackface minstrelsy. Both groups were frequently charged with being disorderly, a term with legal *and* social (and musical) implications. Legally,

then as still today, the term meant "immoral or indecent conduct"; socially, Noah Webster in that time defined disorderly as "contrary to rules or established institutions." The implied opposition in both cases—order—was owned by those in power, and, without subversion through disorderly behavior and disorderly music, lower-class people were trapped at the bottom of an imposed, "orderly" world.[1]

At some point in my work, I peered far ahead from *Demons* to the development of early jazz and wondered about a hypothetical connection between that disorderly point in time and space, with its resulting riotous music, and Jacksonian disorder and its brand of riotous music. This book follows from that moment of reflection, an effort to connect some of the dots between the 1840s, when *Demons of Disorder* left off, and 1917, when jazz hit America.

Many of the same obstacles confronted in *Demons of Disorder* stood in the way of *Everybody's Doin' It*, as did some of the same research strategies I employed to overcome them. Since civil authorities tended to take special note of disorder and attempt to do something about it, my attention has frequently been drawn toward laws, legal matters, police and court records, chronicles of alleged illegalities, newspapers, and the records of organizations devoted to social reforms. In such documents are often found accounts of the disorderly and their behaviors, if not the inner realities of their lives.

In general, "my people" (for I have come to love and admire them) tended to live below what I called in *Demons of Disorder* "the horizon of record." To many of these people, the spoken word weighed more than the written, for they were an oral lot. Narratives were vaporous, and of the moment. Then, too, it is in the very nature of documents and artifacts that they tend to be preserved in a ratio commensurate with the social standing of the subject; archives are seldom maintained for those of low social class. In order to reconstruct the lives of the working-class actors in this book, I have often had to rely on the words of literate middle-class witnesses who, as a group, condescended to those beneath their place. It is likely that their biases are embedded in their accounts. Given that, one should be suspicious, as I have tried to be, of many of my sources' historical accuracy. As a rule of thumb, disparaging views written by urban middle-class reporters about the urban hoi polloi should probably be dialed back a notch or two, sometimes even more. Still—and importantly—enough common ranting across a body of narratives likely indicates some underlying truth.

"Disorder" has often been employed as a code word for prostitution, a social issue writ large in *Demons of Disorder*, as, of course, in this book too. In fact, when I began the research for *Everybody's Doin' It*, I imagined a book that would be a comprehensive treatment of the demimonde's role in the development of American music and dance. I learned, without much effort and contrary to much commonly held wisdom, that prostitution was a large, highly developed urban industry throughout the United States from the Jacksonian Era up to World War I. Furthermore, there was a mountain of documentation (some forty-three, city-commissioned vice reports from across the nation, for example), and I laid plans to climb it. In a pivotal conversation with Wendy Strothman, my agent, she suggested that I focus this book only on New York City. The logic was immediately compelling; I did not require much convincing; and the weight of the world lifted. But I still glance occasionally over more-relaxed shoulders and glimpse yet-unwritten books, articles, and dissertations on sex, music, and dance outside of New York (and some still on sex, music, and dance *in* New York), for it turns out that it's a very big subject. If only the shuffle dance with this mortal coil weren't so damned insistent!

⬦

A word on words. What are today acknowledged as highly derisive, deeply pejorative, bluntly racist terms were commonly used and printed in nineteenth- and early twentieth-century America. Some of these show up here embedded in quotations. Their usage is a form of historical evidence and I have reproduced them as written, but always with a flinch and a silent mark of anachronistic condemnation. Outside of quoted material I have generally opted to use "black" when referring to African Americans, for it was a relatively benign word in common usage during the period of this study and remains so today.

Another linguistic problem arose when referring to those of homosexual orientation. Again, there were plenty of offensive contemporaneous terms to choose from, and several of these regrettably show up in quoted matter. Of the less offensive, "homosexual" (or "homosexualist") received some ink in the 1910s, but usage was halting and infrequent; furthermore, the word was then a quasi-medical term implying sexual deviancy. Given that, it would not suffice, and I moved on to other choices. Derogatory references to a homosexual "queer" were increasingly common in the early twentieth century. It is, of course, a word that today is in the process of shedding its slur, but terms of derision are sticky and, sadly, there's still some molt to go. "Gay" was not a word that alluded to homosexuality during the period of this book. It is, however anachronistic, the term that carries less negative baggage in today's world, and it is the word I ultimately adopted and have used throughout. There is no perfect or easy solution here. Know that I have never wished to offend by my word choice.[2]

Women who rent their bodies for the pleasure of men have forever been degraded and marginalized through the words and terms that mark them. A contemporary effort to address this problem has led some toward "sex worker." Surely that's a more appropriate descriptor of what was going on, yet its modern flair feels inappropriate for my historical narrative and I have veered away from it. Instead, I have fixed here on "prostitute," a word less charged with malice than most other contemporaneous references, yet one that still retains a hint of the salacious, as I believe the subject demands.

As for the spelling of words, standardization was not as common in practice then as Webster might have wished. In quoted material I have modernized spelling silently if the meaning is unclear. Since "contemporaneous spelling" and "typo" are not always mutually exclusive categories, spelling irregularities have also been silently corrected (*"sic"* being essentially disruptive of narrative flow, in my view). Original spellings are maintained if the meaning and context are clear and if the color of what was said is thus more deeply saturated.

⋯❖⋯

Finally, a look at the elephant. Early in my research, I was overwhelmed and appalled by the scant choice afforded women in prostitution during this period. Furthermore, the magnitude of the business was incomprehensible to me, as was my lifelong ignorance of it. How could I not have known about this?—a question often followed by a despairing "What *am* I doing?" After struggling with how to deal conscientiously and sensitively with the issue, I found myself tending toward simple avoidance. It was easier to look past the unending lines of women in the foreground, each offering their bodies for the gratification of men, and toward the corner in back, where the musicians were making the fun music that kept people dancing. At this midpoint in the book project, my inclination was to proclaim that I am no scholar of sexuality or gender in America, and therefore not qualified to deal substantively with the many fraught issues raised by prostitution. At which time, I, an unsullied, innocent musicologist, could state that "Prostitution is what it is! My interest is in the music and dance!"

But that, alas, isn't nearly good enough. I've spent years now trying to understand the world of American commercialized sex from 1840 to 1917. Surely I have something to say on the subject.

In my angst, I am somewhat comforted by the company I keep. Those who have studied seriously the institution of prostitution have all been confounded by its complexity. Along with many of my colleagues, I have come to think that prostitution during the period of this book was seldom unalloyed exploitation nor a way for women to be empowered. It was, rather, demeaning work that for many women was their last best hope. Ruth Rosen, who *is* a scholar on gender and society, confronted this issue at the front of her masterful *The Lost Sis-*

terhood: Prostitution in America, 1900–1918 and laid the blame on those who most enjoyed the golden light reflected by the Gilded Age.

> *[T]hat prostitution offered certain opportunities and advantages for some women, however, should not be interpreted as a positive or romanticized assessment of the life of a prostitute. Instead, it should be as an indictment of the limited range of opportunities that . . . women faced in their daily struggle for economic, social and psychological well-being. Denied access to social and economic power because of their gender and class status, poor women made their choices from a position of socially structured powerlessness.*

The problem then in the foreground of the saloon backroom was gender and class, while in the far corner it was race and class, as poor blacks and whites shared musical ideas. A certain (low) class standing is what the women and the musicians had in common. By understanding some of what the women were up against, it became possible for me to understand more of why the musicians and the dancers expressed what they did. Accordingly, you will encounter here women who hated what they felt compelled to do, but none who hated the music they heard nor any who professed to dislike dancing to it. It was the attraction and power of music and dance that joined oppressed people together into a single mind, enabling distressed lives to be somewhat better in the process, if only for the length of a dance. That is not to say that it has been a stroll for me to get to this point; how much easier it would have been to romanticize despair! But the job before me has been to measure the depths of the pitfalls, then factor those figures into a project to understand more about how an American music born in despondency can sing so loudly of hope. For, to pick up again from Samuel Beckett: "It's a question of voices, of voices to keep going, in the right manner."[3]

EVERYBODY'S DOIN' IT

A "mud-gutter" band in front of one of the dance-halls was making discordant music, while children of all ages, from the babe just out of the mother's arms to the young girl in her teens, jostled each other in a rude attempt at dancing. Bare-headed colored women, in soiled calico dresses, with sleeves rolled up, stopped, before entering the brothels, to join with rough-looking sailors in a "break-down." From a cellar-way leading to filthy underground apartments came the noise of a piano, drummed by unskilled hands, while the painted women at the door tried to induce victims to enter. Crowding my way through, I entered a saloon. The place was filled with the fumes of rum and tobacco, the ceiling was low and dingy, the floor waxed for dancing. At one end of the room was an orchestra including a bass-viol with a bad cold, a fiddle with three strings, and a wheezy accordion; at the other end was a bar, to which, after each dance, the floor-manager invited the dancers to "walk up and treat yer pardners, gentlemen." White and black mingled indiscriminately in the dance. A huge negro swung, with great force, a young white girl who was puffing clouds of smoke from a short pipe.

—HELEN CAMPBELL, *Darkness and Daylight; or, Lights and Shadows of New York Life* (1895)

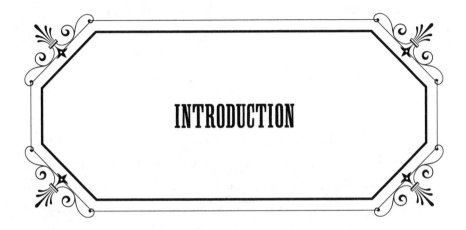

INTRODUCTION

THE *EPIC OF GILGAMESH* is widely considered to be the world's oldest book. Early in the story, Enkidu, a wild man who lives in and with nature, is seduced by Shamhat, the high priestess of Ishtar. By that he is made human. Shamhat then points him toward the Mesopotamian king Gilgamesh, with whom he will form a deep and fateful friendship, and to the capital at Uruk, where he will see on any ordinary day:

> *people singing and dancing in the streets,*
> *musicians playing their lyres and drums,*
> *the lovely priestesses standing before*
> *the temple of Ishtar, chatting and laughing,*
> *flushed with sexual joy, and ready*
> *to serve men's pleasure.*

Thus the very first references to music and dancing in the oldest of stories, embedded in a single sentence that climaxes in sexual joy.[1]

The story told here is at least as old as *Gilgamesh*, was current when "City Missionary" Helen Campbell reported on her experience of a

New York dive in 1895, and is as new as last Saturday night. For when human beings have danced to music and been stirred by the enticing strains of lyres, fiddles, pianos, guitars, mud-gutter bands, and rhythms sounded out by drums, the whiff of sex is ever present.

No effort is made here to chronicle such doings in the millennia since *Gilgamesh*. Rather, attention is directed toward a particularly compelling period in the history of sexuality, music, and dance—from around 1840 to 1917—in a particularly important city: New York.

Everybody's Doin' It explores how the flourishing business of prostitution in New York encouraged dancing made rowdy by wild music, and how that enterprise provided both the reasons for developments in musical style and the economic means to support musicians charged with keeping people dancing. This book promises some answer to a long-standing and fundamental question about how and why American popular music sounds as it does, for the music's energy served well clients-with-coin, all of whom were seeking entertainment, excitement, and ecstasy. It happens that the music followed simply from the complex job at hand.

Threaded throughout the book are characters, many quite colorful, that either made the music and dance or enabled this story's telling. These were musicians, dancers, and dive owners, of course, but they were also madams, prostitutes, bosses, reformers, preachers, reporters, policemen, and politicians. Some of them are well-known and well-documented: George Washington Dixon and Irving Berlin among the musicians; John McDowall, Anthony Comstock, and John D. Rockefeller Jr. among those endeavoring to close down the dance halls and saloons. At the heart of the book, though, are the "routine musicians" whom jazz musician Peter Bocage praised as "the men that didn't know nothin' about [proper] music. They just make up their own ideas." Routine musicians stitched everything together, for over in the dark corners of saloons, dives, brothels, and dance halls they watched the dancers, made up new musical licks, and counted the tips to weigh the results.[2]

The music they fashioned—exhilarating rhythms, a brassy sound, the thumping bass, and sinuous melodies—came out of an improvised, oral tradition, a music-of-the-air that was not published or written down. Finding good descriptions of this made-up music is not easy, for chroniclers typically measured the dive, evoked the people in the space, and waxed about the wildness of the dance, but few of them attempted to put words to ephemeral sound waves, however intoxicating. The best to hope for from most of these sources are descriptions of the band, perhaps aspects of playing style, and references to a song or two. Yet even these accounts are often distortions, for those doing the reporting were generally writing for middle-class patrons who preferred to confirm prejudicial attitudes toward those lower on the social scale than to be challenged to appreciate their culture. Even something so seemingly simple as compiling a list of songs from the sources is also suspect, for although one can usually dig out a title from a sheet-music archive, in actual mud-gutter performance the lyrics would likely have been distorted and parodied and the notes on the hallowed, published page subjected to all sorts of disrespect, even disregard. To analyze reports and commentary for musical style and substance then is somewhat akin to examining a letter in a mirror, for everything is written backwards. If enough chroniclers like Helen Campbell thought the musicians "unskilled," the music "discordant" or "noise," that all accordions were "wheezy," and that the bass viol had a "bad cold," then there is a very good chance that something interesting was going on. Certainly those in the hall dancing so rudely thought so![3]

❖

What can be said meaningfully about a music, obviously everywhere, that left so few marks on the historical record? A sort of historical triangulation suggests some answers. At point "A" are source texts: descriptions, reports, testimony, illustrations, lyrics, sheet music, etc. Although relatively scant and seldom in the voice of those most under study, their utility to any historiographic effort is obvious. Point "B" provides a perspective on the contexts in which the music flourished and what they might suggest implicitly about the nature of music-making. If, for instance, the blood of dancers was said to be "on fire" and images from the time showed "high-kicking" female dancers and leering male dancers, and it was in the best interest of the musicians' livelihood to keep the dancing at a high pitch, then the music was likely to be hot, energetic, tremendous fun, made-up, and open-ended enough in form to keep the dancers dancing.

At point "C" is the issue of class. A reporter in 1866 observed that those living on the impoverished Lower East Side "roll out more lustily their music tasks, and with a purer relish, than their more dainty little friends in the higher walks of life." *Everybody's Doin' It* foregrounds people impoverished in material resources but rich in music. Those lower-class New Yorkers—the "other half," as they were called by Jacob Riis in 1890—often sought through music to bring joy to lives dulled by want. The music provided them the freedom to imagine and express made-up ideas not bound by economic circumstance. From that came an improvised music that emphasized the offbeat accents between regimenting downbeats and prompted provocative dance moves that those who considered themselves respectable considered rude and wildly inappropriate.[4]

An emphasis on class invites a consideration of race. Blacks and whites intentionally intermingled in both "disorderly houses" and in the later "black and tans." Even Mrs. Campbell did not seem shocked by the mixed-race, lower-class culture she observed. In fact, working-class blacks and whites in New York commonly drank together, danced together, and lived and loved together (as well as, on occasion, fought together). They also made music together. As it is impossible to imagine the development of American popular music and culture without considering the central contributions of black Americans, so is it equally impossible to imagine this book without acknowledging the place of New York's black musicians.

There is no single, great life that could trace the central story of

Everybody's Doin' It, nor is there one singular institution that could stage it. A rich gallery of colorful people, institutions, and organizations make up a larger, kaleidoscopic drama. Their bits are acted in chapters that progress in roughly chronological order, with each more or less dedicated to a single decade, going from the 1840s through the 1910s. The focus is always on what can be learned about the evolution of New York music-making by examining the circumstances in which it occurred. Toward that end, each chapter pays special attention to developments that illuminated new sounds and styles, all of which inevitably set the stage for what followed, be it social, cultural, or political.

❖

This then is the story of what Enkidu heard in Uruk, what Helen Campbell heard on New York streets and in saloons, and what all the world discovered at the dawn of the Jazz Age: a dynamic music and dance entwined with expressions of basic human urges. Like most things touched by humankind it is a complicated story, not always an easy one, but sometimes too a beautiful one. Perhaps such must necessarily be the case in an underground world of secret entanglements that nurtured the awesome mysteries of music and dance.

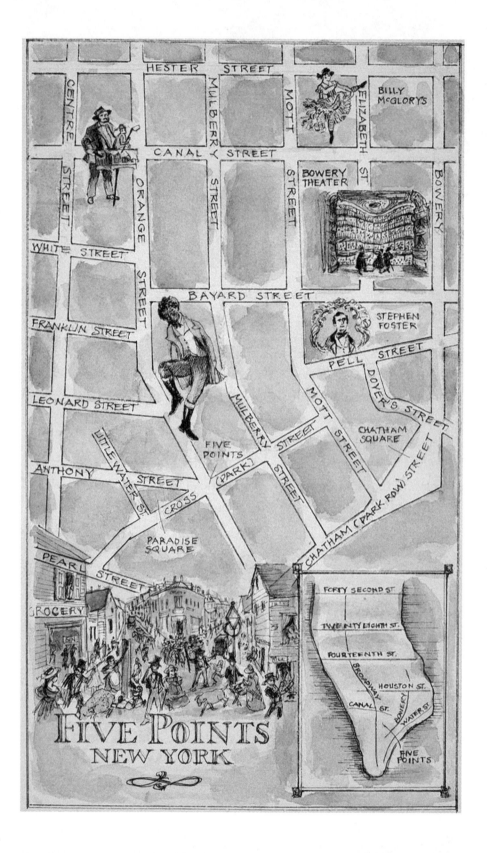

FIVE POINTS
NEW YORK

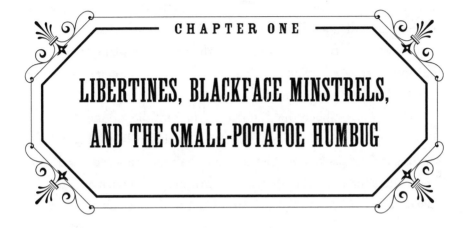

CHAPTER ONE

LIBERTINES, BLACKFACE MINSTRELS, AND THE SMALL-POTATOE HUMBUG

J OHN R. MCDOWALL was a thoroughly righteous, somewhat naive, twenty-nine-year-old student at the Princeton Theological Seminary when he moved to New York City in 1830. He planned to be a missionary among the city's downtrodden. Inevitably he was drawn to the Sixth Ward, with its infamous Five Points and warren of dens, joints, saloons, dance halls, assignation houses, and brothels. McDowall was repulsed by the open prostitution he saw there and branded it an endemic and "gangrenous canker" that was infesting the body and soul of the city. Springing into action, he worked with other like-minded people to forward the mission of the newly established New York Magdalen Society and institute a halfway house (the "Asylum") for the magdalens who wanted to leave their old lives behind. A crusader who was also a writer, within a year of arriving in the city McDowall had edited the *Magdalen Report*, which the Magdalen Society published. There New Yorkers learned that young women were being led to the life through vicious indulgence in drink and capricious frolicking in dance halls or by loss of virtue resulting from malicious seduction. Furthermore, he claimed that "not less than TEN

THOUSAND!!" prostitutes plied their profession in New York, with leading city fathers among their best clients.[1]

The city establishment was not amused. Newspaper editorials, public letters, and meetings at Tammany Hall decried the *Report* as obscene and filled with distortions. Its editor and authors were branded as traitors. Society members received threats, and a majority of them quickly caved. As a result, the New York Magdalen Society folded in late 1831, barely a year after its founding.[2]

McDowall grabbed the gauntlet before it hit the ground, however, revamped the thrust of the *Report*, and quickly published *Magdalen Facts*, a tightly packed booklet of more than one hundred pages that ends with a hymn to "The Magdalen." His life's work back on track, he began editing *McDowall's Journal* in 1833. Emblazoned on its masthead was "Purity and Truth," with the image of a printing press spreading cleansing rays across the globe, while the lead editorial in the first issue laid bare the mission: expose immorality, build public support against it, and destroy it at its root. The *Journal* subsequently published details on techniques employed by seducers, traced the prevalence of prostitution, cited the addresses of brothels, and fingered some of prostitution's patrons by name.[3]

To garner support for the fight against moral contagion, McDowall convened a conference of three hundred clergymen in early 1834. There he shared documents and artifacts gathered during his work: obscene books, sexually graphic prints, lewdly decorated music boxes (some featuring animated nude couples), and more—probably the era's largest collection of what would now be called pornographic materials. The response was not what McDowall expected. The men of the cloth, although initially quite interested, turned against him for polluting their purity of mind. Then, with the patience of the powerful stretched to the breaking point, a grand jury in late 1834 indicted McDowall for presenting "such odious and revolting details as are offensive to taste, injurious to morals, and degrading to the character of our city." Papers filed with the court claimed that McDowall's work produced a result opposite to his stated intentions, for the details he published actually "inflame the passions of the young" instead of quelling them. The indictment was sustained and *McDowall's Journal* was banned for being obscene.[4]

To complete McDowall's fall from grace, the Presbyterian Church defrocked him in April 1836. Psychologically broken and always lacking a strong physical constitution, he died seven months later on December 14, 1836. McDowall was for years afterward celebrated by his supporters as the "Martyr of the Seventh Commandment."

Although viewed by many as something of a fanatic, McDowall did leave a legacy. Organizations that both advocated for moral reform and were aggressively prescriptive on the maintenance of female virtue became a feature of New York life for much of the next century. The most immediately successful of these was the New-York Female Moral Reform Society, which followed directly on the heels of the Magdalen Society. The Society organ—*The Advocate of Moral Reform*, which at its peak claimed to have twenty thousand subscribers—was intended to be read by upstanding, middle-class churchgoers. Articles and columns shared lessons learned from the fallen and advice on how not to become one of them. Attending the theater received constant cautionary attention, for there would be found scantily clad actresses and women of the night in the infamous third tier. Readers were alerted to the dangers of novel reading, since it filled the young (female) mind with useless romantic fantasies. And dancing was certainly bad for the morals, especially waltzing.

> *It consists of a whirling movement, in which the hand of the lady is on the gentleman's shoulder, while his arm encircles her waist. . . . We have heard young ladies confess that they thought this kind of dance extremely indelicate, but "it is so delightful and we love it so, that we cannot give it up."*

Soon, the report warned, the lilting triple meter enchants and "the heart becomes prostituted by unholy sensations." Even music itself could lead to moral perdition. According to the author of "The Use and Abuse of Music," piano music distorted mindful and moral values, for quicksteps and waltzes on the piano both associate the "pleasures of the dance with the witchery of music."[5]

McDowall's crusade, in league with that of the New-York Female Moral Reform Society, forced the consideration of prostitution, promiscuity, and sexuality's effect on an often-resistant public. In this way, his short life's work was not in vain.

⁕

Into the breach left by McDowall's death came a quite different crew, often motley, sometimes brilliant, and always ready and armed (frequently with hypocrisy) to defend the sanctity of womankind. The pen was their sword, and at the head of the brigade was editor and publisher George Washington Dixon, surely one of the most complex, enigmatic, and colorful figures in American history.

Born around 1801, probably in Richmond, Virginia, Dixon entered what he called his "momentous vocation" when he assumed editorship of a Lowell, Massachusetts, newspaper in 1835. From the first he proclaimed that paramount among his duties was to be an "advocate of sound morals." Within a year, Dixon moved to Boston, started the *Bostonian; or, Dixon's Saturday Night Express*, and chased after the moral failings of Bostonians in high places. Already at this early stage in Dixon's journalistic career, a discernible pattern of good intentions followed by overreach to the point of libel was evident. The *Boston Post* in an 1837 editorial noted that Dixon had the tendency to grab hold of the hot end of the poker, and characterized him as somewhat like a cow that gave a pail of good milk and then kicked it over.

Dixon became a New Yorker in 1838 and published the first number of his weekly *Polyanthos* ("many flowers"). In an early issue, he revealed that Thomas Hamblin, a popular actor and manager of the Bowery Theatre, was having an illicit affair with a teen-aged actress in his troupe. Within ten days of the exposé, the actress was dead. A coroner's jury found that she had died as the result of "brain fever" induced in large part by the *Polyanthos* article. Later that year a merchant, Rowland R. Minturn, was censored by the *Polyanthos* for his ongoing liaison with a married woman. Twelve days after that article's publication, Minturn leaped to his death. Nothing if not indefatigable, Dixon then turned his pen on the Reverend Francis L. Hawks, the rector of St. Thomas Episcopal Church in New York since 1831, and charged him with sexual dalliance, graphic details provided.

The Hamblin exposé resulted in Dixon being publicly flogged by the actor. The Minturn scoop did not lead to bodily harm for Dixon, but the family brought him into court on a libel charge. Jailed, Dixon was released when the astronomical bail of nine thousand dollars was provided (in only one of a long string of Dixon paradoxes) by Adeline Miller, a well-known brothel madam. The trial in April 1839 turned into a three-day circus. The press and the masses packed the courtroom in part for the titillation provided by illicit details introduced as evidence and in part simply because the notorious Dixon was in the dock. A hung jury resulted, and the prosecution chose not to retry the slippery defendant.

But only a month later Dixon was back in court, this time to face a libel charge from Rev. Hawks. Astonishingly, Dixon changed his plea to "Guilty" and received a sentence of six months at hard labor in the New York State Penitentiary. There is no convincing evidence why the editor agreed to the libel charge. Dixon did claim two years later that Hawks paid him one thousand dollars to take the fall, thus allowing the reverend to avoid damage to his reputation in a public trial. There might well have been some fire beneath Dixon's smoke, for Hawks was soon removed from the rectorship of one of the largest, wealthiest, and most influential Episcopal churches in the country's largest and most dynamic city and shipped out to a new position in Holly Springs, Mississippi (population about four thousand).

After serving his time, Dixon returned to the publishing fray, seeking to reveal ever yet more egregious immoral behavior among the rich and famous. Fanny Elssler, an Austrian ballerina then the toast of New York's stage, was accused in the pages of the *Polyanthos* of immoral sexual behavior. Words were seldom quite enough for Dixon, so he incited and led a mob against her in August 1840 and subsequently published the incendiary speech he delivered before his enflamed followers. He then turned his attention to the business of Ann Lohman, who worked under the name of Madame Restell performing illegal, backroom abortions for desperate women, many of them married. In Dixon's expressed view, the fundamental function of marriage was the birthing of children, which compounded abortion's sin; and with abortion available, why should women practice abstinence before marriage or remain faithful to their vows afterward?[6]

Madame Restell was indicted and jailed shortly after Dixon's barrage. The editor followed with more articles on Restell, one illustrated with a woodcut of a woman overlaid with the head of death, a skeleton leering in the background. When Restell was convicted in July 1841, Dixon rejoiced in print and then, typically, published a self-congratulatory pamphlet detailing the trial.[7]

William J. Snelling (born in 1804) was initially a publishing partner with Dixon at the *Polyanthos* and contributed columns to the paper for several years. With seeming paradoxical intent, they together broadened the scope of the paper to champion the virtues of New York's prostitution culture. Julia Brown, for instance, ran New York's premier brothel and was royally treated to a "Full Description of Princess Julia's Palace of Love" in an 1841 issue. The "Princess" herself was described—"the rarest specimen of art and nature combined"—along with her brothel, its fine furnishings, and the fetching occupants of the rooms, all of whom were passionate and graced with "downy bosom." The Palace of Love, according to the distorted logic of the *Polyanthos*, was a place where "the evil that flesh is held to" came to know virtue.[8]

Dixon and Snelling spawned a cohort of journalists who followed their line: reveal the titillating lives of New York's prostitutes, endorse generous expressions of male sexuality, and dig for dirt in the lives of New York's hypocrites, especially those of high standing. Cohort members George Wilkes, Thaddeus W. Meighan, and George B. Wooldridge sometimes worked with Dixon and/or Snelling and sometimes against them. Between them they were responsible for a flurry of generally short-lived "sporting" weeklies with names such as the *Flash*, the *True Flash*, the *Whip*, the *Sporting Whip*, the *Rake*, and the *Libertine*. These papers were among the very first to develop a strategy later perfected by tabloids: launch inflaming and moralistic-sounding exposés into the social fray, graced with a brazen, salacious, conspiratorial smirk, adorned by a sly wink, and ornamented on the front page by an image of female dishabille.

The pages of the sporting press paid special attention to prostitution. Brothels, with addresses included, were ranked by the cleanliness and beauty of their women, along with admonishing advice (of course) to avoid them all. The *Flash* advocated in 1841 for making adultery and fornication outside of marriage illegal, and the *True Flash* argued against "self-pollution" (masturbation). All the while they were glorifying New York's male, sporting culture. Satire—often intended to puncture the pretensions of the powerful—was the name of their game.[9]

While hardly serious journalism, the work of Dixon and cohort opened to view important windows on the underworld culture of the times. Perhaps most obviously, if one could cut through the cant, hypocrisy, irony, and personal imbroglios, they established in the public mind a de facto right by print media to investigate and publish findings on the lives of private citizens. Moreover, whereas McDowall seemed most concerned about the philandering of the educated class, Dixon and colleagues eventually widened the lens to include all levels of New York society, high and low. This meant, among much else, that prying eyes now peeked into the basement dance halls of the Five Points as well as offices on Wall Street and the rector's study in St. Thomas Episcopal Church.

Then there is the surprising place of music and dance in the (often sordid) story. And, again, Dixon is the key figure.

He pursued a career in music from early in his life, with records capturing him singing in touring variety shows by 1824. In 1827 Dixon made his New York debut performing some of the day's popular comic songs in a Lower East Side theater. But his claim to fame was made in July 1829 when he first sang "Coal Black Rose." This song features a simple melody, really more of a ditty, that quickly gets out of the way to allow for the theatricality of the lyrics. The story is of Sambo, a slave, who is in love with Rose; everything is fine at first, but in verse eight Sambo spies his rival, Cuffee, in Rose's room, which leads to a tussle and a chase. By the end of the song, Sambo curses "blackka snake Rose."

To perform this song, Dixon applied burnt-cork-and-grease "blackface" makeup to mimic the complexion of the uneducated, comically smitten Sambo. Although white actors at that time commonly applied blackface to play black characters (viz., Othello), this ludicrous, comic song sung to (probably) a folk melody was different. There was no effort here at an accurate representation of black Americans or of their music; the intent was comic ridicule, and audiences in the lower-class theaters of New York's Bowery district loved it. With this stroke, Dixon became, in an honorific coined later by one of his editor colleagues, the "Columbus" of blackface minstrelsy in America.

Thomas Dartmouth Rice jumped on the blackface bandwagon a year later in September 1830 when he first performed "Jim Crow" in Louisville, Kentucky. Rice brought acting and dance experience to the blackface stage with his famous song, opening the fledgling genre to a vivid and dynamic theatricality. Although Dixon also performed "Jim Crow," his lasting mark was made with the blackface song "Zip Coon," which he first sang in 1834. A counterpoise to "Jim Crow," which is a depiction of a southern slave dressed in rags, "Zip Coon" is about a northern, freedman dandy, a self-proclaimed "larned skoler." Together "Jim Crow" and "Zip Coon" represented (and defined) the stereotypes between which most black Americans at that time lived their lives.[10]

Unlike "Jim Crow," "Zip Coon" was graced with an infectious melody, known widely today as "Turkey in the Straw." It is a "fiddle tune" in type or, as it would have been called then, a "jig." Dancing is implied by this tune, which has plenty of rhythmic accents where feet can slap the floor. The tune structure—an A section repeated, followed by a related B section repeated—allows, even mandates, enough repetitions to sustain the energies of the dancers. Like many fiddle tunes of the time, the melody to "Zip Coon" was likely born in a disreputable dance hall or in a lower-class brothel. In fact, the tune has also been known as "Natchez Under the Hill," a reference to the infamous district on the

George Washington Dixon as Zip Coon. *Image from "Zip Coon" [sheet music] (New York: Firth and Hall, [ca. 1834]). Lithograph by George Endicott. From the Sheet Music Collections of the Center for Popular Music, Middle Tennessee State University, Murfreesboro, Tennessee.*

muddy banks of the Mississippi River at Natchez, literally and figuratively "under" the high society "on" the top of the bluff.

In their lyrics, "Jim Crow" and "Zip Coon" both touch on matters of political and social moment that concerned the urban, white working class. Race was one of these issues, and it is clearly the case that white performers in blackface expressed deeply felt fears about black people in a manner that later generations would consider abhorrent. But singers brought up other audience concerns that did not touch directly on race. Verses to both songs were frequently improvised and rendered topically to their place, time, and audience. Some countered elite disdain for President Jackson, who was a hero to many in early minstrelsy's audience; others addressed the oppression of the working class; even specific matters, such as the chartering of the Second Bank of the United States (which was perceived by Jackson and his supporters to favor the rich), were treated.

The constant in both songs is that the music and the texts are

Bowery Theatre. "View of the Stage on the *fifty seventh* night of Mr. T.D. RICE, of Kentucky in his original and celebrated extravaganza of JIM CROW on which occasion every department of the house was thronged to an excess unprecedented in the records of theatrical attraction. New York 25th November 1833." *Lithograph, 1833, 43478, New-York Historical Society.*

expressions of working-class culture and life. An engraving of a performance of "Jim Crow" at the Bowery Theatre on November 25, 1833,
is captioned: "View of the Stage on the *fifty seventh* night of Mr. T.D.
RICE, of Kentucky in his original and celebrated extravaganza of
JIM CROW on which occasion every department of the house was
thronged to an excess unprecedented in the records of theatrical attraction." It shows Jim Crow dancing his jig at center stage while surrounded by the hoi polloi, some listening and watching intently, some
pushing and shoving; a few appear to be enjoying a good fight. Jim
Crow was clearly a man of the people.

In July of the next year, the masses were back at the Bowery Theatre, but this time in an angry mood. A famous English actor who was
performing that evening had allegedly said disrespectful things about
the general character of Americans. In retribution, rioters rushed into
the theater during his performance, threatened mayhem and revenge,
and refused all entreaties for order. But then, according to a reporter
from the *New York Sun*, a newspaper favored by the lower classes:

> *Mr. Dixon, the singer (an American), now made his appearance. "Let
> us have 'Zip Coon,'" exclaimed a thousand voices. The singer gave them
> their favorite song amidst peals of laughter. . . . Dixon, who had pro-
> duced such amazing good nature with his "Zip Coon," next addressed
> them—and they soon quietly dispersed.*

Zip Coon was clearly a man of the people.

The word "minstrel" would not be applied to those who performed
in comic blackface until 1843. But "blackface minstrelsy" was already in
place by 1834. There is no question that the skeleton around which this
popular entertainment was built was the denigration of black people.
There is also no doubt that its muscle consisted of stereotypes of black
Americans, many of which tragically prevail to the present. And—too
often forgotten—there is no question that its enormous, century-long
appeal was because of the music and dance that gave it flesh.

That music and dance, like "Jim Crow" and "Zip Coon," came out of and was an expression of urban, lower-class, dance-hall and brothel culture. To the throngs on the stage of the Bowery Theatre, "Jim Crow" belonged to them. Who would have thought that lower-class music and dance deserved a place on the legitimate stage? And once it was there, the Jacksonian hordes joined Jim Crow in rollicking and roiling solidarity. And to the throngs in the Bowery Theatre in 1834, "Zip Coon" belonged to them as well. The song was of them, and once Dixon sang their song—surely some among the mob danced a jig to it—their point was made: our music; we made it; we belong here.[11]

❖

Over the course of the next decade, American theaters were flooded with songs and dances performed by white musicians in blackface. More than a thousand such performances have been documented, along with many dozens of newly published songs. The songs had titles such as "De Boatman's Dance," "Clare de Kitchen," "Dandy Jim, from Caroline," "Dan Tucker," "Gumbo Chaff," "Jim Along Josey," "Jumbo Jum," "Lucy Long," "My Long-Tail Blue," "Possum Up a Gum Tree," "Settin' on a Rail," "Sich a Gettin' Upstairs," "Walk Jaw Bone," and "Whar Did You Come From." Most of the tunes to these songs appear less "composed" by a single songwriter and more "made" by an involved community, as is the case with much folk music. Almost none of them had an obvious stylistic connection with African or black American music. Most are jigs or other danceable tunes. Most could have been enjoyed and probably were enjoyed in working-class dens, dance halls, and brothels in New York.

Another man of the people, Davy Crockett, described the scene in which this music was rooted in 1835, the year before he died at the Alamo. On his first trip to New York, he headed to the Five Points. Crockett noticed that many of the houses there had cellars and each one was crowded. Underground, "such fiddling and dancing nobody ever saw before in this world. I thought they were the true 'heavenborns.' Black and white, white and black all hug-em-snug together, happy as lords and ladies." And with a dram handy to all.[12]

Crockett's general rendering is confirmed by newspaper accounts from that time. The *Evening Tattler*, for example, published a report of a police raid on Michael Hardy's property at 18 Anthony Street. The watch was looking for signs of organized gambling and to squelch the disorderly behavior that belched out of Hardy's joint. A reporter had apparently been tipped off and was along for the raid. He wrote that the police noticed riotous laughter from the back of the house that was "sufficient to awaken the seven sleepers, or burst a thunder cloud." Proceeding toward that noise, they discovered a saloon occupied by about twenty persons "of all sizes and colors" who were drinking beer, smoking cigars, and playing cards. In one corner, a "little black rascal of twelve years, assisted by two little white ones of eleven or under," was roaring away at a love song, while in another corner a knot of "amalgamationists were applauding the exertions of a bit of a niggar, who was jumping 'Jim Crow.'" The police made their move and instantly the lights were snuffed. Some of the participants jumped through the window, some ran under the officers' legs and out the door, and others shimmied up the chimney. Chaos reigned, and to "crown the whole, two feminine blocks of ebony and a little Irish woman set up a pullaloo that was equal to the keen of a Munster funeral."[13]

Few other papers of the time matched the *Evening Tattler* for its graphic depiction of what the underworld scene looked, sounded, and felt like. But among the select exceptions was the *Libertine*, a sporting paper published during the summer of 1842 by George B. Wooldridge, a protégé of Dixon. The prospectus for the *Libertine* promised editorial content that could be read by the "most fastidious without causing a blush (if not too sensitive)." It stated an intention to publish articles on "celebrated females, illustrated" and exposés of "roués and libertines." In closing: "all the failings of the fair sex will be set forth in glowing colors."[14]

Toward such an end, the first issue contained an account and illustration of a "Dance on Long Wharf." This was a match dance between two Boston prostitutes—"the elegant and bladder-like" Nance Holmes and the sylph-like Susan Bryant. Fiddle music was provided by a mulatto barber. Bryant led off, dancing to "Fisher's Hornpipe," and the way she danced the "big licks was a 'sin to Moses.'" Then Holmes took to the wharf and promised to "make the grease come." She struck up and moved in a way that was "a caution to French bedsteads." If she could keep it up, bystanders thought that the contest between the two prostitutes would be "hip and thigh between them." After a short break, a "Virginia breakdown" was announced. The fiddler lit into "Camptown Hornpipe," then moved on to other well-known minstrel tunes and jigs. "They danced—the sweat poured," but in the end Bryant prevailed, and "Nance was carried home on a cart, procured for the purpose, while Suse footed it, amid shouts of joy from her friends."[15]

There is no knowing if the dance-off actually happened this way, or if there was a contest at all. Susan Bryant was a real person, however, a madam who ran a brothel in Boston, and it is likely there was also a Nance Holmes; Long Wharf existed and the tunes were well-known. But in the world of the *Libertine* the line between fact and fiction was gray; it does not much matter if the scene happened or was only imagined, for even if fictional the piece was intended to distill and express a reality.[16]

Wooldridge was the perfect person to publish "Dance on Long Wharf," for he had deep experience in the worlds of sex, music, dance, and sporting papers. At various times he edited the *Whip* and its successor, the *Whip and Satirist of New-York and Brooklyn.* Furthermore, he was a co-publisher of the *Flash* early in 1841 with Snelling and Wilkes until a libel charge was filed and Wooldridge turned people's evidence. That partnership sundered, he and Dixon banded together to publish the *True Flash.*

As a result of their collaboration, both were skewered by the *Flash*

"Grand Trial Dance between Nance Holmes and Suse Bryant, on Long Wharf, Boston." *Image from* Libertine, *June 15, 1842. Engraving by Manning. Courtesy, American Antiquarian Society.*

later in 1841. One such roasting involved a satirical account of a fancy ball thrown by Julia Brown, who was reported by the *Flash* to be paying special attention to Dixon, for she claimed to have "bought and paid for the melodist, body and soul." Phoebe Doty, who ran a high-profile brothel a few doors down from Brown's brothel at 55 Leonard Street—which was next door to where Wooldridge would come to live—counterclaimed that Dixon was her fiancé and "exhibited a written promise of marriage." Suck Jo and French Celeste, prostitutes, took sides and a tussle ensued during which Brown lost her tiara and Doty was "divested of her bustle." To calm matters, someone requested a song, whereupon Dixon offered up "Settin' on a Rail" and "Jim Crow," the final verse of which went:

> *I've swindled all creation,*
>   *And now I'd have you know,*
> *Lies are nothing but vexation*
>   *And my* Flash *turns out "No Go."*

Peace restored, all present then tucked into the comestibles catered by Wooldridge. The article was signed: "Yours with real respect, Moral Reformer McDowall."[17]

That McDowall had been dead for five years is some clue to the veracity of the report. Still, the other named characters were real, alive, and presumably well. And Dixon singing blackface minstrel songs to calm the unruly has been documented.

Wooldridge suffered through a rough 1842. In early January, after testifying against Snelling and Wilkes, he received special attention from the *Flash*, whose readers learned that he had run the Bank House, the Canvass Back Lunch, and the Elssler Saloon, all drinking and eating establishments that were alleged also to have been disorderly houses. Further, the *Flash* claimed that Wooldridge had been implicated in a burglary, revealed that he had married a prostitute, and that, without divorcing that lady, had since married another. In April he was charged once more with libel against a young woman. July brought an indictment against him for publishing an obscene newspaper—the *Libertine*—after only its second issue. The trial on this charge in September resulted in the jury deliberating for five minutes before returning a guilty verdict. Wooldridge then pleaded guilty to a similar charge against another publication of his (the *Whip*) and was sentenced to sixty days in the penitentiary. To cap his run of trouble, he was indicted again in March 1843, this time for libel against Eliza Trust, yet another target of his self-justified moralizing.[18]

Things did not go well for Dixon that year either. In January 1842, he too was indicted for publishing an obscene newspaper, the *True Flash*. After that, he appeared to turn away from the newspaper business (perhaps because it resulted in too much time on the court docket) and in February embarked on a new career as a "pedestrian" by entering prize-money competitions that involved speed-walking the farthest or longest (up to forty-eight hours, nonstop). But by the end of 1842, again intoxicated by printer's ink, he advertised that his *Polyanthos* would resume publication.

> *When I stopped my nice moral paper and took to stumping it about the Union, a host of small-fry was spawned upon the public, in the shapes of Whips, Flashes, Libertines and Rakes, and now I mean to crush them all.*

But apparently "Dixon, [the] small-potatoe humbug, and literary charlatan," never managed the restart. In March 1843, the *Sporting Whip* published some kindly intended words on Dixon: "George is a queer—noble—erratic—talented—well-meaning, but sometimes mistaken fellow—and when he leaves this nasty little football of clay for a better world, millions will mourn, and the Devil will triumph."

Dixon had other notable misadventures over the next two decades, including commissioning himself a major general, mustering an army of volunteers, and planning an invasion of Mexico (which he never pulled off). When the Columbus of blackface minstrelsy died in the New Orleans Charity Hospital in 1861, "Editor" was listed as his occupation on the death certificate.[19]

⊰⊱

After Dixon's failed effort to revive the *Polyanthos*, other papers arose, including the *Sporting Whip*, whose motto was "Place in Every Honest Hand a WHIP—To Lash the Rascals Naked through the World." The editor, twenty-year-old Thaddeus W. Meighan, was claimed by his (many) enemies to be a male prostitute and to live with a (female?) prostitute who was "fat, fair, and forty." He, like Dixon, also had a strong interest in the popular entertainments of the day, particularly blackface minstrelsy. For instance, his sporting paper followed closely the professional career of John Diamond, a white blackface dancer, and looked forward with great anticipation to a match dance between Diamond and "a little negro called 'Juba.'" The article assured readers that the dancer who could "cut, shuffle, and attitudanize with the greatest facility" would be the winner.[20]

Meighan may even have been the first to write a critical history of blackface minstrelsy. In a *Sporting Whip* article dated January 28, 1843, he cited the pivotal importance both of Dixon's performance of "Coal Black Rose" and of Rice's "Jim Crow." From them, so Meighan claimed, the numerous blackface singers, dancers, and actors that afterward graced the stage were directly descended. Meighan went on in that column to become the first to identify important new developments in blackface entertainment. Until 1843, theatrical blackface entertainers worked by themselves in single acts on programs that might also feature (non-blackface) acrobats, monologues, and comic skits. Instead, at the Chatham Theatre near the Five Points, three blackface entertainers (Frank Kent, Dick Pelham, and Billy Whitlock) were reported by the *Sporting Whip* to have been appearing nightly in enthusiastically received full shows. The next issue of the *Sporting Whip* made it clear that what was afoot was the formation of the first blackface musical ensemble, a turning point in the history of blackface minstrelsy. The band, which had clearly been performing together for some time, was identified by name two days later in the pages of the *New York Herald*.

> *First Night of the novel, grotesque, original and surpassingly melodious ethiopian band, entitled the VIRGINIA MINSTRELS. Being an* exclusively musical entertainment, *combining the banjo, violin, bone castanetts, and tambourine....*

With these strokes, there on the Bowery the blackface minstrel show was born. The world's popular music and culture would never be remotely the same.[21]

Meighan knew the members of the Virginia Minstrels and followed them closely in his columns. He wrote that each played "a negro-like instrument" and called their performances entertaining, essentially musical, and highly original. Meighan also broke the news that the Virginia Minstrels were soon to depart for a tour of England. He was also critical of new minstrel bands that sprang up soon after the original's success, scattered saplings that would soon grow into a forest.[22]

Meighan continued to report on the Virginia Minstrels until mid-March 1843 when he pleaded guilty in the Court of General Sessions to editing the *Sporting Whip*, which had been determined by the court to be an obscene paper. With that, the *Sporting Whip* ceased publication and another window into the life and music of New York's underworld was shut. Meighan's interest in music and the popular theater was long-lasting, however. Later in life, he even tried his hand at songwriting and playwriting, and for a while in the 1850s he managed the Bowery Theatre.[23]

The Virginia Minstrels did indeed travel to England with their blackface extravaganza, as Thomas D. Rice had done with his blackface "Jim Crow" in 1836. When they departed for their six-month tour

The Virginia Minstrels. *Detail from "The Celebrated Negro Melodies, as Sung by the Virginia Minstrels . . ." [sheet music] (Boston: Geo. P. Reed, 1843). Lithograph by Thayer & Co. From the Sheet Music Collections of the Center for Popular Music, Middle Tennessee State University, Murfreesboro, Tennessee.*

on April 21, 1843, they took with them an agent to manage contacts, contracts, and arrangements. That person, surely a friend of theirs, had been an editorial colleague of Meighan, Wilkes, and Snelling. He had operated saloons and hotels that were thought to be assignation houses; he had been rumored to consort with prostitutes; he had an extensive court record and a modest jail record; and he had been indicted for libel less than a month earlier (thus giving him yet more reason to skip the country). The fifth member of the époque-making Virginia Minstrels was their appointed agent, George B. Wooldridge, Dixon's old pal.[24]

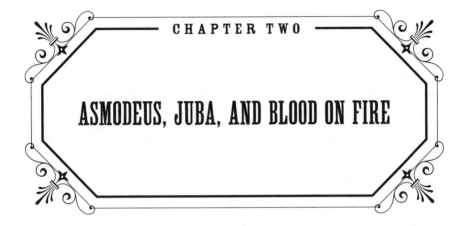

CHAPTER TWO

ASMODEUS, JUBA, AND BLOOD ON FIRE

ALMOST FOUR MONTHS before George Wooldridge published "Dance on Long Wharf," a much better-known writer marveled at a New York tableau that also featured wild dancing, minstrel music, race, class, and the bad side of town. Charles Dickens had arrived in Boston early in 1842, looking to tour the United States and observe and write about its institutions, culture, and citizens. Already famous, he was by then the author of *The Pickwick Papers*, *Oliver Twist*, and *Nicholas Nickleby*. After visiting Boston, he journeyed to New York City, arriving on February 13. There he was greeted by adoring and enthusiastic fans, attention that Dickens soon resented. After more than two weeks of constant feting, he managed to shake the throng and ventured downtown to experience firsthand unalloyed American culture.[1]

Like McDowall and Crockett, Dickens targeted the Five Points. Once there, he encountered a string of cellar dance halls that extended for several blocks, nearly all of similar design. Red bombazine curtains hung over windows and walls and ceilings were whitewashed; benches ran down the sides of halls leaving space in the middle for a sanded dance floor; a bar typically occupied a corner, from which the keeper served beer, porter, and spirits; sailors, firemen, and other working men mingled and danced with women of suspect virtue.

Music beckoned from every Five Points dance hall, with the virtuosic strains from the fiddle of Jack Ballagher ("the black musical wonder") worth the highest fee-per-dance. Among dancers, the Inyard brothers were especially venerated; a contest with rival breakdown dancers could empty all the other "terpsichorean cribs." In addition to dancing, Five Points merrymakers enjoyed comic songs by entertainers, one with the stage name "Jerry Go Nimble." Tom Parsons could rap out lyrics on the spot, rhyming on topical issues and the names of local people. There were also tumblers, jugglers, a "blind man, with a clarionette," a Scotsman with his kilt and bagpipes, and a "dark-skinned Savoyard" organ-grinder, with requisite monkey, who, for those with coin, would grind out "Moll Brooks," "Fisher's Hornpipe," or a favorite waltz of the day. Ballads of the sea, like "Black-Eyed Susan," "Will, the Wild Rover," and "Bay of Biscay," washed out of windows and doors.[2]

Details of Dickens's excursion were published in a *Whip* article by Wooldridge. Readers learned that "Boz" (a nom de plume used by Dickens) turned off Anthony Street, screwed up his courage, and negotiated his way down sets of crazy, tottering stairs. Below street level, he and his small party entered a dance-hall-cum-brothel frequented by blacks, "a wolfish den, where neither ray of light nor breath of air appear[ed] to come." Dickens first stumbled on a pile of rags that, upon closer inspection, turned out to be men and women entwined together and asleep. Appalled at all he saw, he observed that debauchery seemed to have aged the very buildings, which sagged with rotten beams and cracked and broken windows.[3]

After visiting other dens on Anthony Street, Dickens retraced his steps to the intersection of streets that gave name to the Five Points and turned up Orange Street. Braving deep street mud, he passed by yet more cellars filled with dancers and gamblers. At one point, Dickens entered Almack's dance hall, managed by a fellow named Frazer, and was there greeted with a performance of "de Boz Quadrille," a fiddle tune then gathering some interest in New York's underground musical life. The crowd there also danced to "Sich a Gittin' Upstairs" and "Jim Along Josey," to Boz's full amusement. From Almack's, Dickens and his group proceeded on to Roache's, another Orange Street dance hall, where the Englishman delighted in seeing blacks dance "Scotch reels and breakdowns." To close the evening, they took a dark footpath to a joint located at the end of the Cow Bay cul-de-sac, near the corner of Orange and Leonard Streets. There, Dickens took in the scene at the Diving Belle, a dance hall owned by Pete Williams, a black man, which was patronized largely by "genteel negroes." The *Whip* reported that Dickens danced with prostitute Amanda Flagrant until the wee closing hour, but, as a married man, he refused entreaties to revel what remained of the night in the embraces of Julia Simms, Amanda Brown, or Clarissa Brown, three notables among a large group of willing paramours.[4]

When Dickens published his American travelogue in late 1842, which he titled *American Notes*, he conflated the stops on his Five Points slumming expedition. He mentioned only a visit to Almack's, likely a choice intended for the droll effect it would have on English readers who knew that the original Almack's was a high-society social club in London. But the picture Dickens painted of the American Almack's was actually more like the one he found in the Diving Belle. He wrote of the musicians he heard there, principally a fat, black fiddler (Ballagher?) and a fellow musician who played the tambourine, information omitted in Wooldridge's account of the jaunt. Significantly, Dickens paid much more attention to the dancing than Wooldridge. Boz recorded that the crowd called out for a breakdown, and a half-dozen couples rushed to the floor. But then they hesitated since the dancing party was not yet complete, for seated on the bench still was a young, black dancer, allegedly the greatest known. As he rose in his own good time and took to the floor, the dancers rejoiced and the fiddler grinned and played with extra spirit and energy. Even the candles seemed to shine more brightly as the great one began to dance.

Single shuffle, double shuffle, cut and cross-cut; snapping his fingers, rolling his eyes, turning in his knees, presenting the backs of his legs in front, spinning about on his toes and heels like nothing but the man's fingers on the tambourine; dancing with two left legs, two right legs, two wooden legs, two wire legs, two spring legs—all sorts of legs and no legs—what is this to him?

Then, after his "dance of life," he leapt on the bar, laughed the laugh of a million "counterfeit Jim Crows," and ordered a drink.[5]

The dancer was William Henry Lane, known all around New York as simply "Juba." But "Juba" was not just the name of a dancer, for the word also signified a high-stepping, explosive style of black dancing and the music that accompanied it. Juba dancers were common on the minstrel stage of the early 1840s, nearly all of them white men in blackface. A staged dance-off in February 1840 between two blackface juba dancers—John Diamond ("The King of Darkies") and Dick Pelham (who would later become one of the original members of the Virginia Minstrels)—featured minstrel tunes "chawed up" in juba style. Vauxhall Gardens in September 1841 headlined two juba dance-offs, one between Master Miles ("The Catherine Market Rattler") and Mr. Consent ("The Long Island Screamer") and the other between Master P. Keenan ("The Fulton Market Screamer") and Mr. J. Greene ("The Fireman"). As was the case in the competition between Nance and Susan on Long Wharf, the music consisted of minstrel tunes—"Sich a Gittin' Upstairs," "Jim Crow," "Camptown Hornpipe"—many of the same that Dickens heard in the Diving Belle.[6]

Lane was not the first to use Juba as his cognomen. Lewis Davis, a black man who traveled widely "dancing negro extravaganzas, breakdowns, &c., accompanying himself on the guitar," appeared years earlier as "Master Juber." Davis also claimed to be the teacher of John Diamond, the white man who was supposedly discovered by black fiddler Jack Ballagher. According to an anonymous letter published in the *Sunday Flash* in 1841, Lane took over the name in 1840 when a young P. T. Barnum became his manager and put him on the Vaux-hall Gardens stage as a *blackface* dancer (that is, as a black man wearing blackface). To compound and complicate the inversions, in 1841 Barnum advertised Lane as "John Diamond," meaning that Lane was a black man pretending to be a white man pretending to be a black man. To be at the Five Points or even on the minstrel stage at that

"'Juba,' at Vauxhall Gardens [in London]." *Image from* Illustrated London News, *August 5, 1848. TS 952.2., Houghton Library, Harvard University.*

time was to be in a world where the line between black and white was not always clear. "Counterfeit Jim Crows" indeed![7]

⁂

The rendering by the famous Boz brought the Cow Bay notoriety. A petition was even circulated shortly after the publication of *American Notes* to change the name of the cul-de-sac to Dickens Place. Although that notion seems not to have succeeded, by 1845 the Diving Belle had taken on the name, at least informally. Pete Williams, the proprietor, himself became a celebrity thanks to Dickens and assumed many of the airs to match. Ned Buntline, perhaps the era's most popular pulp-novel author, depicted Williams as something of a Zip Coon figure—a black man wearing a plaid waistcoat and an ostentatious cravat, "one of the upper-ten of darky-dom." By the end of the decade, just about anyone wanting to find music and dance among the downtrodden had to head to the Five Points and seek out Pete Williams and his Dickens' Place.[8]

Neither Dickens, Wooldridge, nor Buntline provided more colorful, richly detailed descriptions of the music and dance in and near Dickens' Place than George Goodrich Foster. Born around 1814, perhaps in Vermont or upstate New York, he early fancied himself as some combination of poet, musician, and writer. At times in his life, Foster seems to have aspired toward each of these professions, but finally settled on the (marginal) security afforded a newspaper reporter. Well-read if not perhaps well-educated, he was an urbane writer (with a tendency toward verbosity), a fine literary critic, a published poet, and an insightful observer of New York society. He would also go on to publish an edition of Percy Bysshe Shelley's poetry, edit humor magazines, write books about the 1848 French Revolution and the California gold rush, succeed Edgar Allan Poe as the literary editor at the highly regarded *Graham's Lady's and Gentleman's Magazine*, and compile and edit a *Memoir of Jenny Lind*, the Swedish singer who commanded the full attention of the nation during her Barnum-managed tour of 1850.[9]

Around 1848 Foster was hired at Horace Greeley's *New York Tri-*

bune and assigned primary responsibility for reporting on the city's colorful people and places. The resulting columns, titled "New York in Slices," proved immensely popular. Foster wasted little time in compiling some of his best articles into a book with the column's title, and issued it in an initial run of twenty thousand copies.

Foster acknowledged the draw of the upper crust early in his book, for neither the "beggar's den nor the murderer's cell could vomit forth ghastlier agonies than stalk through the magnificent saloons, and hide behind the silken curtains where gather Fashion's sparkling throng." Reluctantly, though, he turned his pen away from New York's elite and headed out to measure "poverty, misery, beggary, starvation, crime, filth, and licentiousness" among the people whose labor ran the city, "whose brows sweat, and whose muscles ache with the toil which all ought to share." Once among the underclass, his writing acquired special piquancy, for he appears to have known intimately and cared deeply about the people who lived in New York's underworld. He was later to be condescendingly eulogized by the *New York Times* as essentially one of them, a bohemian "hopelessly loose and uncertain."[10]

Foster painted a dark but not patronizing picture of life among his people, which he counted as the ten thousand prostitutes, the seventy thousand paupers, the chain gangs in the city's prison on Blackwell's Island, and the others in New York's underclasses. To cap his reportage, there was the inevitable plunge into the Five Points with its extravagant mix of people. Foster, like others, did not turn a blind eye to the area's squalid buildings and desperate lives. He described one basement cellar in which he was hit first by the stench of cheap drink, stale tobacco, and unwashed bodies, but then, characteristically, saw too a spark of life-affirming joy.

The room looks like a large, dimly-lighted cavern. On a barrel by the side of the bar sits an old negro, tuning his fiddle, while the dancers on the floor have just taken their places. Away they go—a fat and shiny blackamore with his arm around the waist of a slight young girl, whose

skin is yet white and fair, but whose painted cheeks and hollow glar-
ing eyes tell how rapidly goes on the work of disease and death. Oppo-
site this couple, a man naked as at the first moment of his birth, whirls
shouting and yelling away with a brutal-looking woman, once evidently
a queenly beauty. . . . Around the sides of the room in bunks, or sitting
upon wooden benches, the remainder of the company wait impatiently
their turn upon the floor—meanwhile drinking and telling obscene anec-
dotes, or singing fragments of ribald songs.

Almost uniquely among his literary cohort, Foster saw these people
able to "forget for a moment their infamy" through the power of music
and dance.[11]

Foster's interest in music and dance was genuine. As a young man
he had made a living as a professional flutist in theater orchestras. In
addition to his work on Jenny Lind's *Memoir,* his knowledge of music
qualified him to write music criticism for New York newspapers on
subject matter spanning from the minstrel show to opera. Involvement
in the music scene likely factored into his marriage in 1855 to Julie de
Marguerittes, an aspiring opera singer and music critic/historian. (One
of Marguerittes's notable ventures was her edition of composer Felix
Mendelssohn's letters, which she published in 1863.) Marguerittes was
also a playwright and author, who in her sentimental novel, *The Match-*
Girl, used Foster as a model for the handsome newspaper editor, Harry
Rushton—a dynamo endowed with a poetic sensibility and a deep,
abiding love for music. More than perhaps any other chronicler of the
time, when Foster wrote on the music of working people he brought
firsthand experience and compassionate understanding.[12]

The success of *New York in Slices* prompted Foster to publish a
sequel in 1850. *New York by Gas-Light: With Here and There a Streak of*
Sunshine proved even more successful, with claimed sales of upwards of
two hundred thousand copies. Again Foster began uptown, and again
he abandoned that foray for "The Points at Midnight," where "bare-
headed, bare-armed, and bare-bosomed" ladies congregated to drink,

dance, and sell their charms to sailors, negroes, and loafers. A detailed report from one such cellar counted four females on the dance floor, two of them black, while the two white women partnered with "shiny buck negroes." Conventional ballroom attire was apparently not mandatory, for one black female was in her chemise and one of the white women completely naked. In order to take part in the dance, partners roused themselves from their lovemaking on the bunks alongside the room, but did not bother with dressing. Once upright and on the dance floor, they became furious with excitement and spun about and around each other in such profusion that it became difficult to tell one dancer from the other. By the end of the first set, a dancer:

> *feels his blood on fire—all his brutal appetites are aroused, and he is ready for anything. . . . More drinking is proposed—then more dancing—then drink, and so on, until the poor victim loses what little human sense and precaution he is endowed withal, and hurries his partner off in a paroxysm of drunken lust.*

The result was often a pile of bodies "amid such yells, screams and laughter as would mock the saturnalia of hell."[13]

The pull of Pete Williams's place was irresistible to Foster, but it was not simply the drinking and dancing and sex; it was more the music. On a Saturday night, the orchestra consisted of a black fiddler, a trumpeter, and a drummer.

> *[Y]ou may imagine that the music at Dickens' Place is of no ordinary kind. You cannot, however, begin to imagine what it is. You cannot see the red-hot knitting-needles spirited out by the red-faced trumpeter, who looks precisely as if he were blowing glass, which needles aforesaid penetrating the tympanum, pierce through and through your brain without remorse. Nor can you perceive the frightful mechanical contortions of the bass-drummer as he sweats and deals his blows on every side, in all violation of the laws of rhythm, like a man beating a balky mule*

and showering his blows upon the unfortunate animal, now on this side,
now on that.

The dancing reflected the red-hot music-making. To the minstrel
tune "Cooney in de Holler," each gentleman flung his arms around
"his buxom inamorata and salute[d] her whisky-breathing lips with a
chaste kiss, which extract[ed] a scream of delight from the delicate
creature, something between the whoop of an Indian and the neighing
of a horse." They danced; excitement grew; and the dancing became
more inventive, imaginative, and ultimately outrageous. Soon conventional dance steps were ignored altogether and everyone "leaps, stamps,
screams and hurras on his or her own hook." The dancers whirled about
in maddening fashion and finally ended in a disorderly, sweaty heap.
Afterward, some headed to the bar and others to a door in the corner
of the dance hall, which led to a room that served the purposes of
"committee-room, dressing-and-shawl-room, banquet-hall, and some
others of which the muse says nothing."[14]

Surely Foster exaggerated some in his writings. Yet he brought
firsthand experience and knowledge to the reporter's pen. Even dull-
ing his observations a bit still reveals a New York underworld in which
legions of lower-class blacks and whites danced madly to wild music-
making in the search for joy and escape.

Charles G. Foster died a young man in 1856, shortly after mar-
rying de Marguerittes (and after serving a stint in the penitentiary
for forging checks). His obituaries pointed both to his excesses—"the
worthlessness of a brilliant talent unguided by moral purpose"—and
to his better traits—"generous, impulsive, and sensitive qualities which
unfitted him to battle successfully with the world. . . . We admired his
talents and loved his generous heart." History was the loser with Foster's untimely death, for it was denied a rare and articulate observer of
an often ignored, but obviously vibrant, gaslit underworld.[15]

Dixon, Wooldridge, Dickens, Buntline, and Foster were all, in effect if not in name, agents of an ancient but then newly ascendant prince of the underworld: Asmodeus, the demon king of lust. Originated by the Persian Zoroastrians, Asmodeus was adopted early into Jewish and Christian religious narratives. At first wrathful, he was later transformed into a mischievous, joker-like character, with a special talent for exposing the hidden, often salacious lives of the misbehaving by literally peeling back roofs and opening iniquities to public display. By the early nineteenth century he had been fully reconstituted and redeployed. Washington Irving referred to him as did the best-selling British author Edward Bulwer-Lytton, who with his *Asmodeus at Large* (1833) popularly affirmed Asmodeus as one who could magically expose the "mystery that hangs over every house." Of course, Rev. McDowall—an exact contemporary of Irving and Bulwer-Lytton— would have strenuously denied that he was following in the course of a demon king of lust, yet he too felt the era's new license to gape into the dark corners of human experience and presume to illuminate what he found there.[16]

Asmodeus's standing rose further in the 1840s. Alain René Le Sage's 1707 novel, *Asmodeus; or, The Devil on Two Sticks*, was published in English in 1841 and widely read in the United States. That was also the year after *Asmodeus in New York; or, The Devil's Diary* began playing at Mitchell's Olympic Theatre on Broadway. "Something like a French vaudeville," it spoofed manners and customs in the city, made satirical jabs at the era's pretentions, and skewered the high and powerful. On the stage for several years, *Asmodeus in New York* was showing the month Dickens was in New York and he might well have enjoyed seeing it.[17]

Author Harrison Gray Buchanan took up the name of the demon in his 1848 *Asmodeus or, Legends of New York; Being a Complete Exposé of the Mysteries, Vices and Doings, as Exhibited by the Fashionable Circles of New York*. True to his title, Buchanan figuratively peeled back the roofs of brothels, named some of the women who worked there, and hinted broadly at the names of their customers. In that same

Asmodeus. *Image from Alain René Le Sage,* Asmodeus; or, The Devil on Two Sticks *(London: Joseph Thomas, 1841).*

year, "Tom Pepper" (a pseudonym of the journalist Charles Frederick Briggs) offered to the public his *Asmodeus; or, The Iniquities of New York*. Briggs's Asmodeus claimed to have counted twenty thousand prostitutes in the city, fifteen hundred brothels, and two thousand saloons where prostitutes gathered. After reproaching prostitution, Briggs then went after the women who modeled for artists in the nude, to him a sure sign of degeneracy and imminent downfall. His proof included a titillating engraving of a nude model, one who was clearly on the road to perdition.[18]

In 1849, George Thompson, who along with Buntline defined the pulp-novel genre in that time, published his sensationalist exposé, *New-York Life*, the first chapter of which was titled "Asmodeus." In the book's first paragraph, he names Asmodeus as the one who has guided the pens of those who would tell of society's crimes, vice, and moral turpitude. That Asmodeus pursued his intentions while wearing an impish grin partly explained his attraction to Thompson; reform of the debauched and wicked was nominally the book's goal, but the pleasure taken in mocking laughter was just as important. Thompson was so beguiled by the demon king that he was likely the "Asmodeus" who authored *Sharps and Flats; or the Perils of City Life* (1850) and *The Lame Devil, or Asmodeus in Boston* (ca. 1851). Given his abiding interest in the demon and in the affairs of Boston, he might too have been behind the Asmodeus who wrote *The Jenny Lind Mania in Boston, or A Sequel to Barnum's Parnassus*. Bibliographers, however, have thought that this Asmodeus—"king of the regions of song, prince of darkness, Satanic majesty, and grand generalissimo of humbugs"—was more likely Thaddeus W. Meighan, Dixon's former comrade-in-arms from the sporting newspaper days.[19]

The spirit of Asmodeus was seemingly everywhere at midcentury. Initially the Asmodeans focused on mansion roofs and set out to expose the "aristocracy of iniquity, the exclusivism of vice, the upper crust of wickedness, the *bon ton* of profligacy." But public interest in revelations about New York's elite was peaking and would soon fall largely out of fashion. A phalanx of writers, reporters, poets, artists, and social scientists who chronicled New York life quickly pivoted to the roofs under which the "lower million" lived, where they saw and reported on the sordid grittiness of their lives, but where they found as well a vein of creativity, imagination, and energy.[20]

⬥

"Unscrew the locks from the doors! Unscrew the doors themselves from their jambs!" commanded the Asmodean Walt Whitman in his epic poem "Song of Myself" (1855). Whitman expressed boldly for all the world to hear that to be truly unroofed and unveiled was to be joined together in and with full humanity—"every atom belonging to me as good belongs to you." Those atoms included earth and rock and metal and leaves of grass, but were just as much of all things carnal— "Turbulent, fleshy, sensual, eating, drinking and breeding." "I am the poet of the Body and I am the poet of the Soul," blazoned the poet.

Whitman—"a kosmos, of Manhattan the son"—throughout much of his early career earned his livelihood in the newspaper business, which as a trade typically involved some roof peeling. As a young man he had even enjoyed an oblique connection with the Dixon cohort when he served as editorial associate to William Snelling at the *Sunday Times*. Shortly after the publication of *Leaves of Grass* in 1855, Whitman returned to the newsroom as an editor of the *Brooklyn Daily Times* (and as its sometime music critic). One of his first editorial columns there concerned prostitution, but from a perspective foretold in "Song of Myself." He acknowledged how commonplace prostitution was in parts of Manhattan—Canal Street, Greenwich Street, the Five Points, even everywhere. He believed prostitution was so endemic and so ingrained in the city's social fabric that:

> *the plain truth is that nineteen out of twenty of the mass of American young men, who live in or visit the great cities, are more or less familiar with houses of prostitution and are customers to them. . . . [T]he custom is to go among prostitutes as an ordinary thing. Nothing is thought of it—or rather the wonder is, how there can be any "fun" without it.*

To Whitman, the reason this staggering assertion was not ready knowledge had most to do with the refusal of "respectable society" (his term) to talk about it or even acknowledge it. The issue for Whitman was not that commercialized sex had become such a big business, but rather that ignoring it led necessarily to disease among prostitutes and their clients. Much better in his view to accept prostitution as a fact and provide a public health program to ensure hygienic conditions for all. Instead of continuing to cloak sexuality in dark mystery, he called for an unroofed, candid, public discourse on sexuality and the full education of young men and women on all matters sexual.[21]

Some of Whitman's call was met in 1858 when Dr. William Sanger published his 685-page *The History of Prostitution: Its Extent, Causes and Effects Throughout the World*. The first part of Sanger's monumental study surveyed prostitution from ancient times up to contemporaneous practices in Europe, Central and South America, and in areas of the less-developed world. His overview showed that New York was not alone among major Western cities in having a burgeoning prostitution industry. Females found in the celebrated dancing saloons of Hamburg, for example, were mostly prostitutes. To Sanger, Berlin saloons and lower-class dance halls fed bacchanalian excess, with their wild, energetic dancing supported by "ear-splitting music in a pestilential atmosphere."[22]

The last third of his book, though, is devoted exclusively to prostitution in New York City. Sanger held the resident physician position at the prison on Blackwell's Island and observed a steady stream of prostitutes through the gates. Obviously interested in their lives, he developed an extensive questionnaire of forty-nine questions that was administered to two thousand prostitutes (all apparently white). Tabulation, analysis, and annotation of the data formed an important core of his book. Sanger's survey disclosed that half of those interviewed were between eighteen and twenty-three years of age; that 762 were born in the United States and 706 in Ireland; that one-quarter were illiterate; that three-quarters were single or widowed; that half had had children; that three-quarters had been prostitutes for a year or more (with one having been in the trade for thirty-five years); that nearly half had venereal disease; that one-quarter had become prostitutes out of "inclination"; that half admitted to drinking too much; and that religious backgrounds were equally divided between Protestant and Catholic.

Sanger also studied the different social standings of prostitutes in

New York. Among the "first-class" were those found in parlor houses. There the furnishings were lavish and inevitably included a piano "upon which some professed player is paid a liberal salary to perform." The house would be occupied by three to ten women, some well-educated, and among them would typically be accomplished musicians and artists. Sanger estimated the minimum weekly profit for the madam of a first-class parlor house of ten women to be more than six hundred dollars (about fifteen thousand dollars today).[23]

Sanger paid special attention to prostitution in the German parts of the city, which gathered in and around the First Ward at the southern tip of the island. There were to be found lower-class brothels, in which a piano was usually available for performances of German songs. Prostitution also flourished in dance halls patronized by German immigrants. The main room was the ballroom, where a pianist and violinist played waltzes and polkas and were paid through an "appeal to the charitable for assistance" (i.e., the tip jar was in plain sight).[24]

In contrast to the somewhat orderly nature of German dance halls, places on the Lower East Side patronized by the Irish were riotous. There, women dressed provocatively, many in scandalous bloomers, and danced to music made by musicians who played fiddles, banjos, and tambourines. These musicians, in Sanger's view, compensated for their lack of formal training through "vigorous execution."[25]

Sanger did not shy away from putting numbers on prostitution's profile in New York. He calculated that the capital invested in the commercialized sex industry was four million dollars. He figured there were 80 first-class brothels in New York in 1858, 100 second-class houses, 120 third-class, and 78 fourth-class, and that there were 151 dancing saloons associated with prostitution. Furthermore, the money paid to prostitutes and to houses of assignation, along with that spent in dance halls frequented by prostitutes and for liquor in support of prostitution, made commercialized sex the second-largest industry in New York, barely behind textile manufacturing. His realistic estimate that there were six thousand prostitutes in a city of about seven hundred thousand people led him to produce a conservative ratio of one prostitute for every fifty-two males. Another projection led him to conclude that *only* half of the males in New York "have commerce with prostitutes."[26]

Sanger's data also enable some reasonably confident grip on the number of musicians working in the industry. Figure a musician was regularly employed in all of New York's eighty first-class brothels (and none in lower-ranking brothels) and that two musicians worked daily in each of the 151 dance halls. Factored, those numbers yield (very) conservatively about four hundred musicians. The 1860 census counted 1,590 professional musicians in the entire state of New York. At least a quarter of those would appear to have worked in the underground and illegal prostitution business in Manhattan alone.

Prostitution in midcentury New York was an obvious, even accepted, part of the urban landscape. The disciples of Asmodeus revealed it to be big by any measure. Somewhat unintentionally, those chroniclers also opened to display a city filled with wild music pouring out of brothels, saloons, and dance halls made by hundreds of unschooled musicians who were tasked with the primary job of setting "blood on fire." What those musicians produced was an explosive compound of sounds and rhythms that would prove quite impossible to extinguish.

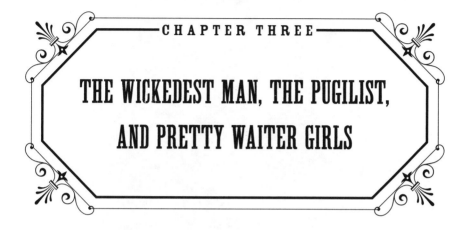

CHAPTER THREE

THE WICKEDEST MAN, THE PUGILIST, AND PRETTY WAITER GIRLS

IN 1868 JOHN ALLEN was about forty-five years old, allegedly worth more than seventy thousand dollars, happily married, and a proud father, especially of his precocious five-year-old son Chester. He had three brothers who were ministers, and a persistent rumor held that Allen himself had once taken the cloth, a story easy to believe for he was an articulate and educated man. Despite his list of seeming virtues, he was singled out in July by *Packard's Monthly* as "The Wickedest Man in New York." Reporter Oliver Dyer, in his new column titled "The Shady Side of Metropolitan Life," made the claim for Allen's supreme infamy by noting that he ran a bar, a dance hall, and an exchange for prostitutes out of his house at 304 Water Street, and, to Dyer, Allen's better qualities were the base issue, for "the best bad is always the worst."

Dyer and companions had visited Allen's place before writing the article and found it at full volume. Thirteen women were in the saloon that evening, seven of whom danced energetically with male partners to music provided by a three-piece band. Allen himself was animated, obviously enjoying the attention and the swirl. To impress his learned guests, Allen sent one of the prostitutes upstairs to retrieve Chester.

"John Allen, the 'Wickedest Man,' and His Son Chester."
Engraving by Stanley Fox, from Harper's Weekly, *August 8,
1868.*

The sleepy-eyed prodigy then demonstrated his preternatural knowledge of ancient history, geography, politics, and more, to Dyer's amaze-
ment. Chester followed with a song, danced (to the manifest delight of
his mother), and recited the Lord's Prayer, all to a counterpoint of lewd
jokes and coarse language from his father.

After the exhibition, Dyer refused Allen's encouragements to dance
with the women and instead sang a hymn, to which at least six of the
prostitutes joined their voices. Astonished that the dance-hall girls
had religious training, Dyer's friends then suggested holding a prayer
meeting in the saloon. The Wickedest Man considered the request but
refused it. His reasoning was that his regard for education, knowledge,
and an openness to hymn-singing already had neighbors thinking him
somewhat unstable, even deranged. If a prayer meeting were to be held

in his dance hall, Allen feared that he might "lose what little character I've got left."[1]

Dyer's piece set off intense public interest, with magazines, newspapers, ministers, and the general public flocking to Allen's place. An unnamed reporter for *Harper's Weekly* was part of that rush. He subsequently published "The 'Wickedest Man' As He Is" in the Saturday, August 8, 1868, issue and in the process countered some parts of Dyer's narrative. Whereas Dyer, for instance, claimed that Allen was especially wicked, *Harper's* retorted that he was simply trying to make a living for his family by providing a service to the community. Allen did not disagree with this point.

We try to entertain each man in the way he likes best; if a minister comes, we can sing hymns with him, and he can hear Chester say his Catechism; but we've got liquor, and there's the women for them as has the stamps [i.e., folding money] to spend that way.

But he did admit to *Harper's* that Dyer had hit a mark.

[T]he business is ruined. I'm overrun by people that come here to look at me, as if I was a wild beast. They bore me to death, and don't spend any money. I have to see hundreds of them a day.[2]

Harper's subscribers expected quality illustrative material. Stanley Fox, one of the popular weekly's best artists, had accompanied the reporter to the dance hall, sketchbook in hand. Allen even extended to him a special invitation to return and make more sketches, and instructed him to "bring plenty of stamps" for the women. Fox did return (although it is not clear if he also brought stamps), and three engravings resulted from his visits. One was a full-sheet illustration of "Sunday Morning in the Fourth Ward, New York," picturing languid citizens lolling about on the sidewalks of Water Street in front of two taverns; sailors smoked while several barefooted urchins looked for trouble, one by prodding a rat with a stick. Another was a portrait of a stoic Allen and a bright-faced Chester. The last was of the dance-hall interior and showed energetic dancing to the sound of fiddle, flute, and double bass. In the deepest back center of this engraving, next to the musicians, Fox drew in an isolated, mysterious, Asmodeus-like character, absorbing what the lower classes did to enjoy themselves at night in a Water Street den.[3]

A follow-up article by Dyer was devoted to ongoing efforts to lead the prostitutes in Allen's saloon away from their sinful ways and to convince Allen to give up the business. Proselytizers eventually claimed to get a promise from Allen that he would change his life's course on "moving day" (traditionally May 1) the following year. But events moved faster than planned and at midnight on Saturday, August 29, 1868, a note was posted at 304 Water Street:

THIS DANCE-HOUSE IS CLOSED!
NO GENTLEMEN ADMITTED UNLESS ACCOMPANIED BY THEIR WIVES
WHO WISH TO EMPLOY MAGDALENS AS DOMESTICS.
John Allen

A half hour after midnight, the dance hall was the site for a prayer meeting attended by clergymen, Dyer, Allen, his family, and many of the now-unemployed dance-hall girls. Dyer soon reported that Allen's dance hall was hosting daily prayer meetings and that the Wickedest Man's conversion had prompted a religious revival that was sweeping through Water Street, saving many a lost soul from everlasting damnation. Huzzahs and hallelujahs resounded from the pages of New York newspapers.[4]

But the conversions of the wicked on Water Street turned out to be a ruse. The *New York Times* reported in late September that Allen's redemption was for show, and that instead of freely volunteering the use of his hall for the purposes of salvation, he had been encouraged along the path of righteousness by a payment of $350. The *Brooklyn Daily Eagle* in October quoted the superintendent of New York City Missions to the effect that not twenty people from the Water Street

"The Dance-Hall at the 'Wickedest Man's' House." *Engraving by Stanley Fox, from* Harper's Weekly, *August 8, 1868.*

district attended any of the dance-hall prayer meetings. "Yet the meetings were crowded—by well-dressed, well-fed, clean, and respectable people from the decent sections of the city."[5]

Allen soon sold 304 Water Street. But the business was in his blood and he afterward attempted (unsuccessfully) to open another dance hall. He also tried to capitalize on his celebrity by going on the lecture circuit. That too failed. Within two years of the exposé the Wickedest Man was dead, leaving little Chester and his family a handsome fortune.[6]

❖

Allen's dance hall was not likely the worst "specimen of Pandemonium" (as writer Matthew Hale Smith described the type). But Allen's plight directed wide public attention toward dance-hall culture. Accounts, for example, showed that 1860s dance halls had changed significantly since the 1840s. Smith noted that the women in Allen's dance hall were now "mostly foreigners," presumably the result of the surge in Irish emigration to America after the potato blight. Fashions changed too, of course, and poor dance-hall girls attempted to dress in something like that day's latest.

> *Immense "waterfalls," made apparently of horses' tails, sit like poultices on the napes of their necks. These appendages are profusely decorated with faded ribbons and sown all over with spangles. Short skirts, frequently of bright tartan patterns, appear to be quite the thing here, showing a good deal of soiled petticoat and cotton stockings. Some of the women have little bells attached to their boots or the bottom of their skirts, which make a wild, savage jingle when they dance.*

But the main difference between dance halls of the 1860s and those of decades before might have been in the music, which was now typically made by larger bands. Dance-hall "orchestras" in Allen's time sometimes included as many as six musicians, although on an average night there might be no more than three. Given the number of Water Street dance halls—Dyer estimated that there were forty of them—there must have been regular employment in them for several hundred musicians. Fiddles, often described as "wheezy," were the melodic instruments of choice in practically all. Nearly as common and more important for establishing and maintaining dance rhythms were tambourines. One "genius" reportedly had such love for his instrument that between sets he caressed it, held it close to his ear, and produced constant, soft purring sounds. A surprisingly large number of reports also placed a string bass in the dance band. The musicians were all practiced and skilled in setting the pace for the evening's fun, with energetic rhythms feeding the joys of the dance, which was most commonly a Virginia reel—"Later in the evening, the reelers will reel more than ever: this many a reel in every bottle."[7]

Despite John Allen's shuttered hall and the push by the evangelicals to convert the Water Street sinners, the New York dance-hall scene was not even close to a state of decline. Indeed, the dance hall would flourish as a nexus of drinking, music, dance, and sex well into the twentieth century.

⁂

But there was competition from a new institution in town, one that would fuel important new directions in music-making: the concert saloon.

The name itself hints at much of the story. At a time when safe, potable water was not always available, the nation's citizens downed vast amounts of cider, beer, wine, and ardent spirits (made mainly from plentiful corn). Much of that imbibing took place in saloons, which were also, of course, neighborhood gathering places, for conviviality and drink have long been of the same piece.

If a saloon was an old, familiar, and traditional establishment, a concert was something quite new. Before the 1830s in the United States, a concert was to most common people an indulgence associated with the higher classes, one that was generally practiced in some far-away European metropolis. For ordinary Americans, music had *function*: it told stories; it was something that one made; it aided worship; it pacified babies; it was to be danced to. Music was not something one much listened to passively for the sheer pleasure derived from just listening. The Hutchinson Family Singers, a quartet of three brothers and a sister from New Hampshire who were foremost among many such "family" troupes, developed and practiced the revolutionary idea of melding the day's popular music with the concept of the concert. As a result, popular music came to large, middle-class concert audiences in the 1840s, making fortunes for performers and forever changing the nature of the nation's music consumption patterns.[8]

In retrospect, it was almost inevitable that an entrepreneurial genius conceived of programing regular popular music performances in a local drinking establishment. With that stroke, the concert saloon was born.

The term appears to have been first used in the United States around

1849. A. McFarland Jr., manager and proprietor, announced to the citizens of Brooklyn that on February 8 of that year the Military Garden would henceforth be known as the Brooklyn Concert Saloon. In all but name the new place was an old-fashioned "pleasure garden"—an entertainment institution that had been around for more than a century, with open, parklike spaces where people could gather and eat, drink, talk, flirt, and listen to music. Like most pleasure gardens, entrance to the Brooklyn Concert Saloon was not cheap, with twenty-five cents the least-expensive ticket and private boxes at two dollars. The music heard there included "the most popular Songs, Glees, Choruses, Solos, Duetts, Refrains, Dances, Manolas, Polkas, &c." McFarland's choices of the term "concert saloon" and of the sorts of music heard in his establishment would resound loudly in New York's musical history over the next several decades.[9]

By the mid-1850s, a division by musical taste and class governed the respective meanings of "concert saloon" and "garden." Perceiving a trend, Niblo's Garden, a venerable Manhattan pleasure garden, actually split into two establishments during that time. Side by side on Broadway at Prince Street, patrons could choose to enter the door to Niblo's Concert Saloon on one side or the one leading to the Garden on the other side. To give some idea of what that choice entailed, Niblo's Concert Saloon in September 1856 featured Miss Emma Stanley performing her celebrated "Seven Ages of Woman," in which she impersonated twenty-four characters, changed costumes thirty times, and sang twelve songs in seven different languages, all against a backdrop of "An Elegant Boudoir Scene." Next door, Niblo's Garden featured "German Opera Nights" on Tuesdays, Thursdays, and Saturdays.[10]

By 1858, the *New York Times* reported that concert saloons (sometimes called "concert halls") were in vogue all over the city. One of the best-known was Canterbury Hall at 663 Broadway. A large building into which five hundred patrons could fit at a time, it was tastefully decorated with mirrors that lined both sides of the hall, enabling patrons to get three different views of the stage. And there was much to see.

The evening a reporter for the *New York Clipper* attended, he enjoyed a program that included comic songs, Roman gladiators, blackface minstrels, "pole exercises," a trapeze act, a flag dance, a ballerina in revealing tights, and several skits (including "Stocks Up and Stocks Down" by a Bull and a Bear). Programs such as this one quickly acquired the term "variety," for they typically featured a wild mix of music, dance, theater, circus acrobatics, and provocative costumes.[11]

Lower-class drinking establishments soon took on the name "concert saloon" but shrank the show. Proprietors realized that a wide range of expensive entertainment acts was not necessary; a small raised platform in a corner manned by a couple of musicians would do. The new approach worked. Patronage increased when music was scheduled regularly, and an explosion of newly wrought concert saloons hit New York.

The numbers of them varied depending on the source. Matthew Hale Smith tabulated seventy-two concerts saloons "of bad repute" in January 1864, and seventy-five two years later. Another source in 1869 counted as many as six hundred of these "immoral mushrooms." A modern-day scholar has estimated three hundred by the late 1860s, which is in agreement with the number cited in *Women of New York* (1869). In short, there were a lot.[12]

Music and drink gave definition to the concert saloons, but it was the bounty of "pretty waiter girls" that gave them zest. Women serving drinks in New York's public constabularies seems to have been rare until the 1850s. Early in that decade city newspapers first started carrying employment ads for "waiter girls," the demand for which increased yearly. Soon, concert saloons were outdoing one another in claims for the exceptional pulchritudinous qualities found only in their bevy of pretty waiter girls.[13]

Not surprisingly, moralists jumped into the fray with charges that pretty waiter girls were only "unchaste nymphs who pour libations to Venus and Bacchus from the same satyr-shaped chalice." The *New York Times* was less poetic and simply identified waiter girls as streetwalkers who found working indoors more salutary than solicitation out in the elements. Another reporter was equally blunt: concert saloons were "little better than brothels." The women who worked in these places were, according to Smith, not all bad at the start, but few were they who did not fall from grace. In his generous view, the inevitable slide into prostitution was greased by the fact that waiter girls earned only five to fifteen dollars a week, which was barely at subsistence level without supplemental "wages of infamy."[14]

New York's concert saloons soon gathered the full attention of high-minded, middle-class, largely Protestant legislators in Albany. So it was that after several months of weighty deliberation in 1862, a bill to "Regulate Places of Public Amusement" (or, the "Anti-Concert Saloon Bill," as it became popularly known) was passed unanimously by the state legislature. It outlawed "wine, beer or strong or spirituous liquors" in the auditorium, lobby, or any adjacent rooms of a place in New York City that offered a public show (which was broadly defined). Furthermore, proprietors of any place of public amusement were forbidden from simultaneously holding a liquor license and one for entertainment. The law did not ignore the role played by the pretty waiter girls either, and it prohibited any female from waiting on or furnishing drinks to anyone in a public place that also mounted entertainment.[15]

With considerable reluctance, New York's police soon began enforcing the new law by conducting raids on offending concert saloons. Almost immediately concert saloon owners and waiter girls fired back with early shots in what would be called the "Concert Saloon War." With some reason on their side, owners pointed out that licensed drinking establishments, musical/theatrical shows, and waiter girls were, independently, all still fully legal, and wondered where the logic lay in banning them only in combination and only in concert saloons. Mustering more than just words and logic, they planned a legal challenge. A courageous waiter girl volunteered to serve a gentleman a glass of lager in Canterbury Hall, purposefully in full view of the authorities. Arrested, her case was brought before the New York Supreme Court and argued vigorously. Unfortunately for the bill's opponents, the court determined that the law was manifestly constitutional and dismissed the case. Another challenge, brought by concert saloons with a German-immigrant clientele, contended that lager beer (and spruce beer and root beer) did not contain alcohol in enough measure to induce inebriation and thus did not fall under the provisions of the law. This argument was upheld on May 20, 1862, and lager beer was shortly back on the menu in concert saloons—but not to be served by pretty waiter girls.

Resistance in the city to the Anti-Concert Saloon Bill was quiet, steady, and endemic. The police could arrest only a handful of law-breakers at a time, and each raid was mostly a symbolic gesture intended to encourage some measure of respect for the rule of law. Most lawbreakers went unpunished. It did not help that the Civil War was raging and New York City was filled with thirsty, randy soldiers who demanded entertainment. One newspaper even editorialized that the Anti-Concert Saloon Bill would lead to the depopulation of New York as citizens abandoned a city governed by such "foolish laws"; it accused legislators and city fathers of behaving "according to the country-village ideas of hypocritical scruplers."[16]

That legislators with country-village scruples considered concert saloons to be such a danger to civic mores is an indication of a wider culture war over the proper place of sex, drink, and entertainment. And that there was as much, or more, resistance as compliance signaled the strength of a common class that refused to be cowed by scruplers. Unified opposition eventually made the law unenforceable, and, within a year, waiter girls were again serving wine, beer, and spirituous liquors to appreciative, music-loving customers, while the police looked on benignly. The only lasting, significant effect of the Concert Saloon War was that variety shows tended now to be found in theaters, while concert saloons focused more on music.[17]

❖

Writers quickly realized that 1860s concert saloons were colorful social touchstones where morality and culture intersected. Somewhere along

Broadway's great length there was always grist for a literary mill. It helped too that there was such a wide spectrum of concert saloons, from the high to the very low.

At the high end were the German beer gardens in Lower Manhattan, where the entertainment and ambience were thoroughly unobjectionable. The orchestras at places like the Atlantic Garden and the Century tended to be quite large (twelve or so players) and might even be all women. The musicians there were often trained in the German classical tradition and the music they played was an expression of that training.[18]

Large, grandiose, even ostentatious concert saloons on lower Broadway occupied the next rung. One chronicler visited Madame B's Arcade at 564 Broadway and upon entering was directly confronted by a large painting of a nearly nude dancing Venus; next in the line of sight was a Colt revolver with a foot-long barrel hung over the bar within easy reach of the barkeeper. Engravings of women in seductive dishabille adorned all the walls. Once seated, his ale order was taken by twenty-two-year-old Ellen, a pretty waiter girl who was dressed in "great scantiness of clothing" and readily admitted to being a prostitute. At the back of the hall was a raised platform holding an "asthmatic pianoforte" on which a shabbily dressed musician thumped, pausing occasionally to call for his glass to be refilled. He played "The Tune the Old Cow Died On," a song perhaps of Irish origin, and repeated it so often that the reporter wondered if that was the only music he knew. Amorous intrigues fueled by drink swirled throughout, and a room at the rear of the hall was observed to accommodate couples—the lady often veiled—for Madame B's also apparently provided rooms for trysting.[19]

When Henry Llewellyn Williams, author of *Gay Life in New York! or, Fast Men and Grass Widows*, wanted to survey human character "in all its Protean phases," he ventured into one of these Broadway concert saloons. There he noted a characteristic of the music-making that was found throughout New York's underworld. A female singer, tall and slim but rawboned, performed one of the day's popular songs, yet graced it with a set of parody lyrics that were slangy and bawdy. For this the audience awarded her prolonged applause and insisted that she sing another, which was even coarser than the first. Meanwhile, stimulated by the entertainments and the wine and liquor, patrons submitted pretty waiter girls to "huggings, squeezings, and amorous pawings."[20]

At the bottom of the concert-saloon scale were the "flash" establishments—"moral Golgothas." These reportedly loathsome concert saloons were clumped together in the Bowery district, principally on William Street, Chatham Street, along the Bowery, and along the East River waterfront—altogether 283 of them by one report. The joints had names like the Evening Star, Kissing Sun, Eldorado, Sailors' Rest, and Good Havens, and were inevitably below street level in dark cellars that had been partitioned into small booths occupied by the "dangerous classes." Rooms off the main hall were common in which men gambled (illegally) at faro and other games. As the dance halls on the Lower East Side had long drawn slumming voyeurs, so now too did the flash concert saloons. A reporter who used the pseudonym "Asmodeus" wrote that only four or five heavily painted waiter girls, whose clothing tended toward "harem" style, served in these small establishments; a common practice among them was to distribute to patrons suggestive photographs on which assignation addresses had been written. Theft and deceit were constants, as were knives, murder, and "a quarter of a dollar for a genuine Havana cigar made out of Jersey cabbage-leaves." Meanwhile, in the corner, musicians played wheezy flutes, murdered pianos, and squalled out ribald songs, all "vociferously out of tune"—noises that only "a lunatic would mistake for music."[21]

Dancing, though, seems not to have been a regular feature of any class of concert saloon. A chronicle of a late-night visit to the Gaieties on Broadway, near Houston Street, suggested that dancing did sometimes occur, just not when the place was legally open. Those still inside the Gaieties when the doors closed at two A.M. were treated to a private, after-hours party (a then-developing tradition that would extend well into the twentieth century). The proprietor of the Gaieties during public hours preferred his concert saloon filled with tables, each with drinking tabs, but the private after-hours were different, and the tables were pushed to the side to make room for "fast and furious" quadrilles. Waiter girls then transformed into dance partners. Furthermore, the women allegedly maintained rooms in the rooming house immediately adjacent to the Gaieties, a broad hint as to the function of those rooms.[22]

There were a few exceptions to the no-dancing practice during regular hours. "Beautiful Anna"—she with the mole on her left cheek—was the keeper of a flash concert saloon that allowed dancing to the "screeching noise" of a fiddle and a banjo, for example. But by far the best-known concert saloon with regular dancing was Harry Hill's. This heavily patronized, legendary establishment was a hybrid saloon/dance hall and sporting and entertainment center that drew clientele from all ranks of society, a must-not-be-missed stop on every tourist's itinerary: "Strangers, ask any Hotel Clerk, Policeman or Conductor, where Harry Hill's is, and they will direct you. If they don't know, then they are not fit to hold their positions in this great city."[23]

Hill made his name early in New York as a pugilist whose matches often brought him substantial purses. A showman at heart, he also dazzled crowds with his virtuosic juggling of heavily weighted Indian clubs. Around 1854 he entered the saloon business and by 1857 was advertising widely his eponymous saloon. (Pugilists opened dram shops quite frequently; boxer Harry Lazarus, for instance, ran the X-10-U-8 ["Extenuate"] near Harry Hill's on East Houston.) A bold, charismatic man who clearly loved company and a good party, for many years Hill organized and sponsored annual steamer excursions in the waters of New York Bay and Long Island Sound. He and several hundred friends and guests would set out (often with a party barge in tow) for a day of fishing, swimming, dancing, music ("by Robertson's Band"), and a chance for those in the party to hobnob with the sporting stars of the day; ladies without escorts (i.e., prostitutes) were admitted onboard at no charge. The intent (and reality) of these notorious parties was clearly something more than fish. By such means and more, Harry Hill wormed his way into the mythology of nineteenth-century New York.[24]

The location of the hall itself at 25 East Houston, just off Broadway in a property owned by none other than P. T. Barnum, was signaled by a large lantern that shed beguiling light through its red-and-blue glass. Patrons passed straightaway into the saloon of the painted brick building, which was dominated by a long, wooden bar. To enter the dance and entertainment hall, men would continue through to the rear of the saloon and up the stairs after paying an admission fee of twenty-five cents. A separate door from the outside allowed women to bypass the male-only saloon and enter directly into the hall, without the need for a ticket. The dance hall itself had been cobbled together by removing partitions between smaller adjoining rooms, leading to a patchwork of ceiling heights. Pictures covered the walls, none of them indecent or objectionable.

Rules of the house were prominently posted and strict: no obscenity, no drunkenness, and no disorderly behavior, with the pugilist himself serving as the enforcer. Legend had it that Hill once broke up a fracas in which Nellie Smith, a prostitute, knocked down a banjo player. Nellie and friends later returned to the saloon, and the proprietor ended up on the receiving end of a knife wielded by Fanny Kelly, another prostitute. Although Fanny left the knife sticking out of the right side of Hill's face, the attending physician deemed the wound "troublesome but not dangerous," and Hill survived to bounce disorderly prostitutes another day.[25]

Everyone in Harry Hill's had to dance. Patrons were permitted to select their own partner, but if they did not one would be assigned; those who would not dance were asked to leave. The band, typically consisting of a piano, fiddle, and bass, kept the energy level high. After each dance set, drinks were ordered and brought up from the bar below, then the women began a new hunt for a dancing partner (and a client for the night).

"Inside Harry Hill's Dance-House." *Image from Matthew Hale Smith,* Sunshine and Shadow in New York *(Hartford: J. B. Burr and Company, 1868).*

Unlike a typical dance hall, Harry Hill's had a stage, from where comedy of the low "Punch and Judy" type was produced. Songs were also sung from there and "each improper allusion, profane remark, the mention of the name of God, or anything that sneers at piety, or what the religious world calls sacred, are rapturously applauded." Such irreverent behavior obviously crossed the moral constitution of reporter Edward Crapsey, who claimed in the pages of a respected literary magazine to have visited Harry Hill's often enough to know its character. He disdained the place and wrote about it with a pen dipped in bile—"wicked," "debauched," "vile" were only a few of his choice pejoratives. To Crapsey (and in some truth), the women were all prostitutes, violence lurked always just below the surface, bubbling up frequently, and the variety show had few redeeming qualities. But he believed the greatest sin was that Harry Hill's and other such concert saloons held the public "in the corroding cords of vice," promoting "ulcers which [were] destroying the moral life of a million people."[26]

Harry Hill's withstood Crapsey's broadside and others like it and established a model that would be replicated throughout the city. And beyond as well. The American West was opening up at this time, and crowds of cowboys, prospectors, railroad men, hunters, and adventurers favored establishments that offered in one place drink, sex, music, dance, and gambling. The archetypal saloon of the wild, wild West was thus born, and eventually fixed in the American imagination by movies and television. In reality, the Old West saloon was not just any saloon, but a concert saloon, an ideal based on Harry Hill's place, far far from the western frontier.

❖

The development of dance-hall and concert-saloon culture came about during a time in which many elite New Yorkers were asking probing questions about the nature of their nation's music. One such was Wall Street lawyer George Templeton Strong, a passionate amateur musician who for some years served as president of the New York Philharmonic Society. A prolific diarist, Strong left accounts of his day-to-day activities and musings that filled 2,250 pages at his death in 1875. Many of his notations reflected his obsession with music. An entry for December 6, 1856, serves as a sample.

> *Mozart's "Jupiter" Symphony [is] perfectly and transcendently beautiful. No music is beautiful in equal degree with his. Sublimity belongs to Handel. The power of Beethoven is in part due to the presence of an uncanny kind of intensity and power—a mighty spirit seeking rest and finding none. Haydn owes much to the goodness and healthiness and geniality embodied in his best works.*

Strong's words idealizing European composers implied his agreement with a sentiment expressed by *Putnam's Monthly Magazine* in 1854:

"Among civilized nations there is, probably, none so little musical as the American." Strong and *Putnam's* were not alone. A whole school of thought found nothing of transcendent beauty in any American music and set out on a project to sacralize the classical music experience through performances of European masterpieces.[27]

There was, however, some resistance to this approach. Composer and critic William Henry Fry called for a "Declaration of Independence in Art" and issued a challenge to the American musician.

> *[He] should not allow the name of Beethoven, or Handel or Mozart to prove an eternal bugbear to him, nor should he pay them reverence; he should only reverence his Art, and strike out manfully and independently into untrodden realms, just as his nature and inspirations may invite him.*

Strong and others in the "Transcendence School" surely never set foot in Harry Hill's, or brought a supply of stamps to John Allen's place. (Fry probably did not either.) They left it rather to Asmodeans like Crapsey, Smith, Dyer, and others of the "Exposé School of Reportage" to peel back the roofs of Water Street dance halls and flash concert saloons and tell about the music they heard there. To these Asmodeans, as it would surely also have been with Strong and those of his class, the sounds made in these places were manifestly *not* transcendently beautiful; they were rather—in some of their own words—out of tune, wheezing, hideous, wild, cracked, thumping, execrable, wailing, wiry, low, squalling, jangling, murdering, savage, and lunatic. Yet there were three hundred or so concert saloons in New York City, and without daily music by the house band each concert saloon would have been just a saloon. There were at least seventy-four dance halls like John Allen's in the city, and without a dance band every night each dance hall would have been just a drinking spot.[28]

New York's musical elite were looking in the wrong places for America's music. In the nether reaches of the city a new music was being made by hundreds and hundreds of professional New York musi-cians, each highly trained in their own way, each striking out "man-fully and independently into untrodden realms," just as Fry had charged them. It was music that was being enjoyed and loved by tens of thou-sands of New Yorkers—overwrought, often hysterical protestations by elite Asmodeans aside. It was down in the lower wards and along the Bowery and the waterfront where a wide diversity of lower-class Americans—black, white, the newly immigrant—were making and sharing inspired music. There the transcendently pertinent question—Where is America's music?—was being answered.

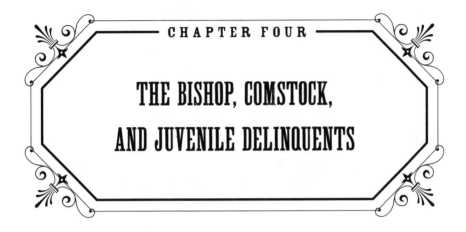

CHAPTER FOUR

THE BISHOP, COMSTOCK, AND JUVENILE DELINQUENTS

NEW YORK CITY was abuzz after Bishop Simpson delivered his January 1866 oration, which he had titled simply, "New-York: A Mission Field." His primary intent was not controversial, for Simpson wanted mostly to draw attention to the bounty of souls in need of salvation throughout the city. As some indication of the potential harvest, he pointed out that the number of his Methodist Episcopal flock barely equaled that of the twenty thousand prostitutes who swarmed through the city's streets, brothels, assignation houses, concert saloons, and dance halls, all presumably unredeemed.[1]

His count (which implied that one of every six young New York females was a prostitute) immediately compelled attention, and authorities joined in a chase for valid statistics. The secretary of the City Mission filed a report in the *New York Times* three days after the sermon that totaled the prostitute population at ten thousand, supported by a business infrastructure valued at five million dollars. (By way of comparison, there were also ten thousand drinking establishments in the city with gross annual receipts of five million dollars, a figure that exceeded the annual police budget by 250 percent.) The heaviest authority to weigh in was John A. Kennedy, commissioner of the New York City Police force. In a lengthy response filed five days after Simpson's sermon, Kennedy declared that the bishop's charge had prompted him to order a census of the city's prostitutes. That study found that there were 621 brothels in the city, 99 assignation houses, and 75 disorderly concert saloons "of ill repute." Prostitutes numbered 2,670; adding in the 747 pretty waiter girls who were likely prostitutes made for a grand total of 3,417. In August, the *New York Times* reported yet another number, this one attributed to the superintendent of the Home for Fallen Women (which was in a building that formerly housed a brothel and was strategically located just across Broadway from Harry Hill's). Although the Home for Fallen Women had already rescued seventy-five women from the streets, work was still to be done, for the superintendent estimated there were four thousand full-time "public prostitutes," something like the same number of part-timers, and an equal number of "kept mistresses and semi-respectable women"; or, in his round numbers, there were about fifteen thousand prostitutes in New York City.[2]

In all likelihood, Kennedy's low number was in the best interest of the police department and Simpson's high number was intended to motivate his congregation. More realistically, an accurate census would have counted somewhere between six thousand five hundred and thirteen thousand, or about one of every twelve young women. Significantly lower than Simpson's ratio, this was still a number that commanded attention.[3]

The issue caught one politician's eye. Elected to the State Assembly in December 1866, John C. Jacobs, a twenty-nine-year-old Democrat from Brooklyn, brought before his fellow legislators on January 8, 1867, a resolution calling for New York City's Sanitary Committee (which consisted of physicians) and Police Commissioner Kennedy to file official reports on prostitution in New York City. Jacobs's move was part of a long-term strategy to legalize prostitution, tax it, and ensure that the women involved underwent regular physical examinations, as was common practice in parts of Europe.[4]

The State Assembly adopted Jacobs's resolution. Kennedy published his report in late February, which contained some of the predictable warnings about how male patrons were being victimized by prostitutes, i.e., trafficking with prostitutes leads to debauchery, then overindulgence, then the shirking of business and family responsibilities, and finally crime. Since Kennedy considered the providers of sex to be the source of the problems, he recommended that heavier penalties be slapped on madams, prostitutes themselves, and the owners of property who knowingly allowed their premises to be used for prostitution. He also attached a new census to his report, claiming that in Manhattan and Brooklyn there were 575 brothels, 93 assignation houses, 38 concert saloons, 2,588 prostitutes, and 336 waiter girls. Conveniently, these numbers represented a decline in prostitution from January 1866, clear evidence (in Kennedy's view) that policing efforts were paying off.[5]

As mandated by Jacobs's resolution, the Sanitary Committee also issued a report, one with far more significant recommendations. Statistics on an epidemic of venereal disease was point one: 8 percent of Union soldiers during the Civil War had venereal scars (only 1.05 percent of such soldiers were from rural areas, but 12.25 percent of those from cities were infected), and Germans were more likely to have venereal disease than Irish or (native-born) Americans. The committee's report then moved on to four recommendations, two of which proposed that the medical treatment of venereal diseases, whether of the client or the prostitute, be made freely and easily available, with program costs to be borne by the city. Next it suggested that all those who managed houses of prostitution or assignation houses be registered, along with all prostitutes; the register, which would be maintained by the police, would not be open to public inspection. Proposal four recommended that all houses of prostitution and all prostitutes be subject to regular inspections by the Board of Health.[6]

Jacobs drew points from both reports and fashioned a bill that he put before the Assembly on March 6, 1867. In the spirit of compromise, it called not for the licensing of bawdy houses but for penalties to fall on those who maintained them and those who owned property used for prostitution. Furthermore, the police would be required to maintain a list of all bawdy houses and the women in them. The bill was amended in committee to mandate medical examinations of all females in the houses and, if found diseased, to provide for tax-supported convalescence in a medical facility.[7]

Heavy lobbying by those involved in New York's prostitution business aimed at killing the bill. Fearing that the bill would pass, they worked with Assemblyman David G. Starr, an upstate Democrat, to frame a different bill that authorized the licensing of all bawdy houses, the appointment of a commission to regulate them, and the empowerment of a board of medical inspectors. The bill had two measures favored by the industry: 1) the de facto legalization of prostitution, and 2) licensing fees set high enough ($500 for a "first-class" house; $250 for a second-class one) that they would presumably drive lower-class houses out of business. Curiously referred to the Assembly's Committee on State Charitable Institutions, it was thought by the *New York Tribune* to be the "cheekiest" bill yet presented that year, and by the *New York Times* as unlikely to pass. In fact, it was never reported out of committee.[8]

Jacobs's bill, however, was reported out to the Assembly, but with a negative recommendation from a subcommittee of the entire Assembly. The Assembly voted the bill down; and the state of New York took a pass on its only serious opportunity to legally recognize prostitution in New York City.[9]

Although nothing much came from these efforts initially (except for the advancement of young Jacobs's political career), media and public attention was now sharply focused on the issue. One result was yet more statistics on prostitution in the city. The *New York Times* counted fifteen thousand prostitutes in the city in August 1866; the *Buffalo*

Commercial soon after reduced that by a touch to only fourteen thousand. The *New York Tribune* in early February 1867 figured a "grand army of twelve thousand six hundred criminal women" and put that number in a telling spatial context: "placed in line [with] two feet of space allowed to each, the painted procession would extend from the Battery to Fortieth-st." Commissioner Kennedy conducted yet another census and this time recorded a mere 2,924 prostitutes and suspect waiter girls. Other numbers thrown about in 1867 were two thousand seven hundred; five thousand; ten thousand; twelve thousand; twenty-one thousand; and twenty-five thousand. The obsession with numbers was not entirely misplaced, for the decade of the 1870s represented the zenith of commercialized sex in New York's history.[10]

The services of prostitutes could be procured in many places. Dance halls, as in the past, were prime locations, especially for the lowest classes and for sailors freshly in port, who were known for seeking the "greatest amount of pleasure within the shortest possible time." Concert saloons during this time were little or no better. In these places the dresses of already scantily clad pretty waiter girls shrank during the decade until they were finally "microscopic," whereupon "immodesty [threw] off as it were the last fig leaf" and celebrated lust and revelry, according to one reporter. And, conveniently, many concert saloons arrayed "wine rooms" around the floor, furnished with a table, two chairs, a sofa, and a door that locked.[11]

And if still unsure where prostitution's business might be found, there was always the *Gentleman's Companion* (1870), fifty-five pages and sized to fit unobtrusively in a pocket. Descended in a line from the sporting press of years before, the *Companion* contained the names and addresses of 150 brothels and concert saloons, ratings for many of them (nine were "first-class"), the numbers of prostitutes in each, and information on any special qualities or skills held by the women. Of course, the *Companion* made emphatically clear that the publication's

"Jack Tar Among the Land Sharks." *Image from Samuel Anderson MacKeever, Glimpses of Gotham and City Characters (New York: Richard K. Fox, 1880).*

purpose was that "the reader may know how to avoid" such places. Readers, for instance, needed to be warned against the second-class house at 127 West Twenty-Sixth Street, which had little reason for special attention but for the fact that a bear was kept in the cellar, the purpose of which "may be inferred." Things were better right behind that house, at 128 West Twenty-Seventh Street, where Madam Lizzie Goodrich's five attractive boarders had dispositions that would "tend to drive away the blues." And if a naive visitor to the house had been overcome and entrapped by one of the prostitutes, a physician was always on hand to tend to any health concerns. Readers also learned from ads about the erotic books for sale at John F. Murray's establishment on West Houston (*Fanny Hill, Fast Young Lady, Annie or the Ladies' Waiting Maid*, among others). And that Dr. Charles Manches, on Broadway, offered great prices on a dozen "French Male Safes," with the buyer given a choice of base materials—skin or India rubber. Clearly, sex and sexuality in that day's New York City as practiced by the many was not at all like the polite prudery widely imagined for them today.[12]

Because of prostitution's proliferation and its ubiquity, many New Yorkers were genuinely appalled by what they saw around them. They felt that to bring a vice epidemic into the blinding light of a more moral day a crusade was needed, one to be headed by a strong-willed, right-minded captain.

Enter Anthony Comstock.

❦

Comstock was of New England Puritan stock, with his moralistic perspectives sharpened by allegiance to many of the period's social-reform movements, particularly abolitionism, temperance, and pseudo-medical reforms involving bodily purity. He had moved to New York City shortly after serving in the Civil War (where he alienated many of his fellow soldiers by pouring his rations of whiskey on the ground instead of sharing them). There he joined the Sons of Temperance in Brooklyn and found a job selling dry goods.[13]

New legislation at both the federal and state level pointed Comstock toward his life's purpose. In 1865, the U.S. Congress passed a law banning the distribution of obscene publications through the postal system. The New York State Senate in 1867 went further and considered legislation to suppress the publication and distribution of indecent images as well. Such a bill was forwarded to the State Assembly and was widely expected to pass, but the document went "missing" from the clerk's desk and could not be brought forth for consideration. Another year and another legislative session, and in January 1868 Senator John O'Donnell introduced into the Senate a bill banning the dealing in or circulation of obscene materials of all sorts and any object or artifact of "immoral character." It was passed by the Senate in March and the Assembly toward the end of April. Within its wording there was no effort to define "immoral," "indecent," or "obscene"—apparently one just knew it when one saw it.[14]

Later in 1868, with those laws now on the books, Comstock's personal diary contained an annotation on how an acquaintance had been "led astray and corrupted and diseased" by indecent literature. The Puritan in Comstock billowed and he immediately sought out the seller of the literature, Charles Conroy. Comstock then bought from him an obscene book. With the evidence literally in hand and a conveniently placed police captain nearby, Comstock had Conroy arrested and his stock of immoral materials seized and destroyed.[15]

Comstock must have been thrilled with his easy victory, for he soon became a vigilante force of one. His method was always the same: identify sellers of immoral literature; incriminate them; get their stocks destroyed; extract legal justice. Among the many he found peddling illegal material during this time was, once again, Conroy, which ended with a result similar to that in 1868. In 1874 Comstock went after Conroy for the third time. Perhaps weary of his antagonist's tenacity, Conroy retaliated, produced a small knife, slashed at Comstock, and cut his face from the temple to the left chin. Undeterred by mere mortal harm, with blood spurting from the cut, Comstock seized Conroy and again had him arrested. He would wear a distinctive scar the rest of his life.[16]

Comstock's success at suppressing obscene materials prompted renewed interest from the U.S. Congress. Encouraged by the Young Men's Christian Association (YMCA) and other organizations to seek stronger federal legislation against the immoral trade, Comstock lobbied in Washington for the "Act for Suppression of Trade in and Circulation of Obscene Literature and Articles of Immoral Use," which was subsequently passed on March 1, 1873. A much-strengthened successor to the 1865 law, it made it illegal for anyone to use the postal service to send obscene materials, any information on obscene materials, contraceptives or information on preventing pregnancies, abortion medicines or information thereof, "rubber goods" (i.e., condoms), even medical anatomy books. For good reason, the Act came to be widely known as the "Comstock Law." In recognition of his vigilance in suppressing obscene literature, the postmaster general appointed Comstock a special agent of the postal service, a position he would proudly hold for forty years.[17]

Comstock's newfound notoriety garnered broad citizen support for the establishment and legal incorporation in May 1873 of the New York Society for the Suppression of Vice, with support from J. P. Morgan and the YMCA. The Society's seal made the mission clear: on the left side, an image of a handcuffed purveyor of obscene materials being taken away by a policeman; on the right, a derby-hatted, upstanding citizen burning smut.[18]

Comstock now had the ways and means to broaden his campaign. Abortion came into his line of sight, and in 1874 he boasted of having arrested eleven abortionists in three days. Then in 1878 he turned his attention to the most notorious, best-known abortionist of the era.

Madame Restell had served out her prison sentence in 1841 after George Washington Dixon engineered her indictment and subsequent conviction. She soon returned to providing backroom abortions, although now with more circumspection. Restell still advertised her services in New York newspapers, but in densely coded language: "A Certain Cure for Married Ladies, With or Without Medicine" and "infallible French Female Pills." Her illegal and dangerous work over four decades had made her an exceedingly wealthy woman but also earned her the title of the "Wickedest Woman in New York." And she was now in Comstock's crosshairs.[19]

His method, as almost always, was to gather incriminating evidence incognito. In this case, Comstock posed as an impoverished husband desperately seeking Restell's French Female Pills for his wife. Once purchased, he brought in waiting police officers and had Restell arrested. Ann Lohman (her real name) was then sixty-five and had battled against police and reformers from even before Dixon. Comstock's pursuit and arrest of her must have been a final indignity. The day after her arrest she was discovered in her bathtub, dead from self-inflicted knife wounds. To Comstock, never the empathetic humanitarian, that represented justice—"A bloody ending to a bloody life."[20]

Comstock liked to tote up and broadcast the results of his crusades. Among his hauls: the destruction of 320,000 pounds of obscene literature, 284,000 pounds of publishers' plates, 4,000,000 pictures (including 186,000 pounds of indecent postcards), and enough people arrested to fill a passenger train of sixty-one coaches. But he seemed to have overplayed his hand when he boasted that Madame Restell was the fifteenth person he had driven to suicide after exposing criminal behavior. Public opprobrium was widespread after this comment, something of a shock to Comstock. Ezra Heywood, an anarchist who promoted free love and was long a special target of Comstock's crusades, wrote tellingly of the man, his mission, and his methods: "This is clearly the spirit that lighted the fires of the Inquisition."[21]

There had been crusaders and societies of crusaders before, of course. By and large these people and their organizations were typically conservative in their actions and reserved in public demonstrations of righteousness. Comstock, on the other hand, realized that citizens and societies of organized citizens might function as aggressive vigilance groups that directed the attention of authorities toward targeted problems and, moreover, could and should lobby lawmakers for strong laws governing personal and social behavior. The influence of Comstock and his aggressive approach would be felt well into the twentieth century. Indeed, one wonders if laws such as the 1910 Mann Act (prohibiting interstate trafficking in sex), the 1914 Harrison Narcotics Tax Act, the widespread banning of prostitution districts (1910–1917), or the 1919 Volstead Act (prohibition of alcohol) would have come to pass without his towering influence.

❖

The Society for the Reformation of Juvenile Delinquents in New York City, although a much older institution, soon adopted some of the methods perfected by Comstock. New York's high-minded had long been concerned about incarcerating young people who had committed petty crimes alongside seasoned, adult criminals. To address this problem, some citizens in the mid-1820s helped establish a House of Refuge for young offenders, an institution that would later be called a reform school and today a juvenile detention center or a halfway house. The idea was to provide juvenile delinquents with a safe and supportive peer-group environment, then train them in a trade that would lead to a meaningful place in society.

Bricks and mortar plus maintenance and staff, the House of Refuge was an expensive proposition. It was initially supported by members of the newly incorporated Society, the federal government (which loaned and later sold an unused building to the Society), the State of New York (which had passed a bill in 1824 offering assistance in the amount of two thousand dollars per annum), and commensurate help from the municipal government. Budget support was modified in 1829 when the State Assembly passed legislation directing the New York City commissioner of health to channel funds to the Society, including a proportion of licensing fees paid by city theaters and saloons. As a result, the Society's ledger sheet in 1830 showed fifteen hundred dollars from fees paid by three unnamed theaters. In addition, the Society that year benefited from licensing fees levied on 2,842 taverns, which accrued to the account books a total of $4,263. A funding pattern was thus established that would prevail for many decades, the policy's rationale being that if entertainment and alcohol provided the soil in which vice, criminality, and juvenile delinquency flourished, let entertainment and drink pay the social costs.[22]

In 1861, funds to aid the Society from "Theatre licenses, &c." amounted to $8,081.80, with an additional amount from the Board of Education of $5,199.60. Then came the Anti-Concert Saloon Bill of 1862, which outlawed alcohol in places of public amusement. This had the effect of severely cutting revenue from licensing fees as theaters and saloons could now seek a liquor license or a theatrical license, but not both. In 1872, for example, the Society received funds from theatrical licensing fees of only $1,365.08, leaving its budget more than two thousand dollars in the red.[23]

It was soon clear that state legislative efforts to regulate vice by removing alcohol and pretty waiter girls from theatrical events clearly had not worked as intended, for many establishments (and the police) simply ignored the law. The legislature addressed the issue on May 22, 1872, when it passed "An Act to Regulate Places of Public Amusement in the City of New York." Among other things, the Act declared that it was unlawful to mount any "interlude, tragedy, comedy, opera, ballet, play, farce, [blackface] minstrelsy or dancing . . . equestrian, circus, or any performance of jugglers or rope dancing, acrobats" without a theatrical license. To obtain a license, a place of public amusement paid five hundred dollars, which amount "shall be paid over to the treasurer of the Society for the Reformation of Juvenile Delinquents in the City of New York, for the use of the said Society." Without said license, each performance was subject to a penalty of one hundred dollars. Then came the clause that gave the Act heft: "which penalty the Society for the Reformation of Juvenile Delinquents in this city is hereby authorized to prosecute, sue for and recover for the use of said Society, in the name of the People of New York." The legislature essentially turned over to the Society for the Reformation of Juvenile Delinquents legal incentive for policing theatrical performances in New York.[24]

To no surprise, the Society soon sent undercover agents into suspect places without theatrical licenses: beer gardens, medicine shows, sponsored balls and parties, museums, dens, and most any other places where illegal performances might occur. There they waited for and documented any infraction of the Act. After passing evidence to the authorities, the Society collected the fines *and* any subsequent licensing fees.

And it paid off. Within a year of the Act's passage, the "Theatrical Licenses" line in the Society's annual report had increased by more than one thousand percent to almost fifteen thousand dollars. By 1878 it was $22,457.56. And in 1880, the Society would benefit to the amount of about thirty-five thousand dollars from licensing fees and fines.[25]

To gather and consolidate evidence, agents were required to file reports with the Society on what they saw and heard. Those reports would then be edited into affidavit form and submitted to the courts. As a result, some details of the investigations have survived in the affidavits, although the reports themselves have not. For example, agent Charles R. Groth visited the Liverpool Variety Theatre at 27 Bowery on September 13, 1881, and testified that it was a "combination of a 'pretty waiter girl' saloon and a theater and is the resort of a low class of people of both sexes." Rudolph W. Faller was with Groth and repeated the testimony in his affidavit. Affidavits in hand, the Society stood to be at least one hundred dollars richer.[26]

The Bowery Varieties Theatre at 33 Bowery received special attention from Society agents. In 1879, one agent described the "concert room and theatre." There was a raised stage, footlights, a drop curtain, and an orchestra of piano, violin, cornet, and drums. Performers included four men and four women, the latter of whom wore tights under their fancy dresses. In keeping with contemporaneous entertainment traditions, the men were in blackface, dressed in minstrel costumes, and played the tambourine and bones. The ensemble sang songs and told jokes that consisted mainly of a string of bad puns. The minstrels were followed by a musical interlude, then another act of three men (one dressed as a woman) took the stage and entertained the audience of about 150 persons with their songs, dances, and acrobatics. A later report noted that there was a female singer who wore a short dress, fancy shoes, and colored stockings, and that she pranced up and down the stage. Her act was followed by a blackfaced clog dancer.[27]

In May 1882, an agent visited the as-yet-unlicensed theater again. He testified that there was no admission charge, which suggests that the Bowery Varieties functioned more as a disorderly concert saloon than a bona-fide theater. "Private boxes" were noted (probably available for use by the hour), and a female singer entertained with "The Pitcher of Beer," a popular song from 1880 by Edward Harrigan and David Braham, a clear violation of the Act.

Each night in the week and week in the year,
With a heart and a conscience that's clear,
I've a friend and a glass for to let the toast pass,
As we drink from our pitcher of beer.

Another woman then launched into "Awfully Awful," a somewhat risqué English music-hall song. The program closed tearfully with a maudlin rendition of "A Violet from Mother's Grave" (1881).[28]

Although the Society did not need to provide evidence of immoral behavior to claim the fee and fine, it seemingly could not resist. The last item on the preprinted affidavit form concerned the size of the audience, which agents then typically used to note the nature of the audience, specifically the women in it: "including many females who sat at tables drinking and smoking with male companions" was a common formulation. Agent Sooney made sure to mention that "about one hundred persons were present" and the "females [were] of loose character." References to the relative virtue of audience females occurred so frequently in the affidavits they strongly suggest that while some male patrons might have been there for the "concert" or the "saloon" aspect, many of them were there for the women.[29]

The agents of the Society for the Reformation of Juvenile Delinquents also occasionally included the names of entertainers in their affidavits, some forty-one of them from 1879 to 1883 alone. Although most of those named were apparently singers or instrumentalists, several were pugilists who boxed in rings installed in many concert saloons, à la Harry Hill's. Only a few names among the musicians left much of an historical mark. Then (as now) many loved to make music and dedicated important parts of their lives to the profession, but the bold impression on music history was infrequent.[30]

Blackface minstrels were almost half of the named musicians. At the Bowery Music Hall in 1879, a quartet of them sang and played the fiddle, banjo, bones, and tambourine, and "besides singing, marked time with their feet, shouted, and the bones and tambourine players

"Interior of a Concert Saloon." *Image from George Ellington,* The Women of New York; or, The Under-World of the Great City, Illustrating the Life of Women of Fashion, Women of Pleasure, Actresses and Ballet Girls, Saloon Girls, Pickpockets and Shoplifters, Artists' Female Models, Women-of-the-Town, Etc., Etc., Etc. *(New York: New York Book Co., 1869).*

did many ludicrous things to amuse the audience." Some of the blackface acts featured performers of some renown. Vocalist and dancer Billy Emerson, for instance, a popular Irish-born minstrel who first appeared on the stage as a twelve-year-old in 1858 and performed throughout the English-speaking world during a long career, gave stopover performances in New York's concert saloons. That blackface minstrelsy, more than forty years old in the 1870s, was still a vital presence on the American stage speaks reams of its centrality to developments in American popular culture, to say nothing of its place in expressing race and society.[31]

In addition to naming entertainers and entertainment genres, agents listed song titles—eighty-six of them from 1879 to 1882—thus providing a useful cross section of the music heard in that day's concert saloons and variety theaters. They ranged from old ballads ("Sally in Our Alley") and eighteenth-century patriotic songs ("Yankee Doodle,"

"Hail Columbia") to Scottish and Irish songs ("Scotch Lassie Jean," "The Irish Fair") and older popular songs ("Old Folks at Home," "What Are the Wild Waves Saying"). But by far the majority of songs noted were the day's most popular, with titles such as "Cradle's Empty, Baby's Gone" (1880), "De Golden Wedding" (1880), "Little Log Cabin in the Lane" (1871), "The Mulligan Guard Picnic" (1878), "Silver Threads Among the Gold" (1873), "A Violet from Mother's Grave" (1881), and "When the Robins Nest Again" (1883).[32]

Many popular songs heard in concert saloons were undoubtedly performed as published, with a vocalist and a pianist respecting the notes on the printed page. Indeed, there were occasional reports of a "gurgling piano, ring-wormed by wet beer glasses" loaded down with a stack of well-used sheet music, implying that something like straight performances was common. But published songs could also be reshaped to fit the situation. Concert saloons had pianos, but musicians also played violins, cornets, French horns, banjos, tambourines, bones, guitars, and more. With such rich musical resources available, songs must often have been "arranged" or, perhaps more accurately, improvised—made up on the spot and never written down. In fact, the urge toward ad-hoc music-making is a long-standing and salient characteristic of American popular music performance. For instance, Stephen Foster (who had died in January 1864 at 30 Bowery) published "Oh! Susanna" in sheet music form in the hopes that there would be profit from its sale. He wanted the song to be performed as printed in thousands of American parlors, generally by middle-class musicians (often female) who had some training in reading music. But Foster also knew that the song might be (and was) performed by minstrel bands, marching bands, solo fiddlers, and a host of others, all without his sheet music in view, and in an era when performance rights were nonexistent. In fact, the sheet music of that time often functioned more like a musical chart than a musical score not to be violated. In that regard alone, "Oh! Susanna" (1847) was different in actual practice than, for example, the rigorously authoritative score to Chopin's "Sonata in G minor for Piano and Cello" (also 1847). Popular music was performed in a manner befitting situation, audience, and the musicians at hand. In that way it lived in concert with its time and place.[33]

Fluidity of performance was also true of the song's lyrics. Many concert saloon performers surely rendered the text as printed. But many others used the sheet music as a set of ideas, situations, characters, and rhymes—a jumping-off place for extrapolation to topical parody. Beyond that, parody could even veer into the bawdy (or "smutty," as one agent described the process). Of course, of the three possible permutations of a popular song—printed, topical parody, or bawdy parody—the form most likely to endure as a historical record is the printed. Parodies are expressions of an oral tradition meaningful in the lived moment, with half-lives rarely chronicled and often only implied.

One well-known song heard in the Opera Concert Saloon gives some idea of how far parody could deviate from the printed page. "Dixie" was performed there in 1864 by a pretty waiter girl named Fanny, who was known for "accidentally dropping her cambric and stooping down to pick it up so as to let the young fellows see that there's nothing artificial about her." Fanny sang Dan Emmett's song to the accompaniment of a piano and a fiddle. But her parody version, quite unlike the published version from five years before, told the story of a young gallant who wooed lovely young Nancy by taking her for a boat ride in Central Park. The boat capsized and in the process the gentleman lost his coat, watch, waistcoat, and cash. He kindly escorted Miss Nancy home "to tea" and learned that she too had suffered losses—her teeth, her heavy makeup, and her wig. Months later, the protagonist bumped into Nancy again, this time with a babe in arms. She had been before a judge and the gallant now learned that he was legally a father. As a result:

"An East Side Jamboree." *Images from Alfred Trumble,* The Mysteries of New York; A Sequel to Glimpses of Gotham and New York by Day and Night *(New York: Richard K. Fox, 1882).*

Three dollars a week I had to pay
To Nancy, Miss Nancy,
I never was there I do declare,
And that's what I don't fancy.[34]

❖

In spite of efforts by the agents of the Society for the Reformation of Juvenile Delinquents and by Comstock and colleagues, the concert saloon sustained its free-wheeling, subversive, sybaritic air through the 1870s. Here, dance-based music long associated with demimonde culture was fluidly conjoined with more genteel popular song idioms of the day, in the process changing how American popular music was made, appreciated, and consumed. Such music gave expressive voice to the voiceless, for deep beneath the dour Comstockian regime, wild music could ignite a jamboree of joy, wit, and camaraderie that revealed puritanical delusions for what they were.[35]

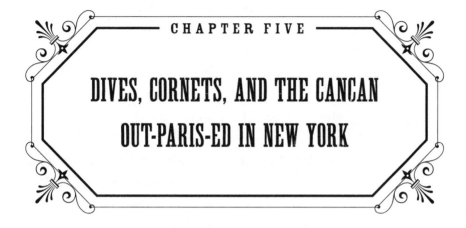

CHAPTER FIVE

DIVES, CORNETS, AND THE CANCAN
OUT-PARIS-ED IN NEW YORK

A REPORTER FOR THE *FLASH* was on lower Broadway in late 1841 and noticed two suspicious characters weaving down the street. One he described as a short, slightly built mulatto of down-and-out appearance; the other was a tall, awkward, thuggish white man "whose hang dog look cried 'gallows' louder than a trumpet." After a long string of disparaging flourishes, the former was identified as George Washington Dixon and the latter, George B. Wooldridge. The editors of the *Flash*, after a recent falling-out with their former colleagues, took obvious pleasure in smearing Dixon and Wooldridge with charges of low-class behavior, criminality, public drunkenness, a general lack of manliness, and blackness (spuriously so, for although Dixon had a dark complexion, no black heritage is known). To conclude the character assassinations, the reporter tracked the pair to the doors of the Elssler Saloon, a popular drinking and dancing den run by Wooldridge, whereupon the companions "gave each other a fraternal hug and dived together into the abyss."[1]

Suspect places like the Elssler Saloon were almost always in below-sidewalk cellars. To get to such joints, where blacks and whites frequently gathered together, people "dived" into them. By the 1860s, the verb, with racial and social connotations intact, had started its slippage toward common noun status. For instance, "a negro 'dive'" was referred to in a Buffalo newspaper in 1860 (the embedded quotes alerting readers to the linguistic arabesque) and was just one among a flurry of such references from that day and place. Dive patronage in Buffalo must also have been racially mixed, for a white man (who was a professional blackface minstrel no less) got into a fight with a black man in a Commercial Street "dive" in 1868, which dispute ended with Washington Smith, the black man, drowning in the Erie Canal.[2]

New York newspapers latched on to the term in the 1870s, with the commingling of blacks and whites almost always an overlay. The *New York Herald* reported a police raid on "a 'dive'"—those quotes again— in a basement on Laurens Street kept by Thomas Kelly, a white man. Twenty-five people were found there, "black and white, of both sexes," many of them being "somewhat under the influence of the tangle-foot [i.e., booze]." Then there was a column on the "Loftus 'Dive,'" a place on Leonard Street that was widely known for its mixed clientele. It measured only ten by twelve feet, but into that small space were crammed twenty-one adults, about equally divided by gender; many of the males were reported to be black and "of the Kentuckian type" (which apparently meant tall and lanky).[3]

The decade of the 1880s is when dives and all their layers of nuance and implications came to full flower. The word even began showing up in songs. "Upper Ten and Lower Five," from 1888, tells the story of an encounter between a New York "Upper" and a New York "Lower."

> NOBLEMAN.—*Well, I belong to the upper ten, the upper ten, the upper ten,*
> *Eight thousand a year is my income clear,*
> *And I manage to spend it too.*
> BEGGAR.—*And I belong to the lower five, the lower five, the lower five,*
> *I live in a dive, and sometimes contrive,*
> *To pick up a copper or two.*

In "The Bowery," a hit from the 1891 musical *A Trip to Chinatown*, a naïf comes into the city and takes in the sights on that infamous, lower Manhattan street:

> *I struck a place that they called a "dive";*
> *I was in luck to get out alive;*
> *When the policeman heard my woes,*
> *Saw my black eyes and my battered nose,*
> *"You've been held up!" said the "copper" fly!*
> *"No sir: but I've been knocked down!" said I;*
> *Then he laughed, though I couldn't see why—*
> *I'll never go there anymore.*[4]

❖

Perhaps the rube would never go there anymore, but New Yorkers certainly did. And to such an extent that when George Washington Walling wrote a memoir of his years as the chief of police in New York (1874–1885), dives were very much on his mind. Walling thought dives the "hot-beds" of New York's vice problem, which might be why he devoted a long, detailed chapter to them. To Walling, "tyrants of the worst sort" owned and operated dives. The dangers of such places were obvious to him, especially when it came to New York's womanhood, for it was in dives that pure womanhood, attracted by the scene and the "carefree strains of music," too often began her "dance of death."[5]

To make his point, Walling took his readers slumming. His tour could have included any of scores of New York dives, which had names like the Burnt Rag, Hell Hole, Shang Draper's, the House of Lords, Owney Geoghegan's, A Bunch of Grapes, Walhalla Hall, the Mozart, Rat Pit, Hole in the Wall, the French Madame's (where, for a fee, the female dancers could be persuaded to perform in an "entirely nude state"), or the Star and Garter. But he chose to visit only a few, most of them among the city's best-known.[6]

Walling began in "Satan's Circus," an area around Sixth Avenue in the lower Thirties. It was the epicenter of a larger area of vice, from roughly Twenty-Fourth to Forty-Second Streets and between Fifth and Seventh Avenues, a swath of New York real estate better known by the expression given it in 1876 when Police Department Captain A. S. ("Clubber") Williams was transferred there; anticipating a bribe bonanza, he allegedly retorted: "I've been having chuck steak ever since I've been on the force, and now I'm going to have a bit of tenderloin."[7]

An early stop on the Tenderloin tour was at the Haymarket, which would become the best-known dive in New York and probably its longest lived. Located in an undistinguished, three-story building at 66 West Thirtieth Street right off Sixth Avenue, it came alive only at night. Swinging doors welcomed prostitutes (free entrance) and their escorts (twenty-five cents) to the "Grand Soiree Dansante," for the Haymarket was unequivocally a dance hall. A platform at one end held the orchestra, which played beguiling dance tunes at full blast. A gallery ran on three sides above the dance floor and was usually crowded with men and women drinking, smoking, laughing, and telling ribald stories. The women in the Haymarket ranged in age and attractiveness as well as in disposition. While Walling considered some to be tastefully dressed, others were tawdry with heavily made-up faces; some were modest in demeanor, some brazen. They ("inmates of disreputable houses") served the Haymarket by running up patrons' tabs, while the Haymarket served them by providing a place to meet their marks. To Walling, the Haymarket (the "Moulin Rouge of New York") was where young men, supposedly many innocent ones, got seduced by "devils in female forms."[8]

Comstock and his agents of the Society for the Suppression of Vice also had thoughts on the character of the place. In December 1885, an attorney appointed by the governor to investigate possible collusion between the Excise Board, which granted liquor licenses, and those seeking them called the proprietors of the Haymarket before him to testify. The Haymarket was charged with being one of the most

immoral and disreputable dance halls in the city and without the quali-
fications necessary for its recently granted license. Comstock verified
its depravity, while a policeman on Captain Clubber Williams's force
countered by assuring the investigating attorney that the Haymarket
was patronized by people both good and bad. That comment prompted
further interrogation by the attorney, who asked if any decent women
went there. The policeman replied, "Oh, twenty, I suppose in the four
years I was on that post." Despite this decidedly unimpressive number
and an official report that confirmed that the Haymarket had serious
problems with disorderly behavior, the license was not revoked. (And,
presumably, Clubber feasted on more tenderloin.)[9]

The Cremorne, on Thirty-First Street just west of Sixth Avenue,
was often paired with the Haymarket. It was named after a famous
twenty-two-acre pleasure garden in London (as, in like manner, the
Haymarket borrowed its name from a well-known London theater).
The Cremorne had not always been on Thirty-First Street, though, for
the name had wandered around the city, changing form and function
as the pleasure-seeking business in New York evolved. It opened first in
1862 as an upscale variety theater, featuring some of New York's finest
classical music talent. Apparently that approach did not spell financial
success, and the following year it moved far uptown to Seventy-Second
Street and Third Avenue, where it reopened as a pleasure garden. Only
in 1877 did the Cremorne Garden move to the Thirty-First Street
location, there to be described as a "beautiful Bijou Ecole Dansante
and Temple of Terpsichore" that showcased sensational dances, well-
turned parlors, nude statues throughout, delightful music by Mons.
Bauer's Parisian Quadrille Band, and "runners" for the brothels in the
neighborhood positioned at each table.[10]

On the same block as the Cremorne was the Sans Souci, the "Resort
of the Elite of New York." More commonly known by its proprietor's
name, the clientele of "Tom Gould's" included prize fighters, sporting
men, and gamblers, as well as merchants, clerks, politicians (Tammany
Democrats, mainly), bankers, and officials; the women found there

ranged from mistresses to prostitutes to "First-Class Lady Artists" (as pretty waiter girls were called in Tom Gould's). The Sans Souci was not uniquely a saloon or a concert saloon or a music hall or a dance hall, but a bit of them all. Patrons entered through a hallway that led into a long room softened by cut flowers and potted plants. Tables were scattered about, attended by First-Class Lady Artists, while skilled black men tended the bar. A platform stage stood at one end of the room, on which "negroes and white men [sang] popular songs and musicians play[ed] the latest operatic airs." People flocked to Tom Gould's for the variety of entertainment and a desire to "not only see the elephant, but pull it by the tail."[11]

Like many dives in New York, Tom Gould's had a history of contesting the fine print in excise and entertainment laws. Specifically, Gould took exception to a part in the ordinance that called for the physical separation of alcohol and staged performance. Tom Gould's had a liquor license but not one for entertainments; caution was thus always in the air since agents of the Society for the Reformation of Juvenile Delinquents were forever on the prowl. When music rang out from the Sans Souci's small stage and agents or the police were known to be around, Gould might allow into the hall only the patrons he knew and trusted. Still, Gould was arrested repeatedly, generally to be let off with a small fine. In 1886 he attempted to avoid even that by declaring that he was no longer the proprietor of Tom Gould's but only managed it under his own famous name. On other occasions he would vanish from the premises when the police arrived, which might lead to the unjust arrests of employees serving the drinks. (Two of his black bartenders received six-month penitentiary sentences in this way.) And if it looked as if jail time was imminent, Gould would simply run off to Canada.[12]

Whatever Gould's flaws, his flair for the dramatic managed to keep the issue of excise and amusements laws before the public. The result of that law, according to the proprietors of many dives, was persecution inversely proportionate to political influence and class standing. A State Senate committee investigation in October 1885 looked into corruption among members of the city's Excise Board, protection money allegedly demanded by and paid to the police, and the law's general and broader effects. One witness before the committee claimed to have abandoned the restaurant business because the open palms of the Excise Board and the police ensured that only well-connected places could succeed. Police Captain Allaire of the 10th Precinct testified that he endeavored to enforce the substance of the law, but if one looked only to its letter then all theaters in the city should be closed, including "Wallack's, the Casino, [and] the Grand Opera House" (all "legitimate" theaters)—"The only difference in the theatres is this, that some are frequented by the rich and others by the poor."[13]

New York's working classes deeply resented both the "amusement" section of the 1883 Excise and Theatrical Law and, perhaps even more, its section 32: "No inn, tavern or hotel keeper, or other person, shall sell or give away intoxicating liquors, or wines, on Sunday." Working people treasured their Sundays, at that time the only free day afforded by the prevailing six-day workweek, and drinking was an important tradition of that day. Saloon keepers disliked the statute since it affected their bottom lines. Accordingly, proprietors and city legislators pressured the state legislature to let New York City set its own "Music and Beer Law." "It is time that the Legislature understood that New York is capable of taking care of itself," blustered U.S. Congressman Ashbel P. Fitch. In support, about two hundred saloon proprietors and others in the beer/wine/spirits business gathered at the Terrace Garden Theatre in May 1887 for a meeting chaired by Chief Justice Nehrbas of the City Court. When some called out for the law to be ignored, Judge Nehrbas countered: "We want all the laws enforced," but "we don't like this law, and we want it repealed." By meeting's end, a mass demonstration against the "no music with your beer and no beer on Sunday" law was organized for Saturday, May 7, at Cooper Union. And demonstrate they did. A "determined-looking crowd of citizens" filled the two thousand five hundred seats in the hall, then jammed the aisles and the standing room at its rear. The meeting opened when eighty members of the Musical Protective Union marched in playing "martial airs." Banners, flags, and posters filled the air: "We Want No Blue Laws," "This is a Free Country," "We Must Love No Monarchial Government," "Musik, Bier, Freiheit," "Give Us Our Beer and Music," and (in German) "He Who Cannot Take Music with His Beer Is a Rogue, and Should Buy a Rope and Hang Himself." After a full program of passionate speeches, the Musical Association Band played "Hail Columbia" to close the meeting. Altogether it was a "grand demonstration by the working classes" against unjust excise laws, proclaimed the *Brooklyn Daily Eagle*.[14]

Protests, speeches, demonstrations, music, and banners proved to be in vain. With upstate Republican politicians dominating the state legislature, no amendments to the excise laws made it to the floor. Those in the entertainment/liquor business were forced to continue balancing between the trouble and expense of a proper license, a sympathetic (often corrupt) police presence, and the baleful gazes of Comstock and the agents of the Society for the Reformation of Juvenile Delinquents. It was a recipe for manifest civil disobedience, bribery, conflicts between law and practice, and a stressed business model.

❖

After Tom Gould's, Chief Walling moved his dive tour downtown to the Bowery and stopped in at Harry Hill's, now getting long in the tooth but still a New York tradition. The decor had been much the same for decades but for the recent addition of electric lights, personally installed by Thomas Edison. As in the past, nothing vulgar or obscene was heard from the stage and nothing obviously disorderly was permitted, all rules enforced by Hill himself. And—unusual for New York dives—theft or robbery simply did not occur in Harry Hill's. Entertainment there had changed with the times, however, and was more varied by the 1880s; it now consisted of:

boxing-matches, ballads, ballets and comedies. Perhaps a homely woman, dressed in radiant colors, sang a pathetic song in a squeaky voice, or a young and pretty girl in short dresses and long hair put life and bathos into a touching ballad. The comedy presented was of the lowest type, and the jokes of the comedians were coarse and flat.

Sometimes a "serio-comic singer," wearing flesh-colored tights, a bodice, and no dress, would declaim on how she "Tickled Him Under the Chin." Female wrestlers, a new rage, frequently appeared on the program, but also worked the room as pretty waiter girls did in earlier times: "Say, baby, can't I have a wet?," as the wrestler plopped herself on the "quivering knee of a weak little fellow . . . and throws her arms around his neck and hugs him to her flabby breast violently enough to disarrange the black curly hair." By design, the crowd held a fair number of "chair sweaters," women who wore revealing short skirts and whose primary job was to work male patrons for drinks. On the side, they sold pornographic photographs. And so it went at Harry Hill's: "drinking, dancing, smoking, chaffing and having a glorious night of it."[15]

Despite Hill's legendary standing, he was not immune to the reach of the law. Convinced that Harry Hill's was a disorderly saloon, the Excise Board denied his application for a license renewal in early 1885. Hill's response was to run his dive in defiance of the law. That got the attention of Society for the Reformation of Juvenile Delinquents agents, who over the next two years provided evidence leading to thirty-four arrests for serving liquor without a license and for mounting theatrical amusements in the same space as liquor. Finally, on October 3, 1887, Harry Hill capitulated and chained his swinging doors shut, ending an era.[16]

⟨◈⟩

A block north of Harry Hill's, on Bleecker Street, was a popular nightspot named after a famous Parisian dancing garden—the American Mabille. It too was better known by its proprietor's name—The. (as in

Theodore) Allen's. More a dance hall than a concert saloon, The. Allen's employed "a few worn-out musicians" who played the popular hits of the day and muscular bartenders who could swing heavy clubs when necessary. The room behind the street-side saloon featured a stage on which women in "gaudy tights dance and sing ribald songs" and where "Anti-Comstockian farces" were presented. But the real action was in the basement dance hall, which was enlivened by musicians who "make worse music than their fellows upstairs." To Walling, The. Allen's drew in the shop and factory girls of Lower Manhattan through its music, dance, and young male patronage, a "slow poison of vice gradually working to the very center of their moral consciousness."[17]

Yet The. Allen's was mild compared to Billy McGlory's Armory Hall at 158 Hester Street. McGlory himself was the undisputed leader of the district, and a "man out of whom forty devils might be cast." Armory Hall featured balconies for taking in the scene, highly frescoed (and much patched) walls, and a waxed floor for dancing; signs

"Allen's Dance House." *Image from James D. McCabe, Jr.,* New York by Sunlight and Gaslight: A Work Descriptive of the Great American Metropolis . . . *(Philadelphia: Douglass Brothers, 1882).*

were hung about that listed drink prices and emphasized that all men were expected to purchase drinks for their partners at the end of each dance. A "bouncing committee" of waiters stood ready to enforce the "No Fighting" policy. Other house rules were more liberal and allowed one to continue smoking cigars while dancing, but, on the other hand, hats had to be removed "in deference to the fair sex." As for the fair sex, most of the women worked as prostitutes and were required by McGlory to go with any man who invited her.[18]

McGlory's was supposedly the largest dance hall in the city (at about 7,000 square feet) and had its own special Bowery culture. The waltzing style, for example, was "not dancing at all, but a slow, rigid, imperturbably stepping around." The quadrilles, however, were energetic and spirited. By midnight, the orchestra—"a black-haired genius pianist, a fiddler, and a cornetist"—would typically hit its stride. The scene then grew more and more raucous, everything building toward the last, climactic dance, which was signaled by a crashing, banging piano medley.

The figures on the floor go reeling off in a mixture of dancing and by-play as fantastic as the music. The pianist seems to get excited and to want to prove himself a Hans von Bülow of rapid execution. The fiddler weaves excitedly over his fiddle. The cornetist toots in a screech like a car-engine whistle. The movements of the dancers grow licentious and more and more rapid.

At Billy McGlory's, just before the two A.M. closing time, the cancan had begun!

Feet go up. Legs are exhibited in wild abandon. Hats fly off. There are occasional exhibitions of nature that would put Adam and Eve to shame. The draperies of modern costumes for a time covers the wanton forms, but as the performers grow heated wraps are thrown off. The music assumes a hideous wildness. The hangers-on about the place pat their hands and stamp and shout. The females on the floor are excited to the wildest movements. They no longer make any attempt to conceal their persons. Their action is shameful beyond relation. It is climaxed by the sudden movement of eight or ten of them. As if by concerted arrangement they denude their lower limbs and raising their skirts in their hands above their waists go whirling round and round in a lascivious mixture of ballet and cancan.

Then, with a sudden crash, the music stopped. The women fell exhausted to the floor. The lights went out. The night was over.[19]

❖

The cancan originated in Paris, probably in the 1830s. Offenbach's famous "Infernal Galop" from *Orpheus in the Underworld* (1858) popularized the dance in Paris and helped spread the infectious and salaciously erotic dance around Europe. By 1868 it had arrived in New York, where dance instructors were offering to teach the polka, the galop, the waltz, *and* the new cancan. Its suspect reputation survived the transatlantic journey fully intact, and crowds in New York were drawn to places where the "naughty Cancan" might be experienced. It was danced on the high stage and in the lowest of dance halls by 1869, where "men and women disport themselves in the wildest and most extravagantly indecent postures that their imagination can invent," presenting altogether a scene of excited dissipation. Critics of the dance pointed to the American propensity for exaggeration and lamented that, while the French managed some grace and wit when dancing the cancan, with Americans it was only "gross, indecent, and demoralizing." One account from 1885 describing the doings in a dive on Eighth Avenue claimed that the dance degenerated into a "drunken orgie"; while two women danced, their companions snatched at their clothes until in the end they "literally danced in nothing except hats, shoes, and stockings." Another reported that women dancing the cancan in the brothels "threw themselves around in the most loose and reckless manner, exposing their persons outrageously and shame-fully," and exclaimed that the cancan had been definitively "out-Paris-ed in New York."[20]

Americans found it easy to make the cancan their own. It was then, and would be for decades after, a dance for both male and female danc-ers, not at all like the female chorus-line version of today. Imagination and innovation gave it zest—a mixture of dancing and sexual play. An observant reporter of a cancan at Billy McGlory's correctly iden-tified its origins: an "old-fashioned quadrille embellished with kicks and capers." Both the cancan and the quadrille employ a two-strong-accents-to-the-measure meter, giving each foot a heavy place to land in each measure. Given the dance figure, it is no surprise that the music that accompanied these dances was also high-energy. Descriptions of the music—wild, hideous, fantastic, thumped, bang, crash—do not suggest subtlety. These were dances more about an uproariously good time than about getting the proper steps just right.[21]

By the time the cancan was danced in Billy McGlory's, it had strong associations with debauchery and the prostitutes who used high kicks as advertisement. (Women's undergarments at this time, then called drawers, were open at the crotch.) Cancan kicks were quickly interpo-lated into walkarounds, jigs, even the waltz; mad kicking became an acceptable embellishment to just about any dance. At the "McGlori-ous Mardi" in December 1882 ("well ahead of Church time"), women "threw their feet toward the ceiling with all their might." One even ripped the seams from her clothing "in a strenuous straining to reach the infinite." While some aimed for the infinite, others aimed play-fully at their partners, sometimes coming within "dangerous proximity to male physiognomy."[22]

McGlory's McGlorious Mardi debauch was in vogue with the times, and not simply because it so centrally featured the cancan. Beginning in the 1860s and reaching full steam in the 1880s, the period around Mardi Gras featured scores of masquerade balls in New York. Some of these were modest affairs, sponsored by, for instance, upstanding German organizations where nothing more lascivious than a well-ordered waltz was allowed. But many others had thousands of revelers and qualified, in the slang of the day, as a "ballum rancum," or a sexually charged ball where nearly all the female attendees were prostitutes, thieves, or both.[23]

At the annual "French Ball" (the largest and most notorious of the bunch), Chief Walling stated that the dance floor would be jammed with costumed New Yorkers exploring extravagant alter egos: a Neapolitan fisherman, a prince of the Caucasus, Little Red Riding Hood, Oscar Wilde (the original of which had arrived in New York in 1882 to much noise), a gaudy butterfly, a nymph in pale green silk, a water lily, a Moorish chief, and an assortment of "Napoleons, Cleopatras, Joan of Arcs, gypsies, nuns, brigands, vivandières, sultanas, Magyars, Bedouins, 'Olivettes,' Indians, fairies and demons, women in black tights, women in red tights, women in blue tights, men and women in every picturesque garb imaginable." Other accounts reported on the unending bottles of champagne consumed at the French Balls, the inevitable result being a bacchanalia that compromised the morals of even the (relatively) modest. Walling believed that this was a formula for moral degeneracy, and his strategy while police chief was to send his forces into the merrymaking with the mission, according to one reporter, of simply preventing anyone from dancing the cancan.[24]

An orgy of reportage on French Ball excesses inexorably followed each year's revel. Suffragist Victoria Woodhull told of a ball in the 1870s after which "one of the oldest and best in the annals of New York society" seduced a fifteen-year-old virgin and then publicly and proudly displayed evidence of his conquest. In Woodhull's words, the French Ball consisted of "three thousand of the *best* men and four thousand of the *worst* women in the city." A report of the 1888 French Ball noted that women in long skirts generally balanced that sartorial flourish with extensive décolletage. One reveler wore a tree-motif tunic and sought out someone to pluck her leaves, a maneuver at which she apparently succeeded. And this was the ball that had been supposedly dampened in ardor by the enhanced presence of 150 policemen, for the mayor had learned from Comstock that previous balls featured "most disgusting and revolting" behaviors. In effect, wrote one wag, the mayor said "can't-can't to the can-can."[25]

As is almost always the case, contemporaneous accounts are much richer on what the chroniclers saw in dives and at masquerade balls than on what they heard. Yet there must have been a lot to hear, for there were many dozens of masquerade balls annually, hundreds of licensed dance halls and concert saloons in New York City, and somewhere around seven thousand saloons, many with at least occasional music-making. Some of the neighborhood saloons would likely have had local patrons willing to entertain their neighbors for a free drink. ("Free and Easy" saloons made a virtue out of amateur performances by organizing and advertising them.) But much of the music in saloons was provided by a citywide army of roving buskers. According to an account in *The Mysteries of New York*, buskers understood "very little music," which likely meant that they played by ear (and thus, in an important way, understood very much indeed about how music worked in actual sound). They would begin their circuits at about nine in the evening and work late into the hours of "beery good nature of the

"Can-Can" at a masquerade ball. *Image from John J. Jennings,* Theatrical and Circus Life; Secrets of the Stage, Green-Room and Sawdust Arena . . . *(St. Louis: Sun Publishing Co., 1882).*

patrons." Tips averaged about $1.50 per night each, a (barely) living wage at the time. Among musical instruments favored by buskers were the fiddle, zither (dulcimer-like, one presumes), and the harmonica. One virtuoso on the latter could produce dazzling imitations of other instruments and render accurately and beautifully the harmonies of complex songs; but, lest one take a harmonica seriously, according to a reporter the musician was "so nearly an idiot" that his little brother accompanied him everywhere and kept him safe. [26]

A special feature of the times were female bands. One trio of attractive young women, who performed on harp, violin, and cello, was noted to have done quite well ("financially," smirked the reporter). A female orchestra at a beer garden on the Bowery was described as dressed all in virginal white and directed by a female conductor with a baton; they regaled listeners with much "wild music," which seemed to offend the chronicler. Whatever the quality of the music-making, if the proprietor of a saloon had access to female musicians he could count on a generous crowd. They were in such demand that "every female who could torture the neighbors with an accordion, scrape the catgut or bang the piano was enlisted in the grand scheme of catering to the musical tastes of Gotham's beer drinkers."[27]

Concert saloons required lots of music-making, although not necessarily of the Academy of Music sort. Some musicians in these places squeezed "discord out of an accordion with [a] flute obbligato of an ear-piercing and peace-destroying kind." At a concert saloon a half-dozen steps below the pavement, a band of a piano, violin, and a "shrill fifer" played "the music that charms and attracts," noted a reporter with deep irony. Another place featured "a fat German with pink-spotted shirt and stovepipe hat playing the piano, while a chap that has the outward appearance of a speculative philosopher is blowing a cyclone through a cracked cornet."[28]

Fiddles, violins, pianos, flutes, fifes, accordions, zithers, harmonicas, harps, cellos, banjos, cornets—a full consort of musical instruments that sounded out the alleged discord of the dives. Of all of these,

"Female Band." *Image from John J. Jennings,* Theatrical and Circus Life; Secrets of the Stage, Green-Room and Sawdust Arena . . . *(St. Louis: Sun Publishing Co., 1882).*

"Concert Saloon Band." *Image from Alfred Trumble,* The Mysteries of New York: A Sequel to "Glimpses of Gotham," and "New York by Day and Night" *(New York: Richard K. Fox, 1882).*

the most striking among them was the loudest—the cornet (and its close kin the trumpet). As noted earlier, a chronicler described a trumpeter who spirited "red-hot knitting needles" through the tympanum; another heard a cornetist who made his instrument screech like a train whistle; and the aforesaid speculative philosopher blew a veritable cyclone through his cracked cornet. The cornet's sound obviously commanded the attention of those who narrated the period's music-making among the lower classes. Without trying to anticipate too much about the future, it was a sound in the process of changing fundamentally how ordinary Americans heard (and still hear) their popular music.

❧

Walling's last dive was into the basement of 151 Bleecker Street, the address of an old, once-handsome brick building that had formerly housed respectable families and doctors' offices. By the early 1880s, however, the building had seen better days, and the cellar earned special vilification for it had become a site of vice that according to the police chief was flagrant, defiant, and unconcealed. The approach to this infamous den of iniquity was through a narrow, dark, clammy hallway that led toward the back main room. There Frank Stevenson, the proprietor—whose appearance was characterized variously as bloodless, brutal, sneaky, and vicious—greeted his visitors. The regulars in the place occupied a social rung in parallel with that of Stevenson: crooks, thieves, and criminals. This dance hall, though, filled a special niche in the city and proudly advertised its difference, for on a typical night there would be twenty prostitutes present and an equal number of men, all jumbled together in a racial mix. Such was the original Black-and-Tan, of which Walling declared that the goings-ons were beyond the moral imagination and the wild commingling of the races "revolting." Blacks and whites were there together, to be sure, but also reported among the patrons were "Malays, Chinese, Lascars, and other Asiatics as well, and on one evening not long ago two American Indians were found there imbibing firewater."

Like many dives, there were multiple attractions to be found in the Black-and-Tan: drink, certainly, also prostitution, and illegal gambling was carried on in a separate, secure room. But mostly, it was a dance hall.

> *From [it] came the sound of cheap music and a shuffling of feet. The music was produced by a strong-armed negro energetically thumping a piano which was badly out of tune, an old gray-haired colored man sawing the strings of a cracked violin, a gay colored youth with distended cheeks blowing a wheezy flute, and another youth with closed eyes and head fallen to one side industriously picking a banjo. However, none of the dancers were inclined to complain of the quality of the music, and the players seem to be entirely engrossed in producing the greatest possible amount of noise.*

The room for dancing was tight. Energetic dancers bumped and jostled one another, while there was a prevailing spirit of fun and good nature among them. But to Walling, at the Black-and-Tan debauchery knew no limit—"dull-sensed negroes" danced until sweat rolled off their bodies, followed by drinking "until they are stupid." The atmosphere was close, hot, reeking of sex, and capped at the end of each evening's revelry by, inevitably, the cancan. "There is a contest among [the women] to see which can kick the highest, and they take their skirts in their hands, and amid the applause of the spectators kick a cigar from the lips of one of the men."[29]

Walling placed his finger on a racial paradox of the time. On the one hand, white men of power were more and more inclined to characterize and denigrate "American citizens of African origin" (a common newspaper phrasing) by employing prejudicial pejoratives ("brutal," "dull," and "stupid" were some that Walling used). At the same time, many American citizens of European origin were seeking out places where the races could mingle and where interracial sex was available. It was also in such places that people both black and white learned new and exciting ways of moving their bodies to music.[30]

And, increasingly, white people sought out the music made by black musicians. Shortly after the Civil War, black musicians donned theatrical blackface in order to entertain white audiences as professional minstrels. (Another paradox: the most racially derogatory of all entertainment genres became the primary vehicle through which legions of black entertainers gained access to the American stage.) In the 1870s, African American spirituals ("slave songs") swept the nation as the Fisk Jubilee Singers and others toured extensively, performing for enthusiastic white audiences. In the 1880s, popular song itself became a domain for black musicians and black musical consciousness.

Some proprietors during this time, such as Tom Gould, actively advertised for black musicians. One dive hired a band of black musicians that performed thrillingly "in full blast." After their performance, a disheveled, intoxicated young white woman took to the piano to sing "In the Sweet By and By" but was overcome by the song's pathos and broke off, sobbing. On cue, the black musicians "square[d] matters with the audience by giving 'I've Just Been Down to the Club, Dear,'" undoubtedly in a full blasting, spirited manner.[31]

❖

"Dives," at first, were multiracial places, but over time the word lost that context and was applied broadly to entertainment places where the races did not necessarily mix. New York needed a new term, and the Black-and-Tan lent its name to the new (but old) social and cultural space, a place that welcomed patrons both black and white, that enabled music enjoyed by both races, and that encouraged the sharing of bodies, both through dance and through sex. The concept spread quickly, and by the late 1880s there were numerous "black and tans" in the city, as there was still *the* Black-and-Tan. In those years the Black-and-Tan named a world of nightspots that endured for decades as pivotal, racially integrated establishments, places that fused bracingly new sounds and rhythms in American music.[32]

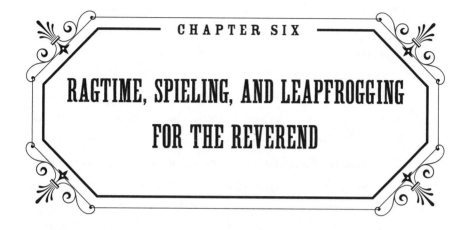

CHAPTER SIX

RAGTIME, SPIELING, AND LEAPFROGGING FOR THE REVEREND

M*AGGIE: A GIRL OF THE STREETS* was Stephen Crane's first novel, published in 1893 when he was only twenty-two. Originally subtitled "A Story of New York," it employs a narrative template used previously by social reformers, poets, and songwriters: an innocent, impressionable young girl is lured down a path to a tragic end by bright lights, music, dance, and a male predator. In Crane's iteration, Maggie Johnson, a Bowery girl, aspires to rise above her condition and class. But she sacrifices her virtue to a dashing bartender, Pete, in whom she sees a way to better her situation (while, in her, Pete sees easy sex). Soon abandoned by her lover and rejected by her family, she spirals downward through a short life of degradation, (probably) prostitution, destitution, and death.

Crane structured Maggie's story in three stages, each associated with a class of Bowery concert saloon. First Maggie and Pete visit a German beer garden, which in Crane's day was generally the most respectable sort. The beer-hall chapter begins with a description of the musicians in the orchestra—"yellow silk women and bald-headed men." The orchestra played a popular waltz, which was followed by a female singer-dancer who wore some half-dozen skirts, "any one of [which] would have proved adequate for the purpose for which skirts are intended." Other widely varied acts made up the program in what was a typical show of the day. After beer and music, Pete takes Maggie home and requests his first kiss, which chaste Maggie refuses.

Shortly afterward, though, it becomes clear that Maggie has succumbed to Pete's charms. Almost in celebration, they venture out to another concert saloon, this one irregular in its shape and scattered about with women wearing heavy makeup who look tired beyond their years. In a dark corner, a disheveled musician heads up an undistinguished band. A female singer, dressed in bright red, sings loudly in brassy voice. She receives two encores, each time appearing on stage dressed in a little less of her outfit. Following this tease, the band fires up some minstrel tunes, in which the drummer "pounded, whacked, clattered and scratched on a dozen machines to make noise." But Maggie enjoys it all, and does not think herself on the road to ruin.

Maggie, by now clearly a fallen woman, soon moves in with Pete. Three weeks later they visit another concert saloon. In this "hilarious hall," Maggie sees twenty-eight tables, a prostitute at each one, all surrounded by a crowd of men puffing out a blue cloud of smoke.

> *Valiant noise was made on a stage at the end of the hall by an orchestra composed of men who looked as if they had just happened in. . . . The chief element in the music of the orchestra was speed. The musicians played in intent fury. A woman was singing and smiling upon the stage, but no one took notice of her. The rate at which the piano, cornet and violins were going, seemed to impart wildness to the half-drunken crowd.*

In the midst of this fury, Nellie enters, the woman that Pete will move on to after dumping spoiled Maggie. The spiral steepens, and only five short chapters later Maggie is dead.[1]

"Me Muthor was a La-dy." *Image by Hy. Mayer, from Rupert Hughes,* The Real New York *(New York: Smart Set Publishing Company, 1904).*

The Rev. Dr. Charles Henry Parkhurst of the Madison Square Presbyterian Church used his pulpit to make many of the same points as Crane, although in a less artful, more political way. He delivered a sermon on February 14, 1892, using as the text for his homily, "Ye are the salt of the earth" (Matthew 5:13). Parkhurst interpreted those words from the Sermon on the Mount to mean that Jesus had charged his flock to heal the world's decay through the application of a moral Christianity. And he had examples of such decay at hand, ready for the salve.[2]

First, Parkhurst called out Mayor Hugh J. Grant, a Tammany Hall Democrat, and his administration for being a "damnable pack of administrative bloodhounds," a "lying, perjured, rum-soaked and libidinous lot," altogether a team of "polluted harpies." Not missing a beat, he railed broadly against their lechery and their patronization of iniquity. To give yet sharper points to his flaming darts, he brought forth the "vile trade" conducted out of Billy McGlory's dance hall, the ruin it brought on young women, and claimed that the dive existed only because it had the protection of the city's district attorney and the police.

Monday's newspapers buzzed with reactions to the incendiary sermon. Not surprisingly, Mayor Grant and his underlings responded stridently to Parkhurst's "intemperate ravings," charged him with bearing false witness against his neighbors, and threatened him with criminal libel. The district attorney challenged Parkhurst to produce proof of his claims and even impaneled a grand jury to weigh them. When the grand jury found the charges to be unsubstantiated, Parkhurst suffered some public rebuke. But he was no paper tiger. Fueled by a desire for retribution and a sense of moral outrage, he determined on a campaign to collect and organize the evidence he needed.[3]

Parkhurst promptly found what he sought, and with it in hand he announced that he would use his pulpit to respond to Tammany and the grand jury on March 13, 1892. On that Sunday, the twelve-hundred-person-capacity church filled quickly: all pews occupied, aisles and gallery overflowing, and the organ loft thrown open to visitors and congregants. Rev. Parkhurst rose to the podium, began his sermon, and soon made it clear that he would pull no punches. As before, his central thesis was that Tammany embraced and profited from vice in New York. Since he had been explicitly challenged to present hard facts, Parkhurst addressed that in his role as the newly elected president of the Society for the Prevention of Crime (SPC), a social-reform organization then active in New York. Parkhurst revealed that the SPC had hired five undercover detectives and charged them with determining if New York saloons were abiding by the Sabbath closing law. On Sunday the week before, between the hours of eight A.M. and midnight, the five visited 254 saloons in New York that were clearly in violation of the blue laws. They had since drawn up neatly typed lists of infractions and been appropriately deposed on their information.

Then Parkhurst turned his wrath—"with as much caution and delicacy as the nature of the subject will allow"—on prostitution. To rapt attention, Parkhurst disclosed that undercover detectives and friends of the SPC had visited thirty brothels. In each of them the men had received solicitations for sex.

To close, Parkhurst waved a stack of depositions containing detailed particulars on vice in New York, each of the 284 pages a challenge to the claims of the mayor and Tammany Hall. Then, in the face of the authorities, he thundered: "Now, what are you going to do with them?"[4]

It turned out that Parkhurst had set about collecting undercover evidence even before the grand jury's snub. Shortly after his February sermon he had arranged for Charles W. Gardner, a private detective, to serve as his personal guide to New York's demimonde. After Gardner groomed Parkhurst in the ways, means, actions, and dress of being "a swell"—apparently no easy task—they set out to visit the "haunts of the elephant."

Dr. Parkhurst and his companion disguised as swells. *Image from Charles W. Gardner,* The Doctor and the Devil; or, the Midnight Adventures of Dr. Parkhurst *(New York: Gardner & Co., 1894).*

Dr. Parkhurst and detective Gardner in a Cherry Street dive. *Image from Charles W. Gardner,* The Doctor and the Devil; or, the Midnight Adventures of Dr. Parkhurst *(New York: Gardner & Co., 1894).*

They entered a dance hall on Cherry Street, where a "most truculent looking ruffian" tended the bar. In the corner of the squarish room, a black musician played a waltz on a wheezy accordion while a half-dozen couples whirled around the floor. Nearly everyone was drunk; men smoked cigars and cigarettes, as did the women—a sure sign of dissipation. While Parkhurst sat at the bar (nursing his untouched beer), a young woman approached: "Hey, whiskers, going to ball me off?" she asked, using street slang to inquire after a dance. After a stammering refusal from Parkhurst, she took to the floor with another man and danced a waltz during which vice "brazen-faced, tried to thrust itself upon innocence." Later, the musician squawked out something like "The Blue Danube" through a thick miasma of vulgar language and the stale smells of beer, whiskey, and tobacco smoke, while Parkhurst calmly sucked on an orange he had bought for five cents.[5]

A few days later, Gardner escorted Parkhurst to the Windsor, a concert saloon at 27 Bowery. Like most such places, admission was free; drink sales provided the margin. From their table, the gentlemen had a view of the good-sized stage, from which female singers and so-called actresses entertained the clientele. One of that troupe, between sets apparently, was stationed at their table. Gardner noticed that she glowed with a complexion that "had been bought at a drug store, and had been applied to her face in liquid form by a fire engine." She wore a skirt that extended only to her knees and a low-cut blouse of "no value as a concealment of her buxom personality." Her job at the Windsor was to encourage patrons to buy drinks. Her job after hours was to entice the reverend and the detective to make up a party in a brothel on Bayard Street, although entreaties to such effect were rebuffed.

Later, Gardner provided a report to Parkhurst on Johnson's dance hall on West Twenty-Seventh Street, "where the lost of the colored and white races nightly congregate."

Fifteen and sixteen-year-old white girls were dancing about with "coons"
to the strains of a waltz, played by an orchestra composed of a piano, harp,

*violin and piccolo. Colored girls of tender years danced with white men,
too, and as all danced in a lascivious way the scene was a startling one.*

Over four weeks, Gardner squired Parkhurst to a wide range of dives,
dens, black and tans, gin mills, saloons, and brothels, each seemingly
worse than the last.[6]

To complete the reverend's education, Gardner took him to Hat-
tie Adams's brothel on East Twenty-Seventh Street, only three blocks
from the minister's church. After being greeted by the madam, the
guests moved into the rear parlor where several prostitutes awaited
their attention. As a special feature, Gardner arranged for a "dance of
nature" at a cost to the SPC of fifteen dollars. First, the "broken-down"
musician who provided the music in the brothel was blindfolded, for
the women refused to dance before the open eyes of "the Professor."
Then the prostitutes removed all their clothes and danced the cancan
to his lively music.

> *"Hold up your hat!" shouted one of the girls, a tall blonde. [Gardner]
> grasped the Doctor's black derby hat, and held it up. The girl measured
> the distance with her eyes . . . then gave a single high kick, and amid
> applause sent the hat spinning away.*

Finally, as the coup de grâce to an evening of unflinching debauchery,
the prostitutes convinced Gardner to crouch on the floor and play the
frog, while they engaged in an extended game of naked leapfrog. After
that particular exhibition, weak-kneed Reverend Doctor Parkhurst
decided to end his "devil chasing."[7]

❦

Parkhurst's sermons hit their marks and would ramify for decades. The
same grand jury that had dismissed his claims in February now lauded
him for his work, while politicians, officials, the police, and Tammany
Hall hurried to protect their backs. Not all succeeded, as the super-

intendent of police was forced to resign. His replacement, Inspector Thomas Byrnes, subsequently directed the force to make hundreds of vice raids (many of them obviously for show).

The November 1893 elections following that March sermon affirmed the force behind Parkhurst's crusade. Republicans swept statewide administrative offices on the slate that year (which did not include the governorship) and flipped control of the state legislature (results likely influenced, too, by general anxiety and widespread unemployment resulting from the year's economic depression).

After Republicans took legislative control in Albany, State Senator Clarence Lexow introduced a bill to investigate corruption in the New York Police Department. Quickly passed, the bipartisan, seven-senator Lexow Committee began its probe on March 9, 1894. Intense political posturing on matters of procedures and protocols followed, forcing the committee to adjourn temporarily in April. Then, in mid-May Governor Roswell Flower, a Democrat, vetoed the twenty-five-thousand-dollar appropriation to support the committee's work, an action that led many to think it would never fulfill its mandate. Not to be denied by a mere executive veto, Lexow, working with the indefatigable Parkhurst, approached New York City's Chamber of Commerce, which promptly agreed to underwrite expenses. Back on track, work began in earnest in late May and, outside of a break during the highest heat of summer, would stretch until the end of the year. Those months of testimony revealed not only the nature and extent of police corruption but also detailed information on what went on in New York's underworld.

The committee received testimony under oath from 678 witnesses. There were others whose testimony was never received, for many potentially valuable witnesses had fled the city, including about one hundred brothel madams who temporarily relocated to Chicago. Still, the committee had plenty of people on its deponent list, of both high profile and low, and provided more than enough pulp for the newspaper mills, whose pages were filled for months with details of committee proceedings.[8]

The committee ultimately published 5,766 pages of minutes, testimony, and relevant documents. Much of the testimony concerned the ways in which the police took money from those being "protected," while other accounts showed that policemen were generally reluctant to move against indecency and immorality.

On this point, witness John H. Lemon identified himself before the committee as one of Parkhurst's agents and confirmed that he had been charged with observing the happenings at the French Masquerade Ball. He testified that he had seen Superintendent of Police Byrnes enter a wine room in the gallery. Lemon told of how scantily clad women in the room were high-kicking to a cancan, of how they allowed their breasts to be exposed, of how they kissed the men, and worse.

> Q. Do you mean to say the Superintendent of Police saw these indecent exposures, and made no attempt to restrain them?
> A. Yes; I mean to say you could not help see it, because he was looking over one of the bannisters when these indecent acts were going on.[9]

A surprising amount of Lexow Committee testimony, like Lemon's, concerned music and dance, whether directly or obliquely. For instance, high-kicking especially concerned the morally minded and was expressly forbidden in licenses issued by the city for events like the French Ball. Joseph Weill, the secretary of the Cercle Français de l'Harmonie that sponsored the annual ball, received pointed interrogation on that very point. In his impertinent reply, Weill maintained that he saw no high-kicking of any kind by anyone at the French Ball, including none by the police.[10]

Near the very end of the committee's work on December 19, Anthony J. Allaire was called to testify. At issue were details of his tenure as police captain in the notorious 11th Precinct along the East River. The committee queried him about prostitution, with the committee's lead investigator, John Goff, attempting to tie this vice to the amount of music made in Allaire's precinct.

Q. Captain, by the way, that was quite a musical district while you were in command; a great deal of music there?

A. It gradually diminished as I went away.

Q. After you went away?

A. No, before I went away.

Q. When you went away there was as much music there as when you came?

A. No.

Q. Isn't it a fact that there was not a house through every street in that neighborhood that you couldn't hear the piano banging every night?

A. I don't think so.

Q. You don't think so?

A. No.

Q. Are you prepared to swear that the piano couldn't be heard in every house in that precinct while you were captain, every night in the year?

A. I have no recollection of anything of that kind.

Q. And the windows full of women?

A. No.

Q. You draw the line at that?

A. I draw the line at that.[11]

On the penultimate day of the proceedings, December 28, a crack opened onto a view of New York's social and cultural life that would widen in time. Police Captain Thomas M. Ryan was called to testify. For three months he had been the captain of the 15th Precinct, and he swore that during his short tenure there he "closed up every disorderly-house, every gambling-house and policy office, and every slide and dive in the precinct." Goff asked him if he knew what a "slide" was.

His response was that on Bleecker Street, in his precinct, there was one of the "most notorious slides in the world." Ryan was referring to the concert saloon at 157 Bleecker Street, whose name—the Slide—now applied generically to a specific class of dive. Tom Stevenson ostensibly owned that establishment, although he might have been only a shadow owner for his entrepreneurial brother Frank, the man who had run the original Black-and-Tan. The Slide had apparently been quietly, almost invisibly, in business for several years, "festering and breeding moral pestilence upon the youths of the city." The nature of the Slide's notoriety became obvious to the committee once it realized that it catered to gay men and women.[12]

The Slide was "morally the lowest in New York," according to a newspaper report from 1892, stating that many of the men there cross-dressed, wore heavy makeup, and called one another by women's names. The reporter (who brought Comstockian disdain to his story) claimed that after midnight on a typical evening the Slide swarmed with "dissolute creatures."[13]

The Excise Exchange at 330 Bowery, which opened early in 1891, was patronized by the "same class of abandoned and depraved beings." Upon entering, a banging piano, a twanging banjo, ribald songs, and loud talk and laughter regaled visitors. As at the Slide, many male patrons wore women's clothing, jewelry, and bleached their hair. A special architectural feature of the Excise Exchange was its upstairs assignation room, where crowds jammed together so that they might witness, for a fee, "the disgusting scenes taking place there." Another slide on East Fifth Street was "so vile that no woman, however low, would go there." Brothels featuring male prostitutes also existed in New York, one of which, the Golden Rule Pleasure Club on West Third Street, had even been visited by Parkhurst and Gardner.[14]

The slides were always under attack. Police action led by Captain Ryan, perhaps prompted by exposés published in the *New York Evening World*, shut down both the Slide and the Excise Exchange in January 1892, just as he had reported to the Lexow Committee. As a result of those raids, Tom Stevenson was convicted of running the "disorderly" Slide and sentenced to one year in the prison on Blackwell's Island.[15]

Doors had been kicked open, however. The following year, Frank Stevenson opened a new dive, the Metropolitan, at 34 Bond Street. There the after-hours party included the sounds of screeching singers and an old piano, while "contemptible" men and "the worst of women" danced the cancan, caroused, and immersed themselves in keen merriment. In 1894, Columbus Hall (probably better known as Paresis Hall and called colloquially the "New Slide") opened at 392 Bowery. There the clientele enjoyed popular songs set to vulgar parodies tailored for the scene. A report identified one of the singers as a Johnnie Spellman who, after leaving the stage, donned a woman's hat and veil and worked the tables, much like a pretty waiter girl would have done decades before. The same report also contained an early reference to a not-in-drag singer who waited tables when not performing, or a "singing waiter," soon to be a common feature of many New York entertainment spots.[16]

Gay New Yorkers did have some access to public entertainment in the decade before the Slide. Most notably, Billy McGlory's Armory Hall welcomed them. A reporter for the *Cincinnati Enquirer* in 1886 told of a young man with the "simpering silliness of a school girl" who sang there. "It jabbered" words that were reportedly incomprehensible but were wildly applauded by the appreciative crowd. "It" had glittery eyes without a spark of intelligence, a white pallor, a large mouth, and "lips as thick as a negro." While "it" performed, four transvestite waiters served drinks and flirted with the men.

While the singer in Billy McGlory's "jabbered," the reporter noted that the crowd "patted juba." By using this term, which is generally associated with black music and dance, he probably meant rhythmic hand-clapping. By conflating the black-and-tan and gay worlds, a burgeoning union of the socially outcast was sketched, an alliance that would be important to subsequent developments in American popular music.[17]

"The Bowery," a concert saloon with singing waiter (largely ignored). *Image by Hy. Mayer, from Rupert Hughes,* The Real New York *(New York: The Smart Set Publishing Company, 1904).*

❖

Although the Lexow Committee was not a grand jury, but an investigation by and for the state Senate, it still resulted in forty police officers indicted on charges that ranged from bribery to neglect of duty. However, by 1897 no indicted policeman remained in jail and all those dismissed from the force had been reinstated. Many disorderly houses quickly returned to their former practices, and saloons continued to buck the blue laws. Life appeared to go on much as before.[18]

Yet, even before the committee finished its work, voters made it clear that they had been paying attention. The November 1894 election was another tidal wave for Republicans. Besides maintaining control of both branches of the legislature, they also captured the governor's mansion, giving them full power in the state. In the city, voters kicked Tammany Hall out of the mayor's office for the first time in twenty years, and by a landslide.

New York's new Republican mayor had campaigned on exercising his powers to shake up the police department, and after his inauguration he promptly set about fulfilling that promise. Significantly, the mayor bore responsibility for appointing the bipartisan police commission that would oversee the administration of the police force. One of his appointees, Theodore Roosevelt (who had run unsuccessfully for mayor against Tammany in 1886), was immediately elected the commission's president. Roosevelt fixed on a progressive reform crusade to clean up the department and control vice in the city, work that was only partially successful yet contributed greatly to his political profile. The Progressive Era was coming to New York City and the nation at large, a movement in no small part the result of the Lexow Committee.[19]

❖

Consolidation of the five boroughs into "The City of Greater New York" became official on New Year's Day, 1898, so victory in the November 1897 city hall election mattered even more than before. When a Tammany Democrat prevailed and became Greater New York's first mayor, many believed that the days of abject corruption had returned. The statewide election in November 1898 was then the next opportunity for Republicans to exert some control over Tammany. Col. Theodore Roosevelt had recently returned from his July dash up San Juan Hill during the Spanish-American War and soon after accepted his party's nomination for governor, running against the brother of New York's mayor. With a national hero at the head of the ticket, voters elected the full slate of Republican administrative office seekers and returned control of both the Assembly and the Senate to Republicans. While Albany belonged to the Republican Party, New York City seemed still to belong to Tammany Hall Democrats.

Within twenty-four hours of the election, whispers were circulating in the capital that there might be a "new Lexow," a clearly partisan effort to discredit and harness Tammany Hall and its allies. That idea went quiet until March 29, 1899, when the new chair of the Assembly Committee on Cities, Robert Mazet (R-Manhattan), introduced a resolution that called for the appointment of seven members of the Assembly to constitute a committee charged with investigating New York City's police force and the "protection" it allegedly offered to saloons and brothels. After six hours of pro-and-con debate, Mazet's resolution passed 87–7. The police department was to be "re-Lexowed."[20]

The Mazet Committee convened within ten days of the resolution and set about work that would stretch into early December. Its published report, similar in poundage to that of the Lexow Committee, took up five volumes and a total of 5,587 pages, including Assembly resolutions, committee proceedings, copies of pertinent documents, and a useful index.[21]

Like Lexow, the Mazet Committee uncovered intriguing details about New York's underground cultural life. Proceedings showed that a new generation of vice dives had since opened—the Empire Garden, the Manhattan, Artistic Club, Broadway Garden, the Trolley Club, the White Elephant, and the Cairo among them. Testimony about what one saw in such places touched on now-standard themes: too-short dresses, suggestive dancing, indecent actresses, women smoking, police involvement in the culture (for instance, a police baton substituted for the sword in a lascivious sword dance), and open solicitation. There was also extended testimony on the possible causes for a rash of suicides and suicide attempts by young women at a dance hall on the Bowery, a dive that was promptly renamed by the press "McGurk's Suicide Hall" (and by which name it became a part of New York's vice lore).[22]

More even than the Lexow Committee, the Mazet Committee pursued an intense interest in New York's gay underground and the music and wild new dances integral to that culture. The issue cropped up on the very first day of proceedings, April 8, in testimony provided by Police Chief William S. Devery. Devery had also testified before the Lexow Committee, which led subsequently to his conviction on bribery and extortion charges and his dismissal from the force, so he was particularly careful in his testimony. (The conviction was subsequently overturned, and Devery was not only reinstated but promoted in June 1898 to police chief.) The committee's head counsel, Frank Moss, a committed anti-vice crusader who had formerly been an attorney for the SPC and an associate counsel of the Lexow Committee, interrogated Devery aggressively from the start. The inquiry soon came around to questions on the Manilla Hall, with Devery's evasive answers surely straying into dissembling.

Q. What about those male degenerates that frequent the Manilla. Did you ever hear about that?

A. Male degenerates?

Q. Do you not know what a male degenerate is?

A. I presume I understand what you mean.

Q. Have you ever heard about their frequenting the Manilla?

A. I have heard about people of that class frequenting those places, yes, sir.

Q. The Manilla?

A. The Manilla.

Q. Have you heard, then, that there are male degenerates upon
the Bowery in sufficient number to be noticeable?

A. No; I have not heard that.

Next, Moss questioned Devery about the dive that had replaced the
Slide as New York's most notorious, then abandoned interrogation for
speechifying.

Q. Have you heard of the Paresis Hall?

A. I have heard of that.

Q. What have you heard about Paresis Hall?

A. Touching upon the degenerates that you spoke about that frequent there.

Q. That is a place that is noticed because it is frequented by those
persons, is it not?

A. That is presumably the reason it gets that name.

Q. And the men that go there are noted characters and are known
by women's names, are they not?

A. I have heard that.

Q. Do you know where it is? Such a thing is a notable thing in
the city, a place where these miserable beings congregate in
the evening; and even you, with your dense condition of mind,
know what I mean? . . . Why do you not, as Chief of Police,
when you hear of a hall notable for these filthy and abominable
practices which have no defender anywhere in human civili-
zation, why do you not go to it and stamp it out? . . . Do you
know what they do is a felony . . . punishable by imprisonment
for twenty years?[23]

Other witnesses were called to testify on gay dives. George P.
Hammond, an officer of Parkhurst's City Vigilance League (a spin-off

of the SPC), acknowledged to the committee that he had investigated Paresis Hall several times and even offered that one of the regular patrons there was what "they call a hermaphrodite." Recalled again before the committee in November, Hammond expressed his strongly held belief that male prostitution had increased dramatically since his earlier testimony and that new places catering to the "dissolute classes" had since opened, six of them on the Bowery alone. He spoke in particular about Little Bucks, across the street from Paresis Hall, which was known for its "circus," a lewd show that featured three or four "of them." Hammond claimed that the generally immoral culture in Little Bucks encouraged male prostitutes to solicit freely and openly. And then he proceeded to make an extraordinary charge.

They danced the rag time there. By the rag time I mean a decidedly immoral dance. That is one of the evils of this thing. You will find the word "rag time" used in high social circles. The people do not know what it means. They do not know where it emanated from. If they did they would blush for shame. It sometimes makes me boil over with indignation when I hear the phrase used.

Hammond was not the first witness to draw a connection between ragtime and immorality, nor the only one to suggest a relationship between the music, the dance, and gay New York. Chief Devery, for instance, confronted by Councilor Moss with an advertisement for Manilla Hall that encouraged people to come "see the rag-time, and the Ki-ki and such things as that," had reluctantly acknowledged that such dancing might "at times become vulgar."[24]

Hammond, Moss, and the members of the Mazet Committee were part of a public avalanche of criticism that questioned ragtime's character and the moral bearings of people who enjoyed it. Chief Devery wrote the year before the Mazet Committee proceedings that ragtime was a "filthy abomination," and others blasted it from similarly high, lofty perches. Arthur Weld, a professor of music at the Wisconsin Conservatory of Music, declaimed while the Mazet investigation was in progress on "The Invasion of Vulgarity in Music." According to the professor, to pass by an open window any night on an American street was to be subjected to music made by the "musical (?) Satan"—"'rag-time,' 'coon' songs, skirt dances, and the rest of the tawdry crew. . . . This cheap, trashy stuff cannot elevate even the most degraded minds." Professor Weld strained to find appropriate pejoratives: "evil," "vulgar," "hideous," "rubbish," "an epidemic," and a "national calamity."[25]

⁂

Will Marion Cook, an eminent African American composer of the early twentieth century, wrote that as early as 1875 black musicians in "questionable resorts along the Mississippi" had begun to develop the idioms that would give form to ragtime. He noted too that the new, still-aborning music received wide and enthusiastic exposure at the 1893 Chicago World's Fair. Cook got his timeline and history more-or-less right. Ragtime did come from black American musical culture; it was a fusion of standard dance forms, marches, the cakewalk, blackface minstrelsy, and much more; and it was nurtured in the brothels, saloons, and dives of the American Midwest. One immediately obvious feature set it apart from other music: its heavily syncopated, "ragged" character that, as Cook explained, "offered unique rhythms, curious groupings of words and melodies which gave the zest of unexpectedness."[26]

Ragtime appears to have first hit New York in 1896. The *Brooklyn Daily Eagle* on September 6 printed a review of the vaudeville show at Hyde and Behman's Theatre, in which the earliest known reference to the term "rag time" is found.

The novelty of the performance is Ben R. Harney, who is out to interest students of American music and should have been seen and heard by Dr. [Antonín] Dvořák. He invents and plays what he calls rag time airs and dances, the effect of syncopations being to make the melody ragged. This is real American music; not of the highest order, but genuine. A brunette from South Carolina is with him, and the dances and cake walks of the two are quaint and good.

Harney, a black man who passed for white, was an early and persuasive ambassador for ragtime who traveled widely and spread this "real American music" to many new audiences.[27]

By 1898 news and tidbits on ragtime filled New York's newspapers. There were horses named Ragtime, ragtime operas, a Ragtime Bowling Club, something (facetiously?) called "Polish ragtime," music from *Il Trovatore* played in ragtime style, and ragtime poems; and the Independent Citizens Party even put up a "Ragtime Candidate" for governor (he got two thousand votes). Ragtime had arrived, and it was big.

Although ragtime has come to be thought of as a piano-based concert music, at the start people expected to dance to its intoxicating rhythms—called "negro dance time" by one reviewer. Ragtime dancing quickly supplanted the cancan as the most sensuous and lascivious dance in New York. As a black American dance form much loved and practiced by gay New Yorkers—not white, European, and straight, like the cancan—it was a target for the authorities on both counts. Indeed, the president of New York's Police Board (Theodore Roosevelt's old position) was unequivocal—"'rag-time' dancing in public halls is to be stopped."[28]

⋅✦⋅

That did not happen. Instead, ragtime dancing grew into such a phenomenon that it became not a single dance, but descriptive of a whole style of dancing. Virtually any moves to syncopated dance music qualified as ragtime dancing, a dance fashion that would last for two decades. The phrase itself, though, had a short life and was soon supplanted by "tough dancing," which better described the wide variety of new moves and steps.[29]

Fundamental changes in the ways Americans danced were signaled even before ragtime by the development of "spieling," perhaps the first of the tough dances. Spieling required a certain attitude. Although based on the waltz's body position, dancers' postures were not graceful but rigid, with the lead arm jutted out straight and aggressively—"like an upraised pumphandle"—which made for a noteworthy style statement on the dance floor. The male leader would slouch up against the female, bend forward and put his chin on her shoulder, while she did the same to him. Then he would plant one foot firmly and pivot his partner wildly, swinging her around in a small circle with such force and speed that her skirts flew up revealing tantalizing glimpses of ankles and legs. In the midst of this frenzy, the male projected a detached cool—"saws wood and gives everybody on the floor the dead face." Songwriters William Jerome and Andrew Mack knew a fresh wind when they felt it, and set it to a waltz rhythm.

> At Walhalla Hall, why she kills them all,
> As waltzing together we twirl,
> She sets them all crazy, a "spieler," a "daisy,"
> For my Pearl's a Bow'ry girl!

"Pivoting" appeared at about the same time as spieling. This dance, especially favored among the lower classes, was also derived from the waltz. In pivoting, the leader planted his feet solidly and swung his partner around energetically; then the follower took the lead and did likewise. A dance floor filled with pivoting couples made for a swirl of colors, motion, and human energy.[30]

The year after notices of spieling and pivoting first appeared in New York's popular press, a new dance grabbed attention. "It is well to say that this winter young people are going to dance the 'two-step' more than anything else." The two-step was an even more energetic dance than spieling or pivoting. As the name implies, partners executed two steps or slides per beat (while the one-step, which would become a feature of later "modern dance," consisted of one step per beat). Not complicated, it invited variation and creative improvisation by dancers who were manifestly unfettered by the "rules" of dancing. High kicks, stops, hops, drags, fancy glides, spieling, and pivoting were all enjoyed while dancing the two-step.[31]

Meanwhile and in the deep background, dancers in the lowest of dives were developing the next generation of fun-filled, sexy moves. One of these—the turkey trot—came directly from black American tradition, like the cakewalk. American newspapers from the 1890s contain occasional mention of it—a "syncopated sensation," according to one. While an article in an 1898 Buffalo newspaper implied that it was widely known, its full notoriety would be in the next decade when it became the progenitor of a field and forest full of "animal dances," the best known of which was the fox-trot.[32]

⋯⋯

The period at the end of the 1890s and the beginning of the 1900s was a social and cultural hinge. Attitudes and expressions that had prevailed before were connected with what came afterward, to be sure, but the articulation was so acute that New Yorkers would inevitably perceive their lives, music, dances, and bodies in new, fundamentally different ways. In dance, before the 1890s most legitimate styles had prescribed steps, moves, and ways of holding partners; afterward, there would be a wide variety of imaginative tough dances, with moves borrowed from the waltz, the polka, the cancan, clogging, jigging, the cakewalk, and others, and put to vastly different effect. And in American popular music, while syncopation had been a feature for decades, highly exaggerated, ragged rhythms now made for a new music that was vibrant, palpably alive, deeply exciting, and soon to be ubiquitous. The Age of Ragtime had begun.

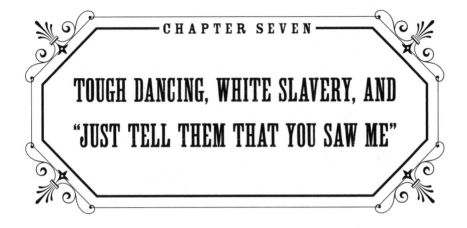

CHAPTER SEVEN

TOUGH DANCING, WHITE SLAVERY, AND "JUST TELL THEM THAT YOU SAW ME"

FUELED BY RAGTIME, New Yorkers went dance crazy. Take, for instance, the real-life story of Annie Donnelly, who was fourteen years old in 1909. Her father drove a horse-drawn cab seven days a week, twelve or more hours a day, yet his fifteen-dollars-a-week pay barely met the needs of a family of five who, plus a lodger, fit tightly in the four small rooms of a rented tenement apartment on the Lower East Side. Annie, cramped for space and with no privacy, lived her social life outside the apartment. As a young girl, that meant walks with her girl-friends or hanging out in the stairwell. But with adolescence and the attention of boys, socializing almost inevitably expanded to include the dance hall. The first invitation flustered her, but after the proper hesi-tancy she accompanied her swain to pugilist Johnny Sullivan's Social Club in a low-ceilinged basement dive. The room was jammed with thirty couples, all trying to avoid stepping on each other while dancing to ragtime. Annie, a bit shy at first, found the music intoxicating and was soon giddy with the dancing. In short order, "modern" Annie felt confident enough to go to a dance hall in the company of a girlfriend or two or even by herself. In fact, to be accompanied by a young man handicapped her pick of dance partners, for, ideally, somewhere in the hall was a skilled and energetic dancer—Annie's first choice. Annie acquired the dance-hall habit, not because she was unusual in the pleasure she took in music and dancing, but because she was normal.[1]

A survey from Annie's time showed that she was far from alone in her interest: ninety-five percent of young working-class women in New York went to dance halls and ninety percent between ages thirteen and twenty-five claimed that dancing was their favorite pastime. Some danced every night, while two hundred thousand made it to a dance hall at least once a week. Annie, like the others of her age, gender, and class, prided herself on becoming proficient in the latest dances and trying them out in the dance hall, up tempo. Dancing, boys, and the drinking of evermore stale beer seemed of a piece with a life that to Annie and friends swirled each day brighter and faster.[2]

Annie, of course, tough danced. The term was descriptively applied to a wealth of dances, most of them with colorful names, many of them probably locally invented, locally named, and since lost to history. Annie might have tough danced to the walk back, the hug-me-tight, the lovers' two-step, the hesitation waltz, the Bowery glide, the slow rag, or any of a number of animal dances: the turkey trot, the bunny hug (sometimes called the bunny hug two-step and even "The Dance of Death"), the kangaroo squeeze, the jackass step, or the newest of these exhilarating dances, the grizzly bear.

Some understanding of what tough dancing actually looked like is possible today, thanks in no small part to Thomas Edison. In September 1897, cinematographer William Heise set up his monster of a camera in Edison's Black Maria Studio in West Orange, New Jersey (the nation's first movie studio), and invited James F. Kelly and Dorothy Kent, members of Waite's Comedy Company, to dance as he filmed. He shot one twenty-eight-second short of them dancing "The Bowery Waltz," which Edison's distribution company quickly released. Not at all like a "proper" waltz, the Bowery version contained, according to the advertising, "many humorous situations." Viewers saw the stiff lead arm of the spieler, gliding leg motions, an awkward dip, attempts (generally failures) at some fancy moves, a clumsily draped embrace, belligerent body postures, and the appearance of deep inebriation. Since Kelly and Kent were for some years an in-demand comedy duo, the film was less likely representational of the way a waltz would have been performed in a Bowery dance hall and more likely something that the Waite's Comedy Company audience would have found funny.[3]

That does not appear to be the case for a forty-five-second film from 1902 titled "A Tough Dance" (and, alternately, "A Tough Dance on the Bowery" and "A Tough Dance at McGurk's"). Cinematographer Robert Kates Bonine, a pioneer in the film business, approached filmmaking as representational of the "actual"; he did not subscribe to the new approach that purported to tell stories through film. In keeping with his concept, for instance, he once set up his camera on lower Broadway in mid-May 1902 and simply filmed the scene: horse-drawn cabs and streetcars (some pulled by horses), throngs of people (many jaywalking), no panning at all, and over in 1'33".[4]

When Bonine filmed "A Tough Dance at McGurk's [Suicide Hall]" on June 19, 1902, he wanted the "actual" thing. Kid Foley and Sailor Lil were featured in the film, although little is known about them. (Foley had a short career in second-tier vaudeville and might have been a middleweight pugilist; Lil's life, career, even her real name, are a mystery.) In the film, Kid and Lil walk into the frame from opposite sides, wearing rags and acting, well, tough. They seem almost to be stalking each other. Kid hits Lil in the face with his open palm (somewhat) playfully; a true tough herself, she seems not to mind. Arm in arm, they strut for a few beats, cakewalk-style. Then they embrace. No fancy waltz posturing here: it's a bear-hug embrace with Lil placing both her hands on Kid's shoulders while Kid sinks his hands into Lil's bottom. They thrust their lower bodies far away from each other and twirl madly about, almost parodying a waltz, while keeping good time to the music (which is unheard by the viewer, of course). They spin more wildly, impress with a few fancy throws (similar to the much later jitterbug), then halt suddenly while Lil appears to grab her crotch and Kid looks on in interest. They resume their bear hug, whirl crazily while Kid's hands slide ever farther down Lil's backside, show off some more energetic throws, spin around some more, and then toss themselves on the floor and roll on top of each other, and . . . "Cut!" (in the nick of time).[5]

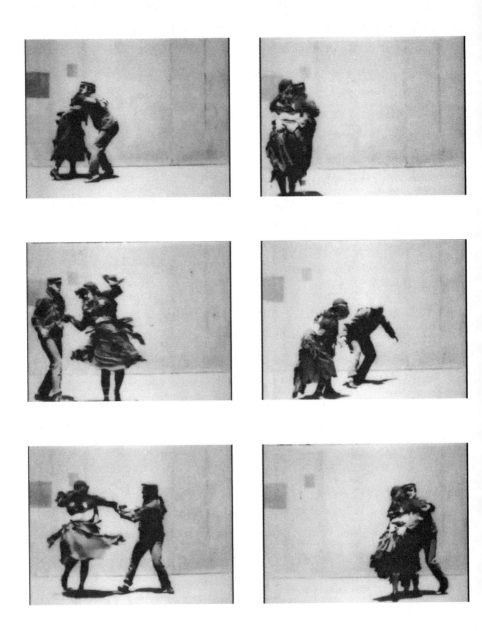

The film corroborates contemporaneous accounts of tough dancing as close-bodied intimacy in which couples wrap themselves in each other and throw restraint and conventional modes of dance decorum to the wind. Shaking of hips, shimmying, twisting, and thrusting of the lower body were all parts of the accepted repertoire of moves.

"A Tough Dance." *Stills from silent film by Robert Kates Bonine. American Mutoscope and Biograph Co., 1902. Courtesy of the Library of Congress, Motion Picture, Broadcasting and Recorded Sound Division, 96520498. Video. https://www.loc.gov/item/96520498/.*

Tough dancing generally required little knowledge of traditional dance steps and encouraged dancers to improvise creatively around the few basics. That tough dancing was so free and loose likely pleased dancers who implicitly rejected rigid middle-class (and middle-aged) ballroom ideals.[6]

✦

As more and more New Yorkers danced, more and more places became available for dancing. Balls, for instance, which had once been for adults and those of some means, now proliferated and threw open their doors to the masses. A club, whose sole purpose might be the sponsoring of private dances, would rent a dance hall, gather a band, and then advertise by handing out "throwaways" on the street, which told when and where, and gave some coded idea of the nature of the dance. These sorts of balls increased greatly in popularity, facilitated by the number of public halls available. A sponsoring society in 1895 could choose to rent from about 130 appropriate spaces; in 1910 the choices numbered 195, exactly fifty percent more. Since many were situated over saloons, access to alcohol was easy.[7]

The weekly sponsored ball became the everyday ball when large dance pavilions, inexpensive public transportation, and a general embrace of leisure time by the public changed the social and cultural landscape. The well-off had long enjoyed summers in Newport, the Catskills, or the Hamptons, where dancing was typically part of the swirl. The hoi polloi had the resorts and amusements at Coney Island or Rockaway, but they did not regularly indulge in beach jaunts until public transportation lines extended out that far at the beginning of the twentieth century. Transportation being suddenly cheap and easy, Annie and friends took the streetcars to the large dance pavilions, danced and partied all day, and dropped into bed at home before their parents' curfews.

Then there were the dancing academies. These had been around for decades, centuries even, and always with the legitimate mission

"The Old Coney Island." *Image by Hy. Mayer, from Rupert Hughes,* The Real New York *(New York: Smart Set Publishing Company, 1904).*

of teaching people to dance. By the turn into the new century, that purpose was not always so apparent. Some academies still taught the steps, both old ones and some of the new, but other newly wrought "academies" functioned more like once-weekly dance halls to which "students" subscribed. To respond to this threatening innovation, legitimate dancing masters across the nation organized themselves into the United Professional Teachers of Dancing in America and gathered together in New York for a conference. Among the resolutions adopted during that June 1906 meeting were instructions for members not to title themselves "Professor of Dancing," as they had in the past: "We stand for dignity, grace and culture, and dignity is first. That's why we are not professors anymore." Furthermore, the one who gave fake lessons or had a bar in the "academy" was, by definition, not a true dancing master—"He is a professor."

> *The fellows that still call themselves professors lay on hands too much. They have a hauling around process that is vulgar. For the modest grace and dignity of the true waltz they have substituted the turkey trot, which is very vulgar.*

The former professors had a point. In 1908, social reformer Belle Israels persuaded the New York Council of Jewish Women to underwrite a survey of dancing in New York, the collected data of which fingered the dancing academies as flash points. She canvassed more than one hundred of these in the city and learned that the total average attendance in a week was one hundred thousand "students," most between fourteen and twenty-one years of age. Some of the academies were legitimate, but many more existed merely to enable unstructured "practicing" of the latest dance steps. According to Israels's research, many of these academies also sold liquor, allowed tough dancing and smoking by both sexes, did not monitor for revealing or suggestive clothing, and even allowed prostitutes to work the floor.[8]

This, of course, paralleled conditions in the nonacademy places where Annie and her friends danced weekly: the local dance hall, of which there were more than five hundred open in the city for regular business. To the moralistic, these places were traps. Israels and her Committee of Amusement and Vacations Resources of Working Girls in New York pointed that out:

> *You cannot dance night after night, held in the closest of sensual embraces, with every effort made in the style of dancing to appeal to the worst that is in you, and remain unshaken by it.*

Furthermore, Israels exclaimed that the period's dancing had become "not dancing at all, but a series of indecent antics to the accompaniment of music"—the result of its birth in tenderloin dives and dance halls. Bacchanalian scenes in dance spots became open spectacle: "Color, light, music, confetti, the dance, together combine to produce an intense and voluptuous intoxication."[9]

George B. H. Swayze, a physician from Philadelphia, took to the prestigious pages of *The Medical Times* in 1906 (the lead article no less) and summarized his cohort's view on causation and prostitution ("the social evil") in a single arabesque sentence of unequivocation:

> *A reeling quickstep through the open gates to the social evil is spurred by the sensual familiarities of the sexes formulated and practiced by rote in dancing-parlors, schools, halls, towed along into late night hours by the suggestive motion-rhythms of beguiling music that rocks mutual desire to the vortex of acute risqué, if not also to the kept-house of actual assignation.*

Progressive-Era moralists were confident that tough dancing to ragtime (if not also reeling quicksteps) in an erotically charged atmosphere encouraged young women like Annie Donnelly down a chute, "which, every year, thousands of girls descend to the way of the prodigal." From their perspective, it was Annie's love of dancing that started

The path to perdition. The dogs are named Disease, Suicide, and Insanity.
Image from Mordecai Fowler Ham, The Modern Dance: A Historical and
Analytical Treatment of the Subject . . . *(San Antonio: San Antonio Printing Co.,
1916). Courtesy of the Library of Congress, Music Division, item 16015355.*

her journey toward perdition less than a year after her first dance-hall experience. And she, like Maggie almost two decades earlier, came to learn that her loss of virtue meant that she was destined for the worst kind of life.[10]

⟞⟐⟝

Israels's study showed that saloon dance halls functioned differently during the time that Annie began going to them than they had only a few years earlier. For, by her figures, about half of all saloon dance halls in New York had become "hotels." More precisely, they had become "Raines Law hotels."[11]

The so-called Raines Law is the poster child for the Theory of Unintended Consequences. The brainstorm of State Senator John Raines, the 1896 law confirmed a view held by a majority of senators that the sale of alcohol on Sundays in New York City should continue to be prohibited. From the perspective of these senators, it was perfectly acceptable to deny the working classes their Sunday glass of beer at the local saloon, but what about middle-class businessmen and travelers staying in hotels? Should they not be allowed a glass with their hotel meals? Accordingly, the Raines Law banned the sale of alcohol throughout the city on Sundays *except* for hotels, which were defined in the law as establishments with ten or more lodging rooms. These and only these were allowed to serve alcoholic drink on Sunday and only then with a meal.

Saloon proprietors quickly exploited the definition of a food-serving hotel. They installed thin walls (or even hung sheets) in unused parts of their buildings and thus made up ten "rooms," into which they piled pallets or cots. They then laid fresh plans to serve food in their newly designated hotel, which often consisted only of "brick sandwiches" (so dry, moldy, and desiccated that they were clearly props). With these strokes the letter of the law was satisfied. Erstwhile saloons had only now to apply for licenses as "Raines Law hotels" and drink would be back on the Sunday menu. Very shortly after the law's passage, New

York City could boast of having ten thousand more hotel rooms than before. Of the 1,407 legal hotels in 1905 Manhattan and the Bronx, about 1,150 were Raines Law hotels.[12]

Lodging, of course, was secondary to the Raines Law hotels, but there were now so-called rooms with beds where there had been none before. Prostitutes, who had heretofore used saloons as places of solicitation with the contract consummated elsewhere, suddenly had on-site accommodation, the hourly or daily rate for which would be paid by the client. Unmarried couples no longer had to seek out assignation rooms, since rooms for rent were easily at hand in any Raines Law hotel. Furthermore, the business side of prostitution changed dramatically. Brothels no longer afforded prostitutes any special advantage, which pushed that institution's market share of the commercialized sex industry into steep decline. And the lines of division between solicitation in saloons, concert saloons, or restaurants became fuzzy, as a contract made in one such place could be easily fulfilled at a convenient Raines Law hotel. By the turn into the twentieth century, the Raines Law hotel had become the primary locus of prostitution in the city.[13]

Prostitutes benefited economically in manifold ways under the new law. Raines Law hotel proprietors typically provided a percentage kickback to prostitutes on rooms rented for their business purposes. And by being an ever-present fixture in Raines Law hotels, prostitutes became assets to the institution's liquor business, for which they received an under-the-table portion of the liquor tabs (usually about ten percent). Plus, of course, their fee for sex. For a prostitute, the Raines Law was a financial windfall.[14]

❦

It was also a good time to be a musician in New York. Nearly all the thousand-or-so Raines Law hotels featured dancing—this in addition to the hundred-or-so dancing academies and the five-hundred-or-so dance halls. Live music by live musicians was required when anyone danced. Then there were concert saloons and theaters, both necessarily with music, and thousands of saloons that welcomed buskers or local musicians who dropped in to play for tips. Whatever the number, a lot of musicians were making a lot of popular music and getting paid to do it.

As is usually the case, the "routine," everyday musicians who did not live in the rarefied (and heavily documented) air of classical music got overlooked by muse Clio. Occasionally a name or a character would bubble up in print and have to represent the unnamed thousands. One such was "Piano Joe." He lived at 96 Bowery and died suddenly of tuberculosis in October 1906, which prompted the *New York Sun* to lament: "Piano Joe Has Passed Away, No More Will He Play in the Dark in a Bowery Café." A widower and the father of an eight-year-old girl, his real name was Joseph Cull, the son of Augustus Cull who was himself a pianist "far above the average." For years, Piano Joe played nightly in the concert saloon behind the Bank Café. Unlike many of his musician peers, Joe loved "Ginney music," or what we would today call the light classics, and the concerts given by the renowned pianists of his day—such as "Paderooski," who might be "the best in the world, now that Joe's dead." The night before his death had been like thousands of others: playing the "pie-anna" until closing time, cracking jokes, entertaining with his renditions of songs like "Waltz Me Around Again" and "Come, Take a Skate Wit' Me, Katie." "He could play anything, Joe could," said barmaid Nell.[15]

"Up in Tinpan Alley the music publishers and their clerks were lamenting Piano Joe's death also," for Joe was a cog in what had become a very big music publishing machine. Music publishers did not charge Piano Joe for sheet music. He could have any song he wanted, for his performances at the Bank Café introduced audiences to new songs and helped pump up the sales of sheet music that, across the whole industry, reached into the millions of pieces per year.

The music publishing business during the time of Piano Joe was concentrated on Twenty-Eighth Street between Fifth and Sixth Avenues, although it spilled out onto neighboring streets as well. The area by 1903 was popularly known as "Tin Pan Alley," named after all the pianos jangling out opened windows onto the street below, which sounded to those of the time much like the "tin pan music" of a shivaree.[16]

Theodore Dreiser, who later came to fame for his novel *Sister Carrie*, left a fine portrait of a typical Tin Pan Alley music publisher in an article for *Harper's Weekly*. A reception room, an office, a stock room, and a music room were all mandatory. The latter might have rugs, divans, and potted plants, all designed to project class and standing; necessarily, there were pianos, perhaps even three or four of them. Salaried pianists pitched the company's latest for any star performer looking for new repertoire, or even wrote down the whistled tune of a songwriter who could not read or write music. "The marvel of the common song" staged everything.[17]

Dreiser even surreptitiously plugged a song. In his article, a vain but talented female singer named "Miss Yaeger" is squired into the music room. The publisher sends Charlie, his stock boy, out to get a "professional copy" of "Just Tell Them That You Saw Me" for Miss Yaeger, in his expressed belief that it would fit her voice nicely. The only real song written by a living songwriter mentioned in the article, it was composed by Paul Dresser, Theodore Dreiser's brother.

❖

Paul Dresser stands as a particularly good study of the relationship between the music publishing industry and the sporting life. Born in Indiana in 1857, he joined a minstrel troupe early, and was soon set on a career as a singer and entertainer. He also began to write songs, mainly tearjerkers about mothers or young girls, the deaths of the undeserving, or some maudlin combination of the types. Such was not the case with his biggest hit, however. "On the Banks of the Wabash" (1897) was an homage to his Terre Haute hometown, and it eventually became Indiana's state song. Its success prompted many to compare his genius to that of Stephen Foster and made Dresser probably the best-known songwriter of his day, as well as one of the best-off. (At least for a while, for he was notoriously impecunious.)[18]

Despite his flair for middle-class parlor sentimentality, Dresser, who had studied for the priesthood when young, was no stranger to the demimonde. While living in Evansville, Indiana, in the 1880s, Dresser maintained an amorous relationship with Sallie Walker, who according to his brother's biographical account was Evansville's most prominent madam. Their relationship came to an end because of his repeated infidelities, including with other prostitutes and perhaps even some of the women in Sallie's house. After moving to New York City, Dresser fully indulged his desires, becoming a frequent habitué of the city's restaurants (he weighed more than three hundred pounds), theaters, Raines Law hotels, saloons, and brothels.[19]

Theodore wrote of his brother that "out of such a world as this he built so many of his songs." "Just Tell Them That You Saw Me" (1895) serves as an example, one that Dreiser said followed from a chance encounter with someone Dresser knew. It is a song about small-village "Madge," who goes to the big city and is sucked into the whirl. Some time later, now pale and thin, she accidentally meets on the street an acquaintance from back home and shrinks away from him. Mystified by her coldness, the hometown friend asks if there is anything he could relay to Madge's mother:

> *Just tell them that you saw me, she said, they'll know the rest,*
> *Just tell them I was looking well you know,*
> *Just whisper if you get a chance to mother dear, and say—*
> *I love her as I did long, long ago.*

This chorus is set to a heart-wrenching melody that expresses beautifully Madge's barely maintained composure in the face of her fall. The song spoke to a zeitgeist and sold hundreds of thousands of copies. The title itself even enjoyed a vogue as a parting between acquaintances.[20]

Other songs by Dresser about innocent village girls gone wrong or the temptations of the city that led to female dissipation include "The Outcast Unknown" (1887), "I Wonder If She'll Ever Come Back to Me" (1896), "The Path That Leads the Other Way" (1898), "Every Night There's a Light Shining Through the Window Pane" (1898), "I Wonder Where She Is Tonight" (1899), and, in 1904:

> She went to the city, 'twas all they would say,
> She went to the city, far, far away,
> And then I heard just the faintest sigh from two hearts that yearned,
> She grew kind o' restless and wanted to go,
> Said she'd be back in a few weeks or so,
> She went to the city with a tear in her eye, but she never returned.

One of the last songs written by Dresser appears also to be of this ilk. "My Gal Sal" (1905) tells of a sweetheart who has been gone only "a fortnight" yet it seemed like "twenty years." But unlike nearly all of Dresser's sentimental sweetheart songs, Sal was no innocent but rather a "peculiar sort of gal" and "a wild sort of devil." In fact, according to Theodore Dreiser, Sal *had* been gone for twenty years, for the song is Dresser's paean to Sallie Walker, the Evansville madam he had loved.[21]

⁜

Dresser's death in 1906 occurred near the time when the sentimental ballad finally went out of fashion. And it was also near the time when a young genius songwriter first pointed American popular music toward an even brighter future.

Israel Baline was born in 1888 in western Siberia, the son of a cantor. He arrived in New York City in 1893 and, like many other recent immigrants, moved with his family into a Lower East Side tenement. Of a decidedly musical temperament, young Izzy worked as a singing waiter in the Pell Street concert saloon belonging to "Nigger Mike" (a dark-skinned Jew). He was a widely appreciated "riot" in the job, which required him to sing while serving tray-loads of beer, making change, and kicking nickel tips along the floor to the kitchen. As expected of a singing waiter, he quickly became adept (and renowned) at providing salacious parodies of the day's popular songs.[22]

In 1907 he branched out and published his first song, "Marie from Sunny Italy." Whether by mistake or intention his name appeared on the cover as "I. Berlin," and Izzy Baline transfigured into the American "Irving" and the cosmopolitan "Berlin."

Once started on a songwriting career that would last into the 1960s (Berlin died in 1989 at 101 years old), songs poured from him. He claimed that he averaged writing four to five songs a week, the majority ultimately rejected. The publishable ones, though, make up a veritable Top 100 of the most-loved and best-known in the history of American music: "White Christmas," "I Love a Piano," "Oh How I Hate to Get Up in the Morning," "Always," "Shaking the Blues Away," "Blue Skies," "A Pretty Girl Is Like a Melody," "Puttin' on the Ritz," "When I Lost You," "Let's Have Another Cup of Coffee," "How Deep Is the Ocean," "Easter Parade," "Heat Wave," "Dancin' Cheek to Cheek," "God Bless America," "Doin' What Comes Natur'lly," "Anything You Can Do," "There's No Business Like Show Business," and many, many more.[23]

Berlin's genius lay in his singular ability to draw from a range of New York ethnicities and express how disparate cultures can cohere in a song. He was an immigrant Jew who married a Catholic and adopted an urbane name while maintaining close friendships and working relations with those of Irish, Italian, German, and African American heritage. His music is of all these and more.

Steeped as he was in the day's song and dance, Berlin could not and did not ignore ragtime. In some of his early ragtime pieces, Berlin added lyrics to previously published piano pieces and republished them; "Wild Cherries" (1909), "Oh That Beautiful Rag" (1910), and "Grizzly Bear" (1910) are of this sort. But by far the greatest number of Berlin's ragtime songs were freshly wrought. Whereas early efforts acknowledged the primacy of black Americans in the music's birth and development (the protagonists in "Wild Cherries," for example, are Jackson and his bride, Lucinda Morgan White, both black stereotypes), Sadie and Yiddle in "Yiddle, On Your Fiddle, Play Some Ragtime" (1909) are Jewish, Tony and Marie in "Sweet Marie, Make-a-Rag-a-Time Dance Wid Me" (1910) are Italian, and other ragtime songs acknowledge the Irish, Germans, and even white Anglo-Saxon Americans, as in "That Mysterious Rag" (1911). Berlin's catalogue at this time was of all Americans, sung large, loud, and ragged.[24]

It was also a ragtime song that cemented Berlin's fame. "Alexander's Ragtime Band," published in 1911, quickly became a big hit.

> *Oh, ma honey, oh, ma honey, better hurry and let's meander*
> *Ain't you goin'? Ain't you goin'? To the leader man, ragged meter man?*
> *Oh, ma honey, oh, ma honey, let me take you to Alexander's*
> *Grand stand brass band, ain't you comin' along?*

Then the chorus, and a burst of Whitmanesque enthusiasm for grand-standing, brassy American music:

> *Come on and hear! Come on and hear! Alexander's ragtime band!*
> *Come on and hear! Come on and hear! It's the best band in the land!*

And to make it clear that Alexander is a true ragged meter man, the bandleader could even take one of America's best-known and most-loved songs by the nation's finest songwriter and rag it.

> *And if you care to hear the Swanee River played in ragtime*
> *Come on and hear, come on and hear,*
> *Alexander's Ragtime Band.*

But to look for the ragged rhythms of ragtime in the sheet music to "Alexander's Ragtime Band" is mostly to look in vain. It appears to be a song about ragtime, but it is not a ragtime song. Berlin's cue—the ragged meter man who can turn Stephen Foster's "Old Folks at Home" into ragtime—makes clear that ragtime is in the performance and not necessarily in the notation. Ben Harney published an instruction manual on ragtime in 1897 in which he provided directions on how to rag just about any style of music, a feat that became something of a fad during that time (and that Berlin acknowledged in his "That Mesmerizing Mendelssohn Tune" of 1909). Harry Von Tilzer, another leading songwriter of the era, wrote that " 'ragtime' is not a type of song; it is a type of song-treatment."[25]

Only twenty-four of Berlin's published songs include the word "rag" in the title or in the lyrics. Yet many, if not all, of his songs from the first decade of his career could be ragged, and most probably were in performance. The dead notes on the printed page did not the music make, but rather the ragged sounds in the air, where, according to Von Tilzer, one could hear "the spirit of the American people, their extraordinary activity, restlessness, initiative, joyousness and capacity for work, and for play."[26]

❧

Annie Donnelly's story was published in an influential book titled *What Eight Million Women Want*, authored by Reita Childe Dorr, a socialist, activist, and suffragist. The "Eight Million Women" were the members in the International Council of Women, a significant number of whom came from the rolls of the General Federation of Women's Clubs in the United States. Dorr's work was emblematic of a new approach to solving urban social problems, which, in her case, partly involved mobilizing an army of women. In the past, the various societies for the suppression of vices developed missions from the ideas or observations of a single person, designed the means to verify a problem's existence, and then attempted to solve it by bringing together the like-minded under charismatic leadership. The method favored by Dorr was bottom-up instead of top-down, with techniques borrowed from the new social sciences: postulate an issue; seek out the affected (like Annie); collect data; analyze; present conclusions dispassionately. This new sociological model applied to urban problems would prove to bring far-reaching, long-lasting change to New York's social, political, and cultural life.

An event that precipitated just such a change occurred on April 26, 1900. Rev. Robert L. Paddock was on Chrystie Street chronicling instances of rampant prostitution, something that seemed to have been an obsession of his. While making his rounds, a policeman suddenly rushed past and shouted out to the women in the doorways, whereupon they scuttled back into their houses. Paddock promptly reported this outrageous breach to the local precinct police station. He testified later that, in response, Precinct Captain Herlihy angrily told him that he disgraced his profession by lying and came at him "with clenched fists."[27]

Paddock conveyed news of the assault to the leadership of the Episcopal Diocese of New York. As a result, in September the diocese requested that Bishop Henry C. Potter investigate the matter and protest in an appropriate manner indignities and abuses suffered by clergy at the hands of the police. Other denominations (including Catholic) and moral reform societies shortly signaled their support for the initiative.

The mayor's office, controlled by Tammany Hall, panicked. Richard Croker, the head of the Democratic machine in New York and a master of misdirection, quickly made public Tammany's full (and cynical) support for eradicating vice in the city. Dive owners, many of whom worked hand in glove with Tammany, were confused and alarmed, and actually closed down in protest for two nights in early October. Resorting to further obfuscation, Croker (and Tammany's charges in the mayor's office and police stations) then orchestrated a media storm denying that any such problem existed, all in patent fear of imminent November elections. But to little avail, for Republicans regained full control of the state legislature, while the city voted for the Republican

Dancing with Annie. *Image accompanies the story of Annie Donnelly in Reita Childe Dorr, "The Prodigal Daughter,"* Hampton's Magazine *24/4 (April 1910).*

presidential ticket (which featured Theodore Roosevelt for vice president). Bowing to pressure, on November 15 Croker appointed from the Tammany Hall faithful a "Committee of Five" (which was quickly relabeled by the press as the "Purity Committee") that he charged with investigating Tammany's cozy relationship with vice and developing a plan to neutralize the protection racket—altogether a perfect instance of the pot disdaining the color of the kettle.

That same day Bishop Potter delivered the results of his investigation to the mayor. In it he skewered the police for protecting the "leprous harpies who are hired as runners and touters for the lowest and most infamous dens of vice." He protested against policemen who not only tolerated vice but shielded, encouraged, and profited by it. The bishop then urged civic authorities toward immediate redress.[28]

Many New Yorkers were justifiably suspicious of Tammany's sincerity in investigating itself. Accordingly, three hundred citizens met on November 27 at the Chamber of Commerce to discuss restraining vice in the city and eradicating the corruption endemic in the police department. Speechifying dominated the meeting, followed by the unanimous adoption of a resolution that called for the formation of a "Committee of Fifteen," which would be instructed to keep close watch on the police and determine if they actually performed their sworn duties. Rather than initiate a reform movement spearheaded by a single, powerful leader, the three hundred mandated that a nongovernmental, extralegal, local-action committee of concerned citizens maintain vigilance and report to the public the results of their work.[29]

The committee was duly appointed (all men, of course) and included prominent citizens such as George Foster Peabody (banker), G. H. Putnam (publisher), and Charles Sprague Smith (Columbia professor), all to be chaired by William H. Baldwin Jr. (railroad executive). By mid-1901 it settled on a strategy of hiring undercover investigators to do the committee's on-the-street work, much as the Society for the Reformation of Juvenile Delinquents had done decades earlier.

Detectives were instructed to report on vice that enjoyed protection by the police, a genteel phrasing that really meant "report on prostitution." The procedures they were to follow included accepting solicitations from prostitutes, paying their fees, and documenting what followed. As a result, reports typically included vivid details.

> *She stripped herself of her clothes, laid on the bed and offered herself to me for prostitutional purposes. She said that she had the monthly but it would be all right for me to stay with her.*

Instructions dictated that an agent was not to consummate the contract but employ a ready excuse—"I told her I would call again"—and leave. Incriminating data collected in agent reports would be analyzed and edited into affidavit form by the committee's executive secretary Edwin Seligman and his assistant George Wilson Morgan, then submitted to the court.[30]

The public report on the committee's work, titled *The Social Evil*, was published in early 1902 and revealed that evidence had been gathered on over three hundred disorderly tenement apartments. Legal action against the occupants had followed in most cases, but even the committee acknowledged that many of the women simply moved on to other places. Streetwalking did appear to be reduced throughout New York though, and several dives closed (or simply changed hands). The committee, however, never managed to generate an estimate of the extent of prostitution, and admitted as much in a telling, if somewhat hidden, footnote. Finally, the report claimed that the police were now under the watchful eye of respectable citizenry.[31]

The Social Evil identified and described a relatively new development in New York's prostitution industry: the pimp system. Before the twentieth century, prostitution largely existed within boundaries defined by establishments. Women tended to work out of a specific brothel, concert saloon, or dance hall and, as a result, received some protection from "her" house. With the coming of the Raines Law hotels, those boundaries blurred as prostitutes often moved across institutions, with the loosely defined and ubiquitous hotels serving to provide convenient beds. Although there was frequently monetary benefit to this arrangement, solicitation was more complicated and protection from physical harm not as assured as in the days of the concert saloon bartender-with-club. Hence, the rising need for the services afforded by a pimp.[32]

A variant of the pimp's job established yet another job category, one that would touch off a firestorm of moral outrage, lead to a powerful new federal law, affect the direction of culture in America, and provide meat for New York's next local-action vigilance committee. Since prostitution was such a lucrative business for brothels, Raines Law hotels, and pimps, the procurement of prostitutes became a specialized skill, one practiced by "cadets."

> By various means—"giving the girls a good time," force, fake marriages, entrapments, threats of bodily harm, seduction, fraud or duplicity—[the cadet] leads women to become prostitutes.

One odious method employed by the cadet was the drugged drink, after which "the girl wakens and finds herself at the mercy of her supposed friend." Ruined and entrapped, the only viable option seemed to be a life of prostitution.[33]

The cadet became a vital cog in what the public came to call "white slavery." Claims were made that thousands of young (white) women were ensnared, trafficked, and sold to the highest bidder—"They are guarded, watched, beaten, threatened, ruined, [and] robbed." The issue first concerned Europeans, who took the lead in bringing white slave trafficking to the full, even panicked, attention of Americans. Delegates from European nations affected by white slavery met in Paris in 1902 and drafted the "International Agreement for the Suppression of the White Slave Traffic," which was signed in 1904. Although the United States was not a party to that convention, it became a signatory to the agreement in 1908 under

President Roosevelt. Public concern over the problem throughout the world led to another conference in 1910 and even stricter international agreements.[34]

In the United States, pressure forced Congress to action as well, and the White-Slave Traffic Act of 1910 (broadly known as the "Mann Act") passed in June. That law made it a felony to transport a female across state or national borders for "the purpose of prostitution or debauchery, or for any other immoral purpose." It subsequently proved useful in interdicting interstate trafficking and is still in effect today.

⌖

The Committee of Fifteen identified issues and developed investigative tactics that would ramify for decades, but its life was short. It boasted that its work had a direct bearing on the results of the November 1901 mayoral election, in which Tammany was thrown out. Once newly elected Republicans were in office, the committee felt that public officials would conscientiously articulate moralistic public policy and control vice in New York. So the Committee of Fifteen wrote its report, washed its hands, and closed the door.[35]

It neglected, however, to turn out the lights.

CHAPTER EIGHT

C XIV, ALLEGED MUSIC,
AND SUPERLATIVELY ROTTEN DANCES

A T ABOUT ELEVEN O'CLOCK on a Thursday evening in early
May 1912, Jack Stockdale, a forty-one-year-old married father of
five, walked into a Bowery saloon at 180 Park Row. A sharp dresser, he
fit right in. In a room at the saloon's rear he noticed eight women sitting alone, likely prostitutes, while at another table three more women
were entertaining sailors. There was a band in the corner made up
of a pianist, a fiddler, and a drummer who played both a bass drum
and a smaller drum. The piano player, who was black, started in on
Irving Berlin's new hit song, "Everybody's Doin' It Now," and two sailors immediately jumped up and started dancing. Goaded on by the
prostitutes, they gyrated about in a provocative manner that Stockdale
thought simply "Rotten."[1]

Having seen enough, Stockdale left and walked a few blocks into
Chinatown where in a dive at 6 Mott Street he observed ten men
around the tables, some of them drunk, plus, in his words, two "fruit-
ers." One of the latter stood and sang a modestly ribald version of the
1910 song "Whoops! My Dear," in which Georgie, "a dainty youth,"

likes to watch "the girls in tights, their figures trim and neat." After enjoying a beverage, Stockdale continued on and entered Madami's on Doyers Street. There he found a prostitute talking with one of the singing waiters, who shortly launched into his take on "I Will Love You If You Only Call Me Papa." A couple soon entered the joint—likely a prostitute and her pimp—and commenced dancing the "everybody doing it" dance. She soon hooked up with a potential client in the room and started to "dance rag time" until the fiddler called out to them that that was not acceptable at Madami's. Another man took up the dance with the lady and when the fiddler was not watching, they "walked backwards," stood still, and did the wiggle.[2]

Jack Stockdale was all pretense. He was not looking for a night on the town, but was at work, getting paid seventy-five cents an hour plus

Excerpt from a report filed by Committee of Fourteen agent Jack Stockdale on May 31, 1912. At 388 Eighth Avenue, Stockdale found couples dancing the everybody doing it/grizzly bear dance to the music from a slotted player piano; he declared the place "Rotten." *Committee of Fourteen Records. Manuscripts and Archives Division. The New York Public Library. Astor, Lenox and Tilden Foundations. Courtesy of the New York Public Library.*

all expenses to provide undercover evidence of immoral behavior to New York's Committee of Fourteen.

The Committee of Fourteen picked up where the Committee of Fifteen had left off and would prove to have a much more significant impact on life in New York City. It was formed on January 16, 1905, in part as a response to Tammany Hall moving back into the mayor's office the year before. Founding members included leading citizens from areas in the city strongly affected by the development of Raines Law hotels, leaders of the city's major religions, and former members of the Committee of Fifteen.

The committee's specific mission was to bring about the abolishment of Raines Law hotels. To accomplish this, detailed evidence on their nature was required. Undercover detectives were quickly hired (or volunteered) and then spread out across the city, visited hotels, and wrote up what they saw or experienced.

J. W. Brewster and A. Whitehouse were typical agents. Together they spent an evening at the Friendly Inn, 116 Mott Street, in May 1905. There they chatted up the patrons and drank beer; Brewster played the barroom piano and Whitehouse sang some songs. At about eleven P.M., Whitehouse solicited a prostitute and went upstairs with her to one of the "hotel" rooms.

> *The girl laid on the bed and pulled her dress up to her waist showing her naked body to the waist. I sat on the edge of the bed and was talking to her and she kept saying hurry up, I have got to go to the other room. There is others that want to be fucked as well as you. I told her that I was not in a hurry and that I did not want to fuck in a hurry. With that she got up and said you go to hell and you won't get your money back.*

The committee eventually investigated twelve hundred places like the Friendly Inn that year and found more than seven hundred of them to be "evil resort" Raines Law hotels. Thanks to the diligence and hard work of Whitehouse and Brewster, the Friendly Inn made the list.[3]

With that kind of information in hand, the committee lobbied the state legislature for passage of the "Prentice Law," which would mandate meaningful inspections before Raines Law hotel licenses could be issued. Passed early in 1906, the new statute required, among other things, that walls separating the ten or more rooms necessary for hotel status be of a certain thickness and of certain materials—sheets separating ten dirty cots would no longer suffice. As a partial result of that law, hotel license applications in New York City fell from 1,304 in 1905 to 650 in 1906.

A fifty percent reduction in applications represented a victory but was far from "abolishment." If a Raines Law hotel conformed to the terms of the new law but was still thought by the committee to be disorderly, options were somewhat limited, for the committee had no legal or policing authority. Recognizing this, the Committee of Fourteen developed a strategy that targeted the infrastructure supporting Raines Law hotels.[4]

At this time, the hotels (which were also saloons, of course) had their libations provided by a sponsoring brewer or distributor, such as Pabst Brewing Company, Anheuser-Busch, or the more than fifty other local brewers then active in Brooklyn alone. More than just the alcohol behind the bar, many saloons depended on their sponsors for loans, mortgages, advertising, and other forms of support. Brewers provided the booze, along with a security net. If a Raines Law hotel/saloon was reckoned disorderly, then the committee would approach the sponsoring brewer, share the damning reports, and press it to rein in the offending sponsoree, lest their support of vice lead to more regulations, fees, licenses, and bureaucratic hassle. If the brewer did not respond accordingly, the committee next turned to the saloon's surety company. This tactic was simple. The excise laws of New York stated that all places with liquor licenses had to be bonded and insured. According to the committee's logic, bonding a Raines Law hotel made the surety company a partner in its business.[5]

Confronted with evidence of disorder, most brewers and surety companies quickly realized that their best business interests entailed cooperation with the committee. Accordingly, they could and frequently did withdraw support from a beyond-salvation saloon, which generally ensured its closing. Only as a last resort did the committee threaten to press charges for code violations (of which there were always a convenient number).

Dedicated volunteers working out of desks loaned by sister organizations managed the committee's work at this time. To be effective in the long run—Would the 654 saloons that did *not* reapply as hotels remove their cots?—the committee needed a long-term plan. Toward that end, it incorporated in 1907 and then sought, and obtained, financial support for its work from some of the city's wealthy elite; John D. Rockefeller Jr., J. P. Morgan, George Foster Peabody, and George H. Putnam, among many others, cut checks to finance the committee's work. Office space was rented at 27 East Twenty-Second Street and Frederick H. Whitin was hired to oversee the committee's mission.

The Prentice Law and the vigilance of the committee, along with its political acumen and clout, eventually spelled the end of Raines Law hotels. By 1910 only eighty-seven of them were left. An unqualified success, the committee had fulfilled its mandate. But rather than disband—as had the Committee of Fifteen after its success—the Committee of Fourteen pivoted and turned its attention to the social evil.

⊰❖⊱

Members of a subcommittee formed in 1908, called the Research Committee, anticipated the new mission when instructed to study "the laws of New York relating to the immorality of women." To some extent, the subcommittee was being asked to respond to the national panic over white slavery and the felt need to do something about it. To help fashion and energize a program, the subcommittee hired George J. Kneeland, a sociologist who would play a major role in Committee of Fourteen activities for years to come. Kneeland subsequently organized the subcommittee's agenda, directed the background research, and oversaw the publication in 1910 of *The Social Evil in New York City; A Study of Law Enforcement by the Research Committee of the Committee of Fourteen*. That report laid the foundation for a tide of committee-initiated social activism that would change New York's approaches to morality by 1917—and even alter prevailing sexual practice among consenting adults.[6]

Kneeland's explosive book (which Anthony Comstock thought obscene) grabbed public attention in ways that Raines Law hotel legislation never could, and financial support for the committee's work grew dramatically from about five thousand dollars annually to fifteen thousand dollars through much of the 1910s. An executive secretary, Walter G. Hooke, was soon brought on, as well as two stenographers; Whitin's position was upgraded to full-time status and retitled "general secretary." In February 1912 the official mission of the Committee of Fourteen became "the Suppression of Commercialized Vice in the City of New York."

The committee's approach to confronting prostitution took a different tack than the one then commonly prevailing, which was to identify prostitutes and jail or fine them. Its strategy, signaled by the word "commercialized," followed from that developed to attack the Raines Law hotels: ferret out involvement by the agents of prostitution and challenge owners and managers of the properties where it flourished. If the committee could destroy the vine, the fruit would soon wither.

Whitin, with Kneeland's professional assistance, led the assault. Gathering compromising evidence of prostitution in New York had begun in earnest in 1911, but it became tightly focused after the new mission charge. The primary means of collecting information was by now familiar: hire undercover detectives to go into saloons, dives, joints, dance halls, brothels, cafés, restaurants, entertainment resorts, assignation hotels, and tenement houses looking for vice and write up reports on what was observed there. With significant available resources, the work ramped up as a corps of agents went to work sniffing out immorality in New York's underworld.

They had lots of places to hit. A grand jury impaneled in January 1910 to investigate the white slave traffic in New York City, headed by John D. Rockefeller Jr., had developed a fifty-seven-page list of more than five hundred "immoral places." Their addresses were passed on to the committee and most of them were visited multiple times. That turned out to be only a starting point, though, as thousands of other places received the attentions of the committee over its life, which continued to 1932. Investigative reports, mostly handwritten, eventually totaled nearly one hundred thousand and are now archived in the New York Public Library, where they take up more than fifteen tightly packed feet of shelf space.[7]

⋯❖⋯

Dozens of investigative detectives eventually took positions as frontline troops for the Committee of Fourteen. On occasion, agents had some training (or at least standing) as detectives, such as did Jack Stockdale, but most did not. Some of them had experience working for the state Department of Excise; others were journalists or had worked in social service organizations. In general, investigators were hired who met job profiles defined by race, ethnicity, and gender, and who could fit in among common people. Stockdale, for example, was white, a native Pennsylvanian, and Catholic, and was sent where he would be most inconspicuous. Harry Sussman, on the other hand, was a Russian Jew who spoke English, Russian, Polish, and Yiddish, all of which came in handy for his work among specific ethnic communities. James A. Seaman, a New Jersey–born medical student, provided free medical advice to some of the prostitutes he befriended (and, ironically, managed to resist solicitations by claiming to have a case of gonorrhea). David Oppenheim, who had a day job in the clothing business, was a German Jew, whose facility in German, "Jewish," and English served him well during his several years of service to the committee. Natalie Sonnichsen (*née* de Bogory) was a married, twenty-five-year-old freelance journalist when she began working for the committee; born in

Russia, she grew up in Switzerland and spoke a range of European languages, which presumably enabled her to pass readily as one among the many immigrant prostitutes in New York. William Pogue and Robert Lewis Waring were African Americans who could easily infiltrate and investigate the black and black-and-tan nightspots.[8]

Their work would not be without danger. Agents were involved in deceiving people who had often taken them into their confidence, people whose well-being might suffer from what the agents would report. Proprietors, managers, waiters, entertainers, and prostitutes soon learned to be cautious around those they did not know, in large part because they were suspicious of committee activities. Reports detail several occasions on which compromised agents had to talk their way out of suspicion, some involving actual physical danger. Inevitably, covers were blown and agents were transferred to a different section of the city or were simply retired.

Whitin was not undercover, but rather served as the visible, public face of the Committee of Fourteen. Also its field enforcer, he was particularly loathed by those in the businesses he monitored. As a result, he carried a police-permitted pistol with him at all times, protection he did not appear to have granted his agents.[9]

Instructions to the investigators seem not to have survived, but some details can be gathered from the nature of the reports. Investigators were always undercover, required to blend in with the sporting crowd, and were dressed accordingly; some even wore disguises. They were expected to size up the joint under investigation and make that assessment a cornerstone of their reports: How disorderly (or not) was the place? If things were disorderly, then investigators were to mix in and gain the confidence of those involved.

Female investigators, of which there were a fair number, were expected to flirt, dance, and count the solicitations they received for sex, all the while employing a range of excuses to turn them aside. Male investigators should buy drinks for the women, dance with them, charm them, and either solicit them for sex or allow themselves to be solicited. If the latter, the agent was to employ a ready excuse: "not enough money," "need to get home," "have another appointment down the street," etc. But if their solicitation was accepted, things could and did get tricky. Accordingly, many reports told of situations in which an investigator ended up in a room with a prostitute, who then removed all or most of her clothing and offered herself to the investigator/client at the agreed-upon price. At that point the investigator typically claimed a problem with his "nature," or that he had had too much to drink, or that he had "the clap" (presumably just remembered), or that he had just discovered that he did not have enough money . . . thus presumably wriggling out of a tight situation with his Committee of Fourteen credentials intact.

On many occasions, male and female investigators were paired to see if they could book an hour at one of the alleged assignation hotels. If they succeeded, they proceeded to the room, ordered drinks to be sent up (also a violation of city code), ruffled up the bedsheets, and used a blue pencil to mark "C XIV" on the undersides of drawers, backs of mirrors, and in other inconspicuous places. Soon after, Whitin and the police would charge into the establishment and claim that the hotel functioned as a disorderly place for unmarried couples to consummate sexual liaisons. If the hotel manager denied the accusations, the proof was to be found on the backsides of the furniture.[10]

Kneeland and Whitin stepped up their investigative work as 1912 went on. At their direction, reports became more detailed than before, with the specifics proving foundational to the publication in 1913 of Kneeland's *Commercialized Prostitution in New York City*. The structure of that book reflected the places where prostitution was found: chapter one is concerned with brothels; chapter two with tenement houses, hotels, furnished rooms, and massage parlors; chapter three treats everything else—disorderly saloons, concert saloons, the streets, public dance halls, excursion boats, parks, etc. Among the findings:

❖ Investigators visited 142 brothels in 1912, each two or more times. Prices in these places ranged from fifty cents to ten dollars per service. Prostitutes in the one-dollar houses had as many as thirty customers each night. Orchestras were a common feature of the thirty-four five- and ten-dollar houses investigated.[11]

❖ Disorder was a special problem in saloon "backrooms," a space partitioned off from the bar area and accessible to women by a convenient "Ladies' door." There the sexes socialized, drank, danced together, and made arrangements for sex. Of the 765 backroom saloons visited by agents, prostitutes circulated in 308 of them. In some of these places the races also mixed freely. The backroom scene, according to Kneeland, was often enlivened by music provided by "a sallow-faced youth" who sat at a piano and "bang[ed] out popular airs in wild, discordant notes." Agents characterized the dancing in backroom saloons as obscene and vulgar.[12]

❖ Large public dance halls were rife with indecent behavior. Of seventy-five dances or sponsored balls investigated, agents judged only five as "decent"; eleven were "more or less objectionable"; and fifty-nine were graded as "wholly objectionable." A female investigator (probably Natalie Sonnichsen) reported on thirty-one dances, and at twenty-two of these she was solicited by fifty-three different men. "Tough" (or "half-time") dancing was common in such places.[13]

❖ Approximately fifteen thousand professional prostitutes worked in Manhattan in 1912. "On the basis of data actually on file," each prostitute on average serviced at least ten men per day, yielding a "conservative" total of one hundred fifty thousand tricks turned daily on an island populated by two million, three hundred thousand people.[14]

Kneeland's book redacted many graphic details found in investigators' reports. No mention is made of agent Samuel Auerbach's August 1912 observation that the dancing he saw was an "imitation of [the] action of sexual intercourse," or that Elsie and Daisy (both in drag and assumed by Auerbach to be gay) sang songs "obscene to the farther limit," or that they danced a two-step and "laid on a table and imitated the sexual intercourse," or that another dance featured "the action of committing Sodomy." Nor does *Commercialized Prostitution* copy the episode reported by Jack Stockdale in which he passed a table in a Broadway saloon and a woman reached out, grabbed him by the pants, and opened his fly; whereupon another prostitute joked, "Don't go try to steal my husband," to which the woman replied, "I just wanted to see if he had anything in there." Clearly disorder was much more rampant than Kneeland could chronicle for polite public consumption.[15]

⟡

On-the-street investigators intuited from the first that the nature of the music and dance in a place gave a strong indication of its character. "Disorderly beyond question. 'Market for women.' The street-walkers were coming in and out. . . . Two negroes making alleged music." To agents, the more "alleged" the music-making and the more modern and erotically charged the dancing, the more disorderly the place. Furthermore, report details on music and dance turned out to be more obviously veracious than observations on, for example, social behavior. What went on in the music and dance might be some marker of the central issue, but it was to the committee and its investigators essentially peripheral. Committee activities would not cease just because agents witnessed no alleged music and rotten dance, but they might well if no vice were found. Accordingly, a cellar-level window into a critical period in American cultural history has been recorded and preserved.[16]

The liveliest music and the wildest dancing occurred in dance halls, which category included everything from backroom saloons to larger public dance halls to the dance halls incorporated into beachside entertainment resorts. Despite long-standing efforts by social activists to shut them down, dance halls remained a tenacious and vibrant feature of the urban landscape. Belle Israels had counted more than five hundred scattered throughout the five boroughs in 1909 and there is no indication that the number had diminished by 1912.[17]

There were several good reasons to pay special attention to the dance in the dance halls, one of which was the practical role of dancing in solicitation. The routine went something like this:

❖ Once a dance began, two prostitutes would start dancing together.
❖ Two men, who were teamed and on the lookout for companionship, would immediate approach the women and "break" them, forming two male/female dancing couples.
❖ Propinquity and the loud music provided the necessary privacy for solicitation, which, if acceptable to both parties, would include the terms, the scheduling, the address, and any other necessary arrangements, all conducted out of the hearing of any police or Committee of Fourteen "flatties" in the room.

"Breaking" was not always in operation, however, and indeed some establishments forbade the practice altogether, a regulation that the committee encouraged.

But breaking aside, there was the very richness of the dancing. Few, if any, decades in the history of American dance featured a wider array of wildly provocative dances than the 1910s. Although some of these had been around a while, others were new and of-the-day. In 1912 alone, investigators witnessed and identified the hoochie koochie, the grizzly bear, the turkey trot, the bunny hug, the wiggle, the shiver, the one-step, the two-step, the Bowery, spieling, hopping, dipping, "skirt & muscle dancing," "knee-cap muscle dancing," the "nigger," clog dancing, buck dancing, and an "exhibition dance" in which a female dancer was twirled around as she clung to her partner's neck, becoming airborne in the process. Agents referred categorically to these "indecent" or "disorderly" dances as tough dances, modern dances, half-time dances, or, ragtime dances.[18]

"A Black Cloud and a Moonbeam, Tearing Cyclonically Through Space." *Image by Wallace Morgan in Julian Street,* Welcome to Our City *(New York: John Lane Company, 1912).*

Most all of the dances featured bodies jammed up close to each other—"hollow to hollow," as Stockdale liked to report. Sonnichsen judged a dance she attended to be "perfectly unrestrained; everybody did just as they pleased," altogether giving her the impression of "one wild orgy." What the investigators witnessed were moments in an especially dynamic time when young people from a wide range of ethnicities were hearing flashy, invigorating, and heavily syncopated ragtime rhythms and moving their bodies to the music in fresh, sexy, uninhibited ways. If a hint of wistfulness sometimes crept into the agents' up-close, firsthand reports (many of them danced the dances too), the moral-bearers back at the offices of the Committee of Fourteen never

once doubted that danced expressions of the new, of youth, and of the
sexual were potent elements in an especially explosive compound.[19]

⬦

Committee reports are rich in particulars on dancing, but agents were
no better than earlier reporters at providing useful details on music-
making. Music and dance are both expressed through performance
though. To a dancer, the music is interpreted in the dance; bodily
movements are performances of the aural experiences of the music. In
an important way, dance is music made manifest. To a musician, the
way the dancers move prompts the way the music is made; playing is
in some part an expression of seeing. So, concomitantly, music is dance
made manifest. Reading about dancing in the reports and visualizing
what it was like is a form of synesthetically hearing the music-making
over in the dark corner. If the agents thought the dancing "vulgar,"
"indecent," "suggestive," "disgraceful," or "utterly and superlatively
rotten," they probably also thought the music "wild," "alleged," and
"discordant"—and often called it just that.

Agents could see the musical instruments in a joint, which made
reporting on them easy. They chronicled pianos, violins and fiddles,
guitars, banjos, harmonicas, a zither (the player of which took exception to derogatory remarks cast his way, started a fight, and ended up
being hauled off to the police station), accordions, harps, drums, and,
according to one report, "a cracked piano in [the] bar & a one legged
coon who plays the bones occasionally." An "orchestra" might mini-
mally consist of a piano and a violin/fiddle or, less frequently, a piano
and a percussion instrument—drums of various sorts, bones, clappers,
a trap set, "anything to make a big noise," in Stockdale's phrasing.
Other frequently mentioned ensemble combinations were piano and
guitar, piano and banjo, guitar and banjo, and piano and harp. Four-
piece orchestras typically consisted of piano, drums, and two violins/
fiddles. Just about whoever was around with whatever instrument was
handy seems to be at the heart of the story here.

Only two piano players have names attached to them in the 1912 reports. Stockdale entered a "Café & Saloon" on West Twenty-Fourth Street in April 1912 and noticed that "Frank" the piano player was playing a ragtime hit. "Pianist Plenny Heath, colored," is the only musician identified by full name in that year's reports. Little is known about Heath other than he ran a music shop on West 135th Street in Harlem and moonlighted as a piano player in Percy Brown's Café on West Forty-Fifth Street in April 1910.[20]

Singers in the dives were commonly noted, but infrequently by their names. Six singers earned first-name status and only one of those received any special attention. "Rosie" sang in William Banks's black-and-tan café on West Thirty-Seventh Street, wore a silver band around her hair, sang an unidentified song, and then lifted her dress over her knees, revealing red garters and black stockings. A mulatto about twenty-two years old, Rosie danced the "Hoochy Coochy movement" for four white men who appreciatively threw money on the floor for her. Details of her physical stature (5 feet 6 inches, one hundred forty pounds) were included because in the agent's view she was likely a prostitute who needed to be profiled for the committee.[21]

Songs had titles and lyrics much more often than musicians had names. However, some of the references are so cryptic that it is difficult to peg the song. Did "Lovy Boy" refer to "Lovey: A Syncopated Love Song" (1909) or "Lovey Girl" (1912) or the highly popular "Cuddle Up a Little Closer, Lovey Mine" from 1908? Did "Band" imply Irving Berlin's immensely popular "Alexander's Ragtime Band" of 1911? (Probably, but who can be sure?) What was the "Circus song," with its suggestive lines: "We have the long rubber neck Giraffe, who they feed peas to / But owing to his long thing he can take only one pea at a time"? Or the title of the song with the lyric: "If Your Father and Mother knew as much as you do—you would not be here"? And who wouldn't want to know more about the "Pimp Song" or "O, That Night of Mystery"?

Fortunately, fourteen songs tagged by Committee of Fourteen

agents can comfortably be identified, providing at least a shadowy profile of the music heard in New York dives during the 1911–1912 period.

- ❖ "Boogie Man Rag" (Terry Sherman/Mort Hyman; 1912)
- ❖ "Casey Jones: The Brave Engineer" (Eddie Newton/T. Lawrence Seibert; 1909)
- ❖ "Everybody's Doin' It Now" (Irving Berlin; 1911)
- ❖ "Finnegan" (A. Seymour Brown/Nat. D. Ayer; 1912)
- ❖ "Meet Me Tonight in Dreamland" (Leo Friedman/Beth Slater Whitson; 1909)
- ❖ "My Name Is Morgan, But It Ain't J.P." (Halsey K. Mohr/William A. Mahoney; 1906)
- ❖ "Parisienne" (Lew Brown/Albert Von Tilzer; 1912)
- ❖ "Roll Me Around Like a Hoop My Dear" (Fred Fischer; 1912)
- ❖ "Row, Row, Row" (James V. Monaco/William Jerome; 1912)
- ❖ "Steamboat Bill" (Ren Shields/Frank Leighton/Bert Leighton; 1910)
- ❖ "That's My Personality" (Lew Brown/Albert Von Tilzer; 1912)
- ❖ "There'll Come a Time" (Charles K. Harris; 1895)
- ❖ "There's a Ring Around the Moon" (Alfred Bryan/H. Blanke-Belcher; 1911)
- ❖ "When I Was Twenty-One and You Were Sweet Sixteen" (Egbert Van Alstyne/Harry Williams; 1911)

There are some easy observations to draw from this list. For instance, all the songs save one were published between 1906 and 1912, suggesting that then, as now, the day's current hits were the most popular. Also, although many of the titles do not make this clear, the rhythms of ragtime accent nearly all the songs. Several of them actually mention ragtime dances. "Parisienne," for instance, is explicitly a dance song, which the sheet music cover makes clear, and cites in the lyrics the glide, the slide, the "Grizzly Bear," and the "Turkey trot."

To study the sheet music to these songs does not necessarily tell how they did their work. Sheet music was clearly available in the night-spots; photographs sometimes show that, and one agent reported that he went to the piano to look at some sheet music, from which vantage point he could better peer into a disorderly backroom. But in keeping with a long-standing tradition, performances freely deviated from the notes and words on the page. Take the oldest song in the group, Charles K. Harris's "There'll Come a Time." In its published form, it is a sentimental song in which a daughter whose mother has died is counseled by her father that

> *There'll come a time someday, when I have passed away.*
> *There'll be no father to guide you from day to day.*

However, entertainers in Marshall's Hotel on West Fifty-Third Street—"well filled with both white and colored people"—sang "very low songs," one of which included the lines "There'll come a time when a whore won't need no man, lordy, lordy." "Roberts" and "May," both white women, began dancing to the song, punctuating their steps with kicks high above each other's heads and raising their skirts so high that "their person could be seen." One dancer reportedly wound her legs around the neck of the proprietor (who was a black man) and went through dance motions that were "outrageous." Charles K. Harris, who wrote his song before the age of ragtime, could hardly have imagined such.[22]

"My Name Is Morgan, But It Ain't J.P.," a "coon song" (i.e., a minstrelized ragtime song) from 1906, featured a published chorus lyric that went

> *My name is Morgan, but it ain't J.P.*
> *There's no bank on Wall Street that belongs to me. . . .*

But on June 1, 1912, Jack Stockdale entered a backroom saloon on Seventh Avenue at 12:35 A.M. and found there a few drunken people, one of whom, "Jeanie," staggered over to the piano and sang a song with a verse that Stockdale transcribed loosely as "My name is Moriarty, I keep a hoar house & fuck for charity."[23]

Natalie Sonnichsen reported on a 109th Street dive she visited at the end of 1912 and noted that "Ada," who was reading a romantic pot-boiler novel by Victoria Cross between sets, sang songs that were "very vulgar and full of allusions which made the company laugh." Her second song was the ragtime hit "Row, Row, Row." The published chorus to this song is about a young man taking his beau on a Sunday afternoon boat ride.

> And then he'd row, row, row,
> Way up the river he would row, row, row.
> A hug he'd give her, then he'd kiss her now and then,
> She would tell him when. He'd fool around and fool around,
> And then they'd kiss again. And then he'd row, row, row,
> A little further he would row, oh, oh, oh, oh!
> Then he'd drop both his oars, take a few more encores,
> And then he'd row, row, row.

The printed lyrics are suggestive enough, but Ada's parody lyrics went further and "left nothing to the imagination." Imagination was given some substance in the committee files two weeks later when Jack Stockdale heard the same song in a Brooklyn joint, sung by a different singer, and included a loose transcription in his report.

> He rowed rowed &c then he hugged & kissed her; her saying when, where &c then they left the boat, got on the grass and he loved her & hugged her, when she said &c then he was over her & he rowed & he rowed of course when she said &c.

It would appear that consenting adults who enjoyed salacious songs

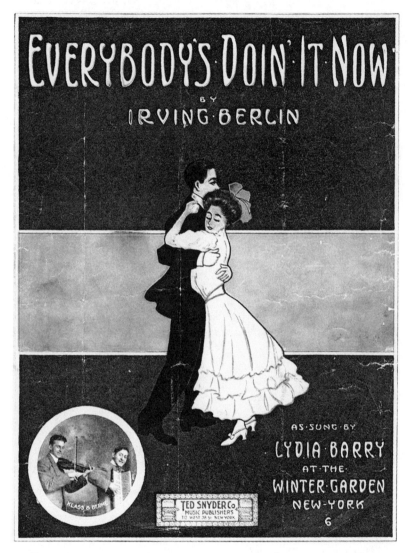

Sheet music cover to Irving Berlin, "Everybody's Doin' It Now." *New York, Ted Snyder Co., 1911.*

in Brooklyn dives did not hold copyrighted verses sacred. Nor did anyone else.[24]

The one song that seems *not* to have been parodied is the one most frequently mentioned in the 1912 reports. Irving Berlin copyrighted "Everybody's Doin' It Now" on November 2, 1911, and it almost immediately exploded in popularity. The Indestructible Symphony Orchestra recorded it by the end of the year, and at least eight more recordings were made in 1912. It was sung and played in places high and low, public and private. People also danced to it. The fetching rag-time rhythms compelled dancing in part because the song's narrative is *about* the joys of dancing ragtime. Verse 1 gets the dancers on the floor.

> *Honey, honey, can't you hear?*
> *Funny, funny music, dear.*
> *Ain't the funny strain,*
> *Goin' to your brain,*
> *Like a bottle of wine, fine?*
> *Hon', hon', hon', hon' take a chance,*
> *One, one, one, one little dance.*
> *Can't you see them all,*
> *Swaying up the hall?*
> *Let's be gettin' in line.*

Verse 2 speaks of the energy required to keep on doing what everybody's doin'.

> *Baby, baby get a stool,*
> *Maybe, maybe I'm a fool.*
> *Honey, don't you smile,*
> *Let us rest a while,*
> *I'm so weak in the chest, best.*
> *Go, go, go, go get a chair,*
> *No, no, no, no leave it there.*

Honey, if the mob,
Still are on the job,
I'm as strong as the rest.

Meanwhile, the chorus—always where the music is most compelling—spells out exactly what everybody's doing and how they do it.

See that ragtime couple over there,
Watch them throw their shoulders in the air,
Snap their fingers, honey, I declare
It's a bear, it's a bear, it's a bear. There!
Ev'rybody's doin' it, doin' it, doin' it.
Ev'rybody's doin' it, doin' it, doin' it.

The "bear" is a reference to the "grizzly bear," among the newest animal dances in 1911, where dancers stretch out their "claws" above their heads and dance aggressively and provocatively. All sorts of variations

"Everybody's Overdoing It." *Image by Wallace Morgan in Julian Street,* Welcome to Our City *(New York: John Lane Company, 1912).*

on the steps were possible. Stockdale noted that while dancing to the song, two women "rub[bed] against each other, shaking and grunting [and] making a noise." In another report, dancers were doing "the G.B. &c. in the toughest way" while "some sang everybody is doing it &c." On June 1, 1912, at a dance held at the Mandarin Club on Doyers Street, the "music was of the 'Everybody's Doing It'" style. The dancing there was "as bad as it could be," with one of the women entertainers pressing her dance partner "against one of the posts in the room" and lingering against his body. One writer noted in August that the song had become the "national hymn" of the modern set, a notion that had been suggested a few months earlier by journalist Franklin P. Adams in his critique of the "fury and craze of these musical days," for he thought "Everybody's Overdoing It."[25]

⁕

The work of the Committee of Fourteen did not cease with the publication of *Commercialized Prostitution* in early 1913. If anything, it accelerated, in part because media attention increased the profile (and the budget) of the committee. In addition, the forms and expressions of prostitution and sexuality were changing rapidly in New York and needed to be tracked. And among them were new modalities that relied directly on vital roles played by music and dance.

There is only a single reference in *Commercialized Prostitution* to the cabaret, which Kneeland suggested is sometimes found in disorderly establishments as a "poor imitation" of the entertainments often found in upper-crust restaurants. Little did he or the committee then realize that New York was under invasion.[26]

The entertainment weekly *New York Clipper* first sighted what was on the horizon when it published a column in 1910 written by its Berlin bureau editor: "'Cabaret' Becoming an Important Factor in the European Amusement World—Its Origin and Progress." The writer, a Mr. P. Richards, thought that many readers of the *Clipper* might not be familiar with cabaret, so he provided a brief history. Cabaret's birth,

Richards wrote, was in the Montmartre district of Paris, where from the first it had a bohemian, "free and easy" air. It was essentially a rough melding of the informal music-making heard in bars and dives and the more formal program of song, dance, and comedy common in vaudeville theaters. Significantly, it was aimed at a more downscale crowd and thus occupied a niche below vaudeville houses. Salaries for cabaret work were lower than in legitimate vaudeville, but the satisfaction gathered from the work and the prospect of long-term employment made it worthwhile—"[performers] didn't make much money, [but] they had a deuce of a time."[27]

"'Oh, You Babylon!': A Taxi-cabaretta," which was "Cabawritten" by Julian Street with "Cabagraphs" by Wallace Morgan, appeared in the August 1912 issue of *Everybody's Magazine*. A piece of clever whimsy, it was nevertheless among the first writing to recognize that the European cabaret had landed in New York.

> *From Little Hungary in Houston Street, to Pabst's vast armory-like restaurant in One Hundred and Twenty-Fifth, we will find them everywhere: rag-time, turkey-trotting spots upon the city map; gay cabarets, jay cabarets; cabarets with stages and spot-lights, cabarets without; cabarets on ground floors, in cellars, and on roofs; cabarets where "folks act gen'l'mumly," cabarets where the wild time grows. . . . Can this be death? No, Kid, this is Life! You can't escape it! You can't escape the cabaret! . . . The town is cabaridden! Cabarotten! And you, poor devil, you're stark, staring cabarazy!*[28]

Cabaraziness could not have arrived at a better time, for New York's larger restaurants were just starting to provide entertainment along with their food and drink. By 1912, "we hear her screaming everywhere, . . . we masticate our morning egg to rag-time, lunch and dine to the strains of the pseudo-passionate waltz." Everything was thus in place for the cabaret, and a rich and varied night out for customers.[29]

There was also the issue of tone. Cabarets in Paris and Berlin were deeply subversive of high-minded mores. So too in New York, which made it an ideal fit with a demimonde that had lost its beds in the Raines Law hotels. Prostitutes, pimps, and clients poured into the cabarets, for as a waiter told David Oppenheim, "all the cabarets are known as regular whorehouses." Harvey, the proprietor of the saloon at the Park View Hotel, acknowledged that "90% of [the cabarets] cater to that trade," and that without prostitutes many saloons could not make a go of it.[30]

The Committee of Fourteen soon recognized cabaret's true face and made it its main focus from 1913 to 1917. Among much else, this meant that agents were hitting a wider range of entertainment places, for cabarets could be made to work just about anywhere. Large restaurants continued to mount cabarets, but soon downscale cafés and saloons were also adding a cabaret a night or two a week. Even dance halls programmed cabarets to supplement the dancing. A stage was not even necessary, for the form depended on a degree of intimacy between patrons and entertainers; indeed, singers were expected to circulate among and around the tables while performing. Personnel requirements were meager and inexpensive. In a backroom saloon, a piano player and a female singer would be sufficient to advertise "Cabaret tonight." The manager of the Manuel da Silva Café told Oppenheim that all he had to do was hire a "couple of Creole girls" and he had a cabaret. And they did not even have to be very good. Seaman reported that a woman singing "What Do You Want to Make Those Eyes at Me For" went around to each table, patted cheeks and whispered "any old thing" to the patrons; but "SING she cannot." Stockdale reported that one cabaret performer "made noise with her mouth in trying to sing."[31]

Although small was just fine, big productions worked too. The continuing development of New York's subway system and a burgeoning automobile culture opened up the development of pleasure resorts on the outskirts of the boroughs, where land was cheaper. These resorts were often called "casinos," a term that at the time did not imply blackjack, roulette wheels, and slot machines. (In fact, as throughout much of the United States, gambling for money was illegal in New York.) Casinos hewed closer to their original, etymological meaning, as in "house" (i.e., *casa*), and offered a range of social activities that might include dining, drinking, music, dancing, vaudeville, movies, bowling, roller skating, and cabaret.

Many of the casinos were adjacent to amusement parks (such as those at Bronx Park, Van Cortlandt Park, and Clason Point) or around beaches, many of which also had amusement parks (Coney Island, Brighton Beach, Rockaway Beach, Canarsie, and parts of Staten Island). They had names like Arbor Casino, Harlem Casino, Manhattan Casino, Dietrich's Fairyland Casino, Gilligan's Palace Casino, and Reisenweber's Casino. These places were generally large, with dance floors that might accommodate a thousand couples. Given the scale, casinos could afford to hire cabaret ensembles of seven or more singers (many of them highly accomplished performers), a comedian, and a small orchestra. So when the summer heat smothered Gotham, legions jammed the subways and trollies and headed to the end of the line at Coney Island or Bronx Park. There cabaret, dancing, drink, food, sport, and a good time beckoned. Among the crowd were prostitutes who knew they would easily find clients. And a squad of detectives charged with the mission of keeping an eye on them was directly on their heels.

Cabarets shifted the attention of patrons (and the reportage of committee agents) away from the drinking and toward music and dance. Accordingly, reports from the cabaret years are rich in information on both.

Agents in 1913 mainly tagged dance steps that had been around a while, like the "Everybody's Doin' It"/grizzly bear, the "nigger," and the Texas Tommy ("Tommy" was slang for "prostitute"). A new style did surface that year, though. Agent Charles S. Briggs inquired about the name of a dance in which a couple "proceeded to go through all the movements of sexual intercourse"; the response from a tablemate was,

Reisenweber's Casino, Brighton Beach in Brooklyn. *Postcard, postmarked in 1914.*

"That's what they call the dry or Kentucky fuck." In 1914, more new dances emerged: the lame duck, the kitchen sink, and ball the jack. The exotic and erotic tango also was first chronicled by agents that year. All these were energetic dances that featured suggestive moves; "sinuous as serpents," one wrote. The dancing of two couples especially repulsed Briggs, for the moves included picking female partners up and flipping them upside down—"when their clothes fell around their shoulders their private parts were clearly exposed to view." He was confounded that such dancing was wildly applauded by spectators. Another agent from that year confessed that he was so shocked by the sensuous gyrations of the dancers that he refused to write a description of it. Ever a good investigator, however, he promised to demonstrate the moves in the offices of the Committee of Fourteen, provided they "will stand for it." (There is no evidence that his offer was taken up.)[32]

The following year marked the first mention of "the Salome," an obvious reference to the "Dance of the Seven Veils" in Oscar Wilde's

1891 play, likely colored in popular consciousness by a scandalous production of Richard Strauss's *Salome* at the Metropolitan Opera in 1907. David Oppenheim reported on a 1917 cabaret performance in which the dancer "with bare legs and body uncovered from the waist line to the hips danced a Salome dance with all the suggestive motions of sexual intercourse."

In 1916 there appeared a reference to the "St. Louis" dance, about which nothing seems to be known; perhaps it is an allusion to W. C. Handy's "St. Louis Blues," one of the first published blues songs (1914). That year also saw a craze for Hawaiian music and dance, specifically the hula. In cabaret, the hula was often danced by (white) women wearing only a grass skirt, since any more covering would (obviously) not be true to the traditional dance. Seaman observed one hula dancer who appeared to be "clad for her bath"; she wiggled the midsection of her body in such a way that it appeared to him as a "universal joint." Prostitutes quickly adopted the dance; one woman promised an agent that she would do the "Gula-yula dance" naked for him if he would go with her.[33]

Rich information on songs performed in cabarets shows up in the reports, including titles.[34] Characteristically, almost none of the songs were reported sung as published. "The Angle-Worm Wiggle," for instance, is an animal dance, but of a different degree of anatomical suggestiveness than the grizzly bear or the fox-trot, an allusion not missed by Chicago authorities when they removed the famous singer-comedian Sophie Tucker from a 1910 stage for singing it.

> *When I dance that wiggling dance,*
> *I simple have to giggle with glee.*
> *So hold me tight, don't let me fall,*
> *Sway me round the hall to that angle-worm crawl.*
> *Oh babe, tell it to me, can you do that angle-worm wiggle with me?*

"With my little wiggle waggle in my hand" was the clever new lyric sung in a 1913 New York cabaret, surely far surpassing the grace embedded in Tucker's singing.[35]

"Chinatown, My Chinatown" received bracing new lyrics during a rowdy evening at the Washington Inn on 155th Street, when "Hearts that know no other land / Drifting to and fro" became "Where you can get a hump / For fifty cents a throw." The agent added only that "this song was supplemented by others equally as indecent." "Some Girls Do and Some Girls Don't" became "Some Girls Will and Some Girls Won't" in 1916. Bawdy parody even trumped national politics in January 1917, when two "nice young American girls" in a dive on Third Avenue joined a piano player in singing "I wouldn't raise my skirt to any soldier" instead of the antiwar lyrics "I Didn't Raise My Boy to Be a Soldier."[36]

Agent Oppenheim discovered the mistress of ribald parody in Brooklyn the evening of August 18, 1915. He was in the Bard & Berl when she struck up: "Yankee doodle went up town riding on a pony stuck his fingers up his a__ and found a macaroni." Oppenheim complimented the singer on her muse, to which the bartender rejoined, "Oh that's nothing. . . . Wait till I get her to sing 'Cock Eye Reilly.'" Oppenheim liked "Cock Eyed Reilly" so much (a song better known today as "One-Eyed Reilly" or "Reilly's Daughter") that it brought out the quiescent folklorist in him. He proceeded to transcribe her version of this old Irish bawdy ballad in full and included it in his report. (See Appendix 2.) But not until after the singer entertained him with her version of "Tip-Top Tipperary Mary," which she renamed "Tip It Up Mary."[37]

❧

In the Committee of Fourteen reports from 1906 to 1912, only two instrumentalists, six singers, no dancers, and no other professional entertainers were identified by name, and only rarely by their full name. In the committee reports from 1913 to 1917, thirty solo instrumentalists or bands, thirty-five singers, ten dancers, and twenty-seven other professional entertainers are named, generally by full name. To some degree, the dramatic increase in identifications reflects the greater number of reports. But, in the main, the Committee of Fourteen came to realize that musicians, dancers, and entertainers in the shows and cabarets were not there just to provide the ambiance *behind* the business of commercialized sex, they were, rather, critical agents *in* the business of commercialized sex and therefore worthy of being marked.

One reason—no surprise here—was simple livelihood, for "like so many girls and women on the stage" they made "extra money on the side with their prostitution." Take the case of Connie "Peggy" O'Neill. She grew up in Pittsburgh, a loved member of a large and prosperous family—"Used to having everything [she] wanted." Like many girls during that time, she learned to dance, enjoyed it, and discovered that she was good at it. When her family's finances suffered in the Panic of 1907, she thought that with her looks and dancing ability she could support herself on the stage, lessening the burden on her family. She got a job in vaudeville but was soon raped by her tour manager. As a result, she "began her life as a careless girl." She continued to dance professionally when a job was available, but she told agent James A. Seaman that it was impossible for a girl to live decently by just working on the stage. So she became a part-time prostitute.

O'Neill was bright and inquisitive—she spent one evening querying Seaman (a graduate of Amherst College) about Buddhism and requested a reading list from him. She also had a moralistic perspective on what she had become and confided in Seaman that "she felt like forgetting all about every man she had been out with and being as she used to be." The following week she began dancing in the cabaret at the Pré Catelan restaurant and somehow managed to make ends meet through that job alone. Six months later, in July 1917, Seaman ran into O'Neill again and learned that she was no longer working regularly as a prostitute, but "just parties" occasionally.[38]

The economics of prostitution as a supplement to a stage income were manifest in a detailed report filed in February 1917. Investigator D. W. Ashley teamed up one day with a Mr. Nugatt, who did not work for the Committee of Fourteen. That afternoon, Ashley solicited Anne Lisard at the Pré Catelan (coincidentally at about the time that O'Neill went to work there). He reported that she was "good looking and well dressed and danced in a most lascivious way." Through her Nugatt was introduced to Mabel White, a dancer in the Ziegfeld Follies. White quickly made it clear to Nugatt that her terms were "ten dollars." She agreed eventually to five dollars and told him to have the next dance with her to set up the arrangements. Lisard wanted Ashley to agree to the same terms, but he claimed to be "in a bad way" (i.e., he had gonorrhea). She thanked him for that information and asked him to pass the time with her still. At 7:30 P.M., the couples gathered in Lisard's boardinghouse. "Miss White undressed and got on the bed with Nugatt and she wanted to do it '69' but he refused." While Ashley and Lisard looked on, the couple consummated their arrangement. White got her five dollars; Lisard received two dollars for the use of her room and a private "hoola" dance demonstration. One woman who performed in the Ziegfeld Follies confided to a committee agent that there was not a "pure girl in the whole company."[39]

Another document, submitted by David Oppenheim, contained yet more lurid details on how the system worked. Oppenheim had been in the Snug Café in Harlem the morning of March 5, 1916. The after-hours party there included fifteen couples, plus ten men, eight women, a lady entertainer, a piano player, a drummer, and the dive's manager, Frank Nolan, all of them black. Although Oppenheim was Jewish, he was dark-complected and sometimes passed as a light-skinned African American. The lady entertainer, Mamie Sharp, went over to Oppenheim and introduced herself by sitting on his lap. She then lifted one of her breasts out of her dress and invited him "to kiss my Titty." According to the agent's report, she was soon "bobbing up and down" on him and told him that he could "scuttle me now if you want." The manager said, "Go ahead, Dave, take her upstairs; she's steamed up." Oppenheim refused the invitation, but Sharp still encouraged him to phone her any night before eight P.M. and she would take the night off to escort him to some of the "buffet flats" in the area, where a range of sexual shows could be purchased, including one "where the women will dance naked for you and also show you how two women bulldike each other."[40]

Outside of working hours, women entertainers like Mamie Sharp and Mabel White could solicit clients directly, but a more circuitous ritual was necessary in the workplace. A standing citywide regulation mandated that a woman could not enter a saloon unless accompanied by a man, a provision intended to deny prostitutes easy access to backrooms and cabarets. But an exception was made for women cabaret entertainers, who were, naturally, allowed to go to work, even if by themselves. That amounted to a loophole, however, if a woman entertainer was also willing to prostitute herself.

In general, potential clients knew that direct solicitation in a joint was not appropriate. To do so would bring attention from any observant undercover policeman or committee agent. But they also knew the workaround: get friendly with the piano player or a singing waiter, arrange to be introduced to the lady entertainer, and then enjoy a nice, friendly, quiet chat over a drink. At the Triangle, in March 1916, the singer had just finished a song when a singing waiter pointed out an elderly man who wanted to meet her. After a drink and a fifteen-minute conversation between them, the man left, the assignation set. Agent Daniel Ogden got to know piano player Steve Hayes at Bobby Moore's place in early 1917. Ogden expressed to Hayes an interest in a cabaret singer there and was soon introduced to Carrie, who it turned out was married to Hayes but also hustled for him. Singing waiters and other male entertainers also pimped for women who were not entertainers. Buddy Reid, a black singer and pianist of some renown performing in John McClary's Café, was identified in a report as a pimp. Oppenheim wrote that Reid did not really need to keep performing because he had plenty of women feeding him cash: "he only holds this job so that the police can have nothing on him." Agent B. J. Cunningham stated in one of his reports that a majority of male cabaret performers live with women who turn "the proceeds of their labor" over to them.[41]

The focused attention given cabarets by the Committee of Fourteen affected the ways entertainers secured their livelihoods, as it did also those who ran the joints in which they worked. Proprietors and managers generally had to get committee approval before even commencing the process of procuring a cabaret license. Accordingly, Chris Traynor of the Village Inn, with a pledge of one thousand dollars in support from a brewer, approached Whitin with a proposal to mount a cabaret, but like most others was refused endorsement. Traynor claimed to undercover agent Daniel Ogden even to have spoken with Mayor John P. Mitchell, who, it turned out, felt powerless to countermand the committee's decision. It is not clear whether Whitin and the committee intended to shut down cabarets throughout the city, but that is what Traynor and others in the business came to believe. The proprietor of Harvey's at the Park View Hotel told detective Oppenheim that the committee wanted to do away with cabarets because "they claim all cabarets are whore houses"; it even, according to Harvey, wanted to disallow any kissing in the saloon backroom. Another manager informed Oppenheim that the committee dictated seating arrangements—men and women were required to sit across from each other at tables, not side by side. On some occasions, fed-up proprietors simply attempted to stage a cabaret outside the committee's oversight; investigator Harry Kahan learned from a waiter that his joint planned to start up a cabaret "in a few weeks, when everything will be quiet." That was a ploy that seems to have been infrequently successful because "the Committee of 14 have men out watching," a belief with some obvious truth behind it since one of those doing the watching wrote the report.[42]

Committee actions such as these led to loud venting about overreach, intolerance, and injustice. Mrs. Forester, who ran Hunter's Hall on Wyckoff Avenue in Brooklyn, confided to Oppenheim that Whitin himself came to her establishment on September 22, 1915, and physically removed her license. She subsequently had to promise to give up the "Hotel business" (which likely meant renting assignation rooms) and to quit serving women in the backroom saloon. When she did not live up to the agreement, Whitin and her brewer literally nailed shut the door to the ladies' entrance. Forester swore that no one could touch Whitin because of Rockefeller's connection to the committee, although she claimed to know for a fact that Rockefeller himself was no paragon of high virtue: "he has a yacht and takes new girls on it for 3 or 4 days then ships them back but forms committees [against] the poor people." Mr. Wagner, who ran a place in a German neighborhood, "kept on cursing Mr. Whitin and calling him the vilest name he could think of." He got so excited that his fluency in English failed him and he reverted to cursing in German. According to Oppenheim, "I think if he had W[hitin] here he wouldn't be a bit squeamish about committing murder." Another proprietor more quietly thought that the Committee of Fourteen wanted to "make a church" out of his nightspot.[43]

Still, the committee's work went on, and with considerable success. The cabarets, like the Raines Law hotels before them, had been a boon to prostitution, since they were relatively safe public places open late in which men looking for women congregated. As the Committee of Fourteen forced the shuttering of cabarets or, at least, the closing of their doors at one A.M., prostitution came under stress. Agent Samuel Auerbach reported on a 1915 conversation with some Swedish sailors during which they despaired over how difficult it was in New York to find a prostitute; one declaimed that "if he had to remain permanently in N.Y. he would have to cut his b__s out." Seaman swung by Times Square at eight P.M. in June 1917 and was surprised to find streetwalkers soliciting on the sidewalks, "like a return to the old way." He reported that the girls, many who had never been on the street, felt they had been forced there by committee action.[44]

There were also outside forces bearing on the business. Telephones were becoming more common, signaling the era of the call girl, which had the effect of scrambling decades-old solicitation methods. Furthermore, social mores and sexual behaviors were undergoing rapid change. Many post-Victorian young women discovered that sex had intrinsic rewards. For these so-called "charity girls," a dalliance with a favored date became a perfectly acceptable cap to an evening out.

After the United States entered World War I on April 6, 1917, the Department of War became concerned about doughboys and their access to prostitutes (and the venereal diseases that afflicted about thirty percent of servicemen). Section 10 of the Selective Service Act of May 1917 required that all known prostitution districts within five miles of any military camp be shuttered. The effect was that many tenderloin districts were closed, not only in New York City but across the nation, most famously Storyville in New Orleans. Altogether, the business of American commercialized sex was due to undergo a major reshuffle.

⟞⟨❖⟩⟝

Then there was the matter of the city's racial climate and the role of the Committee of Fourteen in it. New York City, with some justifiable pride, had had no legal color line throughout much of the previous century. The first emancipation law in New York was passed in 1799, although it was limited in what it accomplished. All New York–born slaves, though, had been freed by 1827. A civil rights act, passed in 1873, guaranteed to all "full and equal enjoyment of any accommodation, advantage, facility or privilege furnished by public conveyances, innkeepers, theaters, public schools, or places of public amusement." The language of that statute was subsequently strengthened so that by 1909 all citizens enjoyed "full and equal rights and privileges," whatever their race. Lest there be any equivocation on the point, in 1913 new legislation established that civil rights could not be withheld from anyone on the basis of "race, creed, color, or national origin."[45]

Many patrons of New York's nightspots appear to have been fine with no color line at all. "The place was doing a rushing business. The backroom being so full of those of both sexes and races that there was no vacant place." An agent scouting the Douglas Club on West Twenty-

Eighth Street admired the girl dancers, who joined in a "free-for-all" dance enjoyed by both white and black young people, "with no suggestion of a color line." At the many black-and-tan nightspots throughout New York, investigator reports show that large, racially mixed crowds gathered peacefully together, flirting, loving, dancing, and listening to "Good music & latest."[46]

In the view of the Committee of Fourteen, however, the mixing of the races, especially among the lower classes, led necessarily to immorality and vice. The issue from the committee's perspective was simple: keep white women away from black men, white men away from black women, and New York would become a more orderly place. Part of its mission thus became establishing and enforcing a de facto color line. Black-run and -patronized hotels, clubs, cafés, and saloons that attracted a measure of white patronage were subsequently targeted. Baron Wilkins' Café, William Banks', Percy Brown's Café, Young's, Diggs', Welch's Café, the Criterion Club, and Marshall's Hotel, all in midtown and among the most popular entertainment places in the city, were hounded by committee investigators, as were other black and tans throughout the city. Racially biased action usually followed.

A typical middling black and tan was Welch's Café at 317 West Thirty-Ninth Street. An early visit by agents, in March 1910, did not go well for them. Both patrons and waiters were startled by the strangers' presence and deeply suspicious. A visit by another agent in June 1911 went better. He counted there nineteen white women, thirty-one white men, and about the same number of "colored." The agent also witnessed "vulgar dances," many black prostitutes soliciting white men, and an argument between a black man and a white woman. Welch eventually signed a note forced on him by the committee in which he promised "not to permit white persons and colored persons to be served at the same table, nor will I serve a white woman without a white man as her escort at any time of the day."[47]

The large and famous café in Marshall's Hotel at 127–129 West Fifty-Third Street was several steps up in scale from Welch's. Even the Committee of Fourteen acknowledged in 1910 that it might have been the most popular nightspot in town. Proprietor James L. Marshall had fashioned a vibrant black and tan that was at the epicenter of New York's black bourgeois life, with clientele that made up a virtual Who's Who of accomplished black Americans: author James Weldon Johnson, musician James Reese Europe, poet Paul Laurence Dunbar, among others, along with intellectuals such as W. E. B. Du Bois.

Despite the prestigious patronage and the fact that all licenses and permits were up-to-date, the committee sent waves of agents into Marshall's. Predictably, reports soon chronicled "orgies and revels" that were supposedly nightly events. Most damningly, investigators spoke of how white women met their "colored lovers" there and of the easy race mixing. By September 1912, enough evidence of disorderly behavior had been gathered that Whitin confronted Marshall with it, leading to an extensive exchange of letters between them. Finally, and in capitulation, Marshall sent Whitin a promissory letter in which he agreed that his main dining rooms would henceforth be "exclusively for colored people" and that two other dining rooms would be converted to one large room for "private dancing and entertainment exclusively for my white patrons only." Marshall added meekly that he hoped that this met with Whitin's approval.

W. E. B. Du Bois, although only a patron of Marshall's, wrote letters to Whitin in which he attacked the committee's actions in the Marshall's Hotel matter. He pointed out the gratuitous conflation of race mixing with immorality and condemned the committee's push toward racial segregation. But to no avail. Although the arrangement forced on Marshall was technically not a violation of New York state statutes, since this was a legal case of "separate but equal," the spirit of Jim Crow started casting its long, dark shadow over New York's social, political, and cultural life.[48]

By 1915 the committee's racist perspective was affecting proprietors and patrons in Harlem, Brooklyn, Coney Island, and throughout Greater New York. An agent noted a sign in a Brooklyn café in July that read: "By request of the Committee of 14—No couples of different color will be served together." And by later that summer the proprietor was refusing any admission to the backroom by white men. Another black proprietor, Mr. Rickey, told David Oppenheim that Whitin himself often dropped into his place on a Saturday night and if he observed a white man here "he would get mad." Rickey claimed that Whitin did not mind his café being open late "as long as there are no whites mixed with the blacks." Frank Nolan, the manager at the Snug Café, informed Oppenheim in March 1916 that the Committee of Fourteen had black investigators working constantly throughout Harlem who reported back to Whitin on "everything that goes on." According to Nolan, Harlem joints typically received several warning letters a year from Whitin detailing happenings about which no one but the boss and a few waiters should know. Manager James Gould at the Lincoln Hotel in Coney Island was direct about the work of undercover detectives: "they are prejudiced on account of color and hound a black man."[49]

Even if Whitin did not directly confront race mixing in a black-and-tan establishment, proprietors quaked that he might, for repercussions could include shuttering the place. One result of committee action and intimidation was that reports filed in 1917 are strikingly absent references to race mixing. The issue just seemed to have disappeared. In August 1918, David Oppenheim got to chatting with one of the black entertainers in the Remsen Café, a "colored bar" in Coney Island. He asked if there were any places around that still stayed open all night, implying black and tans—"like in the olden times." The entertainer noted that the White Cannon Inn in East Rockaway was a lively place open until the early hours, but then added, "it's a high toned place, white people." The color line had become a color wall, one not easily breached for decades to come.[50]

❖

Music has always been good for nightspot business. Martin Heilbutt of the Court Square Café told Oppenheim that his place in 1916 used to be slow until he brought in a piano and that business had since picked up. A fundamental problem for Heilbutt and others who kept an instrument in their backrooms, though, was that you could hope for a walk-in patron who would play the instrument or you could hire a musician. The former was free but not a dependable source of quality music-making; the latter was much more a sure thing but required payment out of proceeds. A solution to this conundrum for many proprietors turned out to be electricity. After 1911, more and more saloon owners and managers bought electric player pianos fitted with coin-slot attachments and placed them in their backrooms. And not only pianos, for they also installed slot harps, slot organs, player pianos with mandolin attachments, and at least one "German band orchestrion."

Much more than a novelty, the purchase of a player piano was a rational business decision. By the mid-1910s, hundreds of the latest ragtime hits could be bought on inexpensive player-piano rolls. Loaded in a player piano, well-played and great-sounding music was available on demand, at any hour, without rest, and did not call for free beer. Furthermore, with the slot attachment, patrons—not the proprietors—paid for the music. And apparently that revenue could be substantial. Trommers, the proprietor of an unassuming joint on Seventh Avenue, told an agent that he paid three hundred dollars per month rent on his place and that the slot instrument in his backroom made that much alone.[51]

It seems that dancers had no issue with the devices and simply brought the old dance ethos with them into the new machine-made aural world. A complaint filed by the Committee of Fourteen with the City Magistrates' Court in July 1912 concerned disorderly behaviors at Selig's Hotel, where an agent observed dancing to an "automatic piano . . . in a manner suggestive of sexual intercourse." One female dancer reportedly placed her hand on the crotch of a male dancer and announced, "Hey, girls, feel the hardon this kid has." Other female dancers cautioned her, "Florence, you better not be dancing with that

kid any more; he'll get such a hardon he will F___ the whole lot of us."
All this to canned music.[52]

Oppenheim, in August 1916, learned that the backroom saloon at
the Arlington Hotel used to hire a band each Saturday night but quit
that practice and installed a player organ. With slot-operated instruments more and more common in backroom saloons throughout New
York, the employment picture for musicians became progressively grim.

Actions by the Committee of Fourteen did not help. Whitin
believed that the backroom was a primary source of the city's immoral
behavior. One of his innovative solutions was to oppose the renewal of a
liquor license until the piano was removed, while another simply forced
proprietors to clear out instruments on the basis of reported disorderly
behavior. Where there had once been music and dancing, there would
now be only the sounds of people talking and drinking, a sure way to
eliminate a measure of jollity (the step before immorality) from a backroom. And with each piano removed, another job or two was lost.

Once agents marked a place where singing waiters served as the
go-betweens for men seeking prostitutes, it became a committee
target. Forced to sign promissory notes, proprietors frequently were
required to relieve singing waiters of their jobs. And with each promise to the committee that was kept, musician unemployment went up
another tick.

The committee held strongly to the requirement that cabarets close
by one A.M., severely curtailing the long-standing after-hours partying.
Eddie, a singing waiter at the Boulevard Inn, complained that business was rotten because of the enforced closing hour. He claimed that
the place now had only three waiters each making about fifty dollars
a week, which he compared to the five or six waiters in the past who
were all good for ninety to one hundred dollars per week. Edda, the
singer at the Village Inn, lost her job because the place could not make
enough money before one A.M. to pay her. She became yet another
number among the newly unemployed.[53]

It is not easy to project how many musicians were making livings in the New York City places that the Committee of Fourteen targeted, or to know how many of them were affected by the tightening labor markets for musicians from 1910 to 1917. But gray estimates on the situation in Manhattan alone give some general indication.

- ❖ *Brothels*. Committee agents visited 142 brothels during 1912. Parlor houses of any standing employed a "professor." Figure that at least one hundred brothel musicians had steady employment in Manhattan at that time.
- ❖ *Backroom saloons*. Kneeland's 1913 report surveyed and documented 765 backroom saloons (a fraction of the total in Manhattan). Many of these places provided steady employment for at least one musician and up to five or six if there was a cabaret. A workable, conservative average would be two musicians in five hundred such places.
- ❖ *Dance halls*. Agents visited seventy-five public dance halls in 1912, but there were surely more (as many as five hundred according to Belle Israels). Assume that about one hundred operated nightly. Each hall typically had a band of two to three musicians, sometimes more and sometimes only a single piano player. Figure that at least two musicians enjoyed steady employment in each of the one hundred dance halls.

That makes for around thirteen hundred musicians in pre-cabaret, 1912 Manhattan who had regular jobs requiring a firsthand understanding of the relationship between music-making and human sexuality.

For comparison purposes, extrapolation from U.S. census data suggests that there were about 4,088 professional male musicians in 1910 Manhattan. That number included symphony orchestra members, pit players, conductors, composers, songwriters, opera singers, vaudeville, and the stars in *Naughty Marietta*, but not music teachers. It also included the thirteen hundred musicians in the brothels, saloons, and dance halls. Musicians employed by the vice business then would appear to make up something on the order of thirty percent of the total male musician population of Manhattan. These were the "routine," mainly anonymous musicians who supported an underground cultural economy based largely on liquor, dancing, and sex, and all were under attack by the Committee of Fourteen by 1913.[54]

Big changes were directly ahead. The 1910 U.S. census had counted fifty-six percent more "musicians and teachers of music" in Greater New York than in 1900, while the general population increased "only" thirty-eight percent. The 1920 census showed that the general population in Greater New York grew by eighteen percent over 1910, but those who claimed employment as musicians increased by *less than two percent* during that time. The number of musicians in New York City had always before (and after) tracked (or exceeded) population changes. But not during the decade of the 1910s.[55]

⋯❖⋯

The year between the way things had been in New York for decades and the way they were going to be in the future was 1917. Ragtime was getting stale after its two-decade run. Tough dancing was being tamed (or sterilized) by the likes of the slick, well-known dancing team Vernon and Irene Castle. World War I began for Americans and the War Department banned tenderloin districts. In order to avoid pressure from the police and the Committee of Fourteen, private "nightclubs," such as the Cocoanut Grove, began requiring nominal "membership" fees to enter. For musicians, jobs were hard to get and harder to keep.

And that was also the year that jazz came to New York City and to the world. On January 27, the Original Dixieland Jass Band opened at Reisenweber's "400 Club" Café at West Fifty-Eighth Street and Eighth Avenue. The *New York Clipper* greeted it with a one-line review: "Its weird music must be heard to be appreciated." And quickly appreciated it was. In February, the band recorded for the Victor label "Dixie Jass Band One Step" and, on the B side, "Livery Stable Blues" This became the first jazz record ever released. Wildly successful, it signaled that the Jazz Age had arrived.

Detail from a witty advertisement for the Circe and the Swine dance in Greenwich Village, January 4, 1918. Note the "Nude Ascending the Staircase" at bottom left, a reference to the 1912 modernist painting by Marcel Duchamp, "Nude Descending a Staircase." Drawing by Clara Tice, well-known at the time for her erotic art, which subsequently came under the disapproving scrutiny of Anthony Comstock in March 1915. *Committee of Fourteen Records. Manuscripts and Archives Division. The New York Public Library. Astor, Lenox and Tilden Foundations. Courtesy of the New York Public Library.*

Agents surely heard the ODJB but none appear to have commented on its music. Reisenweber's was a large place, with a dining room, cabaret, and dancing on one floor, while the top floor, called the "Paradise," held another expansive dining room and entertainment stage. An unnamed agent visited the Paradise on February 1 but said nothing about the music heard there, while James Seaman mentioned only the "Cohen Revue" in his February 5, 1917, report. But jazz was certainly in the air. An agent at the Van Cortlandt Park Inn in August heard a jazz band of black musicians perform (not the ODJB, whose members were white). And an advertising flyer for the famously licentious Greenwich Village "Christmas Costume Party" boasted that at one A.M. "the original Dixieland Jass Band will come down all the way from the Rich Mr. Reisenweber's in a Fleet of Taxicabs."

The explosive arrival of jazz in New York has generally been ascribed to developments in the recording industry and to the arrival in the city of "Great Migration" black musicians. A more immediate explanation would be to take note of the legions of black and white musicians long in New York. Already practiced in an energetic, syncopated dance music—ragtime—they had lost easy access to a secure, demimonde musical economy and so necessarily moved into a new and insecure public economy. There they naturally played for dancing, music-loving patrons the noisy music they had long known how to make, but now inflected by a closely related, jazzy new idiom.

Even as consequential as this moment proved to be, as exciting as this music surely was, and as lovingly as it was embraced, in the deep counterpoint could be heard—if one really tried—distant cornet caterwaulings crying out a dirge for a colorful era that had spanned decades. Dancers have never particularly fancied dirges, however. So they called for some champagne, turned to one another, and raised a toast to that past. Then, in keeping with traditions long maintained by the young, they playfully taunted the sour faces of the moralistic, drained their glasses, smiled to the musicians, kicked high, and got on with their superlatively rotten dancing to an enflaming new alleged music.

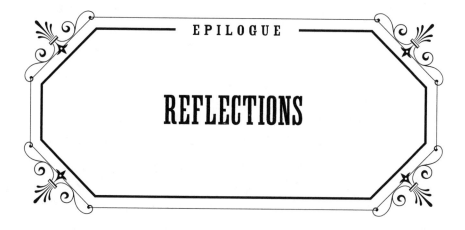

EPILOGUE

REFLECTIONS

THE CITY COMMISSIONERS of Paducah, Kentucky—my home-town—voted on February 17, 1916, to appoint a civic commission and charge it with investigating vice conditions in the city. The commission subsequently contracted with a chief investigator to do the detail work, one George J. Kneeland, the very same sociologist who had conducted similar studies in New York City and Chicago. He, in turn, hired two undercover investigators and instructed them to seek out and report on prostitution in this small city of twenty-three thousand people.

Sixty-six houses of prostitution were subsequently identified by the agents. These places were even mapped at the front of the published report as "Some Sore Spots of Paducah Today." The report also counted 174 full-time prostitutes in the city. Under the heading "What Prostitution Means to Paducah," the shocking extrapolation was that one in every thirty-five adult women in the city worked in prostitution.[1]

Later in the report, Kneeland turned to agent accounts for what actually went on in Paducah's vice scene.

The first thing on entering one of these houses, is to be importuned for dimes for the piano. This begging is constant and repeated, the girls even

trying to get money out of your pockets if you are reluctant. Next is the
begging of a quarter for a drink—then follows the soliciting to go to bed.

The rest of the richly detailed, sixty-three-page report followed the
well-developed Kneeland formula: analyze and edit the reports, redact-
ing where necessary; print a good number of investigator reports along
with commentary; discuss medical implications and law enforcement
issues; make recommendations.[2]

The Paducah report is inherently interesting to anyone from that
fair city. But, implicitly, it also suggests a possible answer to a question that has long vexed one of its musicological progeny. Fate Marable
was a fellow native son of Paducah. Born in 1890, he left town in his
late teens for a gig as pianist/calliope player on steamboats plying the
Mississippi River. Marable quickly worked his way up to bandleader
and subsequently hired many players out of New Orleans to fill chairs
in his highly regarded dance band. Baby Dodds, Johnny Dodds, Red
Allen, Jimmy Blanton, and others were trained under his baton and
later became prominent in jazz history. Most famously, Marable hired
a young cornetist, Louis Armstrong, mentored him in reading music
and the art of ensemble playing, and encouraged his improvisational
skills. Marable's protégé, of course, went on to become the key figure
in the early development of jazz.[3]

So what kind of musical training could Marable have received that
prepared him for such a career? Well, as the vice commission report
suggests, there were sixty-six brothels in Paducah, many of which must
have provided jobs for black piano players with ragtime chops. The
professors might have served as teachers to young Fate, or as role models, or perhaps even included him among their number. Speculation?
Sure, and probably unprovable. But there was a network in place to
support Marable, and his subsequent career certainly fits the pattern.[4]

Paducah's vice study is introduced here not only so that I might
postulate about my hometown's music history, but also to show that
cities other than New York had "Some Sore Spots" in which prostitutes

and their clients danced to alleged music. Furthermore, there were a lot of such cities. One estimate is that by 1900 nearly one hundred American cities—north, south, east, west; large, medium, small—had tenderloin districts (several with multiple districts) and one hundred thousand prostitutes lived in towns and cities scattered across the land. Then came social reform movements and the campaign against commercialized sex, which also stretched across the nation. The Paducah report mentioned that the American Social Hygiene Association had coordinated vice investigations in 105 cities, nearly all of them between 1910 and 1916. In 1917, Howard B. Woolston, an urban sociologist, visited forty American cities that had already published vice reports in order to conduct a follow-up survey of conditions. There is no reason to suppose that there were not parallels in these cities to New York's culture of sex, music, and dance; in fact, it would be harder to imagine the contrary. *Everybody's Doin' It* then is not just New York's story or Paducah's. It is America's story.[5]

⁘

It's also the story of many thousands of routine and anonymous musicians in New York, Paducah, and throughout the nation. The 1910 census counted 39,163 professional male musicians in the United States. An earlier calculation in this book projected that approximately thirty percent of Manhattan's professional male musicians made their livelihood in the underground vice economy, or about one of every seventeen hundred citizens. A comparative analysis of population and musicians in Chicago suggested a ratio there of about one in two thousand. To take Chicago's more conservative number and factor it against the population in the fifty largest American cities in 1910 (where just twenty-two percent of the nation's citizens lived), yields 10,152 professional full-time male musicians working in places that harbored prostitution. Since some of the other thirty thousand musicians throughout the nation were surely employed in the commercialized sex industry outside those large cities (remember little Paducah, with its sixty-six sore spots), a rough but conservative estimate is that one in three professional, full-time male musicians in the United States in 1910 made music in direct support of commercialized sex.[6]

To state the obvious, that's a tremendous number of musicians working night after night throughout the country refining a musical language intended to heighten an atmosphere of loosened sexuality. But by the end of 1918, a hundred tenderloin districts had been closed down, raising the question of musicians' welfares. Inevitably, as was the case in New York, many musicians in the United States around this time abandoned hopes of a music career altogether. Whereas the 1920 census showed that the number of musicians/music teachers in New York was about the same as in 1910, the situation was much worse across the nation as the numbers declined by 9,045.[7]

Musicians who managed to retool and rise to the challenges of a new world shaped by new social expectations did so in a vastly different musical environment than ten years before. A typical tenderloin dance band in 1910 was two to four musicians, suitable for the smaller concert saloons, dance halls, and dives, many unlicensed, that hoped to avoid wide public scrutiny while maintaining their patronage, which was often multiracial. By the 1930s, combos would feature five to seven musicians and big bands were even larger, better numbers for the grand restaurants, theaters, and nightclubs that sought wide public attention, places like the Apollo Theater and the Cotton Club, where the performers were black and the audiences white. Music as an intimate, backroom, black-and-tan experience was in rapid decline; music as a public, big-space, segregated experience was in high ascendance. This was a track that would have broad ramifications for subsequent developments in American popular music and its consumption.

In 1871, Charles Darwin addressed a fundamental conundrum that underscores much of this book: "Why music?"

[I]t appears probable that the progenitors of man, either the males or females or both sexes, before acquiring the power of expressing their mutual love in articulate language, endeavored to charm each other with musical notes and rhythm.

He continued on to suggest that humans, like songbirds, enhance their chances of reproductive success if they are musical.[8]

One does wish, though, that Darwin had applied more of his prodigious analytic skills to the last word in his observation. He, like many middle-class Victorians, seemed to assume that rhythm served a role in music-making but that it was perfunctory and less important than "tones and cadences," or melodies and harmonies. In his section on music in *The Descent of Man, and Selection in Relation to Sex*, which he titled "Voice and Musical Powers," rhythm as a critical component in dance music is not mentioned at all.[9]

Yet from deep in our human history up to the present in many parts of the world, "to enjoy music and to dance to it are virtually synonymous." Although the English language has never developed a word that articulates that fundamental "music/dance" overlay, other cultures have been more comprehending and found their word. For instance, among the hundreds of millions who speak the bantu languages, *ngoma* can mean either music or dance or theater or some elision of the three. To expound a bit from Darwin, men and women have sometimes endeavored to charm each other with song and symphony to be sure, but mostly they have done so with something very like *ngoma*, even when they did not have a word for it. Furthermore, there are plenty of personal stories suggesting that this kind of charming can and often does lead to sexual expressions of mutual attraction.[10]

Geoffrey Miller, an evolutionary psychologist, has framed the issue:

Music is a biological adaptation, universal within our species, distinct from other adaptations, and too complex to have arisen except through direct selection for some survival or reproductive benefit. Since there are no plausible survival benefits for music production, reproductive benefits seem worth a look.

That look has begun with some recent scientific studies offering provocative (but still tentative) support to both Darwin's postulation and the veracity of common anecdotes. Experiments from 2005 and 2007 suggested that hormonal levels and genetic makeup could be communicated to potential mates through dancing. Research out of a laboratory dedicated to dancing and psychology concluded that men who had high levels of testosterone danced differently than men with low levels, and that heterosexual women of childbearing age were most attracted to the high-testosterone dancers. On the other side of the mating game, work published in 2012 propounded that forty-eight young heterosexual women subconsciously expressed late follicular ovulation through their dancing and that males, viewing video clips alone, were capable of detecting danced cues that signaled female fertility. Much more work remains to be done, of course. But when it comes, scientists and musicologists must resist the easy wisdom that music-making and dancing are necessarily separate human activities, a notion that was not the case in human evolutionary history nor with the many whose engagements with *ngoma* have made up this book.[11]

⋅⋅❖⋅⋅

Miss Lee, a singer then enjoying a flourishing career in cabaret and vaudeville, joined Committee of Fourteen agent S. F. Lieb's table one evening in 1915 at the Broadway Rose Garden. After some casual chit-chat, she asked Lieb if he danced. After he confirmed that he did, she invited him onto the floor with her. According to Lieb, Miss Lee's dancing, like that throughout the Rose Garden, was in a "particularly vulgar fashion." She wiggled herself while dancing and rolled her eyes around. Lieb asked her if she was enjoying herself. She replied that there was nothing quite so nice as dancing, except for "the real thing."[12]

It is not clear from Lieb's report if Miss Lee was a part-time prostitute trying to procure a client, or even if solicitation was made or implied on anyone's part. In any case, such questions miss the bigger point. *Everybody's Doin' It* is, to be sure, a book about how a huge, profitable industry provided an infrastructure supporting important developments in dancing and music-making in America. But that formulation unfortunately suggests that the narrative can be broken into largely discrete, discipline-specific components that don't, or only barely, touch one another: sexuality and gender studies; dance history; musicology. In the end, that's not how I have come to see this book, and I don't think Miss Lee, or even agent Lieb, would have seen it that way either. Miss Lee wiggled in a vulgar fashion to alleged music that naturally and seamlessly put her in mind of sex. The sensations that she enjoyed so much, surely among the better things in life, quite likely resulted from complex codes deeply embedded in the biological and psychological constitutions of what makes us who we are. In this way, she had kinship with the many millions before her and after, whether prostitutes, charity girls, johns, committee agents, gays, straights, blacks, whites, ordinary people, extraordinary people, editors, reporters, philosophers, dance historians, musicologists, perhaps even a social reformer or two who hadn't forgotten how to dance. Yet even more than the richness of sensual experiences involving sex, music, or dance is an elemental humanity that joins all of us together in all these things. For that's the *real* "real thing."

ACKNOWLEDGMENTS

IT'S A STRANGE THING about putting "sex" and "musicology" in the same sentence. Many seem not to think at first that the two can coexist in a mutual frame of scholarly mind. But after the initial shock and an additional explanatory sentence or two, everyone seems to brighten with something to say about music or (sotto voce) about sex or both, whether it ranges from "too narrow a topic" to (more commonly) "Well, yes, I remember once when . . ." Everything said to me by everybody along the way has been valuable; their thoughts, ideas, and responses have kept me going (or pausing for reflection) during the years of researching and writing this book. "Each has his or her place in the procession," to return once again to Walt Whitman. And a very long procession it is, indeed.

I have chewed on this topic for more than two decades, sometimes vigorously, sometimes slackly. And sometimes hesitantly, for what would my friends, family, and colleagues think of a tweedy musicologist alone in his study pondering sex (and, oh yes, music and dance, but people tend not to get past the sex part of the equation). Finally, I girded my loins and presented some of my early research at a conference of the Society for American Music. Maribeth Payne, then a senior editor at W. W. Norton, was there and grabbed me afterward, insisting that the work should be developed into a book that Norton would want to publish. She refused to let the wild notion go and exchanged countless emails with me through several years to refine the topic (along with stimulating disagreements on the relative merits of smooth and smoky Kentucky bourbon and medicinal-tasting scotch, discourse still in need of mediation). Maribeth was the one who put me in touch with Wendy Strothman, whose keen eye for topic, narrative, and detail enabled, first, a proposal and then a credible book. With always helpful Wendy at my elbow, I then began working with Norton senior editor Amy Cherry, assistant editor Remy Cawley, and editorial assistant Zarina Patwa. If there is any lucidity of thought, poetic turn of expression, or structural logic in this work, credit Amy, Remy, and Zarina. Then if there is any graceful flow to this book, credit the superlatively wonderful (and meticulous) Nancy Palmquist for her copyediting. What a joy they've all been, and how much I have learned. Bouquets to each of these smart, gracious, exceedingly helpful professionals.

From here the procession gets really long and crowded. Bill Brooks and I have hashed (and sour-mashed) this project back and forth for years, and I have always been grateful for his interest and insights. Chris Ballantine, as always, has been an enthusiastic and supportive friend while maintaining his superbly focused critical eye on the tenuous, tedious, and wrongheaded. George Harris, philosopher, writer, and soul brother, has kept my horizons broad (even constantly expanded them) and has taken word-by-word critical interest in this project (and graciously allowed me to out-fish him when I needed a break). Tim Gilfoyle, whose masterly *City of Eros: New York City, Prostitution, and the Commercialization of Sex, 1790–1920* sits on my desk and open always, years ago encouraged me toward this project, one for which he doubted he had the musico-cultural chops. (I questioned that then, and question it still.) Ellie Hisama has encouraged me in this work and tried to guide me over some treacherous shoals. My ragtime buddies Ed Berlin, Gene Jones, and Terry Waldo have given freely of their extensive knowledge of ragtime and made sure that its sounds remained fresh in my ears. Greg Barz, ethnomusicologist extraordinaire, has richly supported me in this work and helped keep my modest ethnographic chops up to (even) modest speed. Joe Horowitz reminded me often, always to my benefit, that there's a great deal more to music in New York than that covered here. Deane Root kept me going at times when I was close to wavering. (Not sure he knew that!) Charles Hamm, who did not live long enough to see this work to completion (How I miss him still!), provided gentle encouragement over the years, garnished with always sure advice. And Rich Crawford, the consummate musicologist, has made sure that this horse doesn't bolt—"evidence, evidence, evidence." Finally, to friend, neighbor, and artist extraordinare Janet Fredericks, whose work of art poses as a map of the Five Points at the front of this book, how wonderful it has been to find such a talent and kindred spirit in my own backyard. A pocketful of posies to each of these fine colleagues and friends.

I could (and should) sing songs of praise to yet many more in the procession, but I'm not sure my voice would hold out. Note that all of these added something important to my work: Alice Sparberg Alexiou, Gillian Anderson, Vanessa Blais-Tremblay, Renee Camus, Mark Clague, Susan Cook, Dan Czitrom, Sarah Gerk, Daniel Goldmark, John Graziano, Gail Henry, Nathan Lynn, Susan McClary, Petra Meyer-Frazier, Carol Oja, Sam Parler, Ron Pen, Guy Ramsey, Tom Riis, Gillian Rodger, Stephen Shearon, Chris Smith, Judith Tick, George Todd, Rob Walser, Joe Weed. There are many more unnamed here, none of you forgotten. On the final, crashing cadence, a distribution of nosegays to all.

And the libraries and archives, without which . . . The American Antiquarian Society, both collections and staff, helped me lay the foundations for this work more than two decades ago. In the time between then and now, the fine, friendly, and helpful staff at the Wilson Music Library, Vanderbilt University, dug out interlibrary loan after interlibrary loan, as well as provided a great library platform. The wondrous collections at the Center for Popular Music, Middle Tennessee State University, have sustained my scholarly life for decades, and do so still; thanks Greg, Rachel, Lindsay, Yvonne, Martin, and all the rest. After moving to the extraordinary place called Vermont, the Middlebury College Library has been a great asset. A special and gaily colored clutch of blossoms to colleagues Marvin Carlson, Bruce McConachie, and Don Wilmeth, who together came up with the ideas that led me to the Shubert Archives, the Society for the Reformation of Juvenile Delinquents papers there, and Sylvia Wang, the collection's greatly helpful archivist. Finally, a super special thanks to the wonderfully supportive staff at the Division of Manuscripts and Archives at the New York Public Library. After two months of working through the ofttimes unseemly and (almost) always undecipherable Committee of Fourteen investigative reports, I needed their omnipresent examples of how to maintain quiet psychological, emotional, and professional balance; they came to feel like family. Let the florist be summoned!

Always and forever, there's Lucinda and Enkidu (the twenty-five-pound black Pomeranian, not the wild man from Mesopotamia). Lucinda has put up with more than a spouse should bear: times when I went down the rabbit hole of fixation, untold hours spent with "my ladies" and not with her, dragging her to New York for yet more research (when she'd rather be here in this Vermont paradise), lurching shifts of focus as I suddenly thought to reconsider a nearly forgotten turn of phrase . . . just way too much neglect. A garden of perennial blossoms for her, the love of my life! And Enkidu . . . well, it's time for a smelly, soul-righting walk! And another. And another. A garland of dog bones for him!

I no doubt deserved my enemies,
But I don't believe I deserved my friends.

(Whitman yet again.)

With all the quality help I've had along the way, you'd think I would have gotten everything right! There's not a chance of that, of course. As I have tried throughout this book to bind an interest in sex, music, and dance to a basic humanity, please extend to me forbearance for my errors, which stem from my own flawed, basic humanity. In truth, however, I know that that which I got wrong was really Enkidu's fault, for he failed to be insistent on the walk that would have cleared my mind. Or maybe it really was that damned squirrel that directed Enkidu's attention toward his basic dogmanity and away from his more altruistic responsibility to heal me of my so manifest human foibles!

SONGS IDENTIFIED BY COMMITTEE OF FOURTEEN AGENTS, 1913-1917

1913

"The Angle-Worm Wiggle" (I. Maynard Schwartz/Harry S. Lorch; 1910)

"Home, Sweet Home" (John Howard Payne/Henry R. Bishop; 1823)

"I Love It" (E. Ray Goetz/Harry Von Tilzer; 1910)

"I'm Alabama Bound: A Rag-Time Two Step" (Robert Hoffman; 1909)

"In My Harem" (Irving Berlin; 1913)

"Keep Away from the Fellow Who Owns an Automobile" (Irving Berlin; 1912)

"When I Get You Alone To-Night" (Fred Fisher/Joseph McCarthy; 1912)

1914

"Ballin' the Jack" (Jim Burris/Chris Smith; 1913)

"When I Come Back" (L. Wolfe Gilbert/Kerry Mills; 1914)

1915

"Back to the Carolina You Love" (Grant Clarke/Jean Schwartz; 1914)

"Chinatown, My Chinatown" (William Jerome/Jean Schwartz; 1910)

"One-Eyed Reilly" (traditional)

"Rocked in the Cradle of the Deep" (Emma Willard/Joseph Philip Knight; 1853)

"Tip-Top Tipperary Mary" (Ballard MacDonald/Harry Carroll; 1914)

"Yankee Doodle" (traditional)

1916

"Hesitation Blues" (traditional)

"Some Girls Do and Some Girls Don't" (Howard E. Johnson/Alex Gerber/ Harry Jentes; 1916)

"The Streets of Cairo, or the Poor Little Country Maid" (James Thornton; 1895)

"There's a Little Bit of Bad in Every Good Little Girl" (Grant Clarke/Fred Fischer; 1916)

1917

"After the Ball" (Charles K. Harris; 1892)

"The Bowery" (Charles Hale Hoyt/Percy Gaunt; 1892)

"Hello! I've Been Looking for You" (John L. Golden/Raymond Hubbell; 1916)

"How Can Any Girl Be a Good Little Girl When She Loves a Naughty Little Boy?" (Howard Johnson/Alfred Jentes/Harry Jentes; 1917)

"Huckleberry Finn" (Sam M. Lewis/Joe Young/Cliff Hess; 1917)

"I Didn't Raise My Boy to Be a Soldier" (Alfred Bryan/Al Piantadosi; 1915)

"Sweet Rosie O'Grady" (Maude Nugent; 1896)

"What Do You Want to Make Those Eyes at Me For?" (Joseph McCarthy/ Howard E. Johnson/James V. Monaco; 1916)

⇥ APPENDIX 2 ⇤

"COCK EYED REILLY"

I was walking down the street,
        I was peeking into the dutchman's corner.
I walked into his Tavern,
        I asked him for a glass of gin and water.
Then back for the day skinny idle lay quack for the skinny idle Cock Eyed Reilly.

When I was drinking my gin and water
        who shipped in but the landlords daughter.
A serious notion came into my head
        I thought I'd like to take a feel of her hindquarter.
Then back for the day skinny idle lay quack for the skinny idle Cock Eyed Reilly.

She took me up to her bedroom,
        politely threw her left leg over.
She sang a song I played the tune,
        we danced and sang till the tune was over.
Then back for the day skinny idle lay quack for the skinny idle Cock Eyed Reilly.

I came down stairs to drink my gin & water.
        When who came in but her damn old father.
He had a bunch of pistols in his hand.
        Are you the man that f_____ my daughter?
Then back for the day skinny idle lay quack for the skinny idle Cock Eyed Reilly.

I shoved the pistols up his a__
    I dumped him with a pail of water.
I told him I would go and F__ himself
    the same as I did with his God D___ daughter.
Then back for the day skinny idle lay quack for the skinny idle Cock Eyed Reilly.

Transcription made by David Oppenheim, August 18, 1915, Bard & Berl Saloon, Brooklyn, New York. (C14, Box 29, Folder: Brooklyn—Inv. Reports & Rel. Mats, 1914–15.)

THE PEOPLE &C. AGAINST
WALLACE W. SWEENEY

WALLACE W. SWEENEY, who ran an ostensibly private club named the Independent Repiners Young Men's Association at 111 West Thirty-First Street, was brought before New York's Court of Special Sessions on January 29, 1912. He was there to answer for events that occurred the evening of November 12, 1911. Sweeney faced a charge of "Keeping and Maintaining a House of Ill-fame (prostitution, lewdness, nuisance . . .) in manifest destruction and subversion of, and against good morals and good manners." A second count lodged against him was for "Keeping a Disorderly House (drinking, tippling, gambling, rioting, disturbing the peace, fornicating, whoring and misbehaving themselves . . .)," while a third was for "Maintaining a Public Nuisance."[1]

The case hinged on testimony provided by Officers Joseph M. Gaffney and Martin Walsh, and was concerned largely with the types and styles of dancing in Sweeney's club. Gaffney and Walsh had, on the evening under investigation, entered the place incognito, accompanied by two unknown women they had picked up on a corner of Thirty-Fifth Street and Broadway.

Gaffney was the first to be interrogated by James E. Smith, the deputy assistant district attorney.

Q. Describe the room which you entered at that time.
A. We entered a hallway and the hallway is about 50 feet long, and we went through this hallway into the dance hall. This dance hall is about 25 feet by 50, and on entering there we saw a number of persons seated

around this room drinking, and the middle of the floor was cleared for dancing, and women and men were smoking and drinking.

Q. How many people were there?

A. About 150 in the place at the time. . . .

Q. What did the woman say to Sweeney at the time she called him?

A. She said, "I am going to get Sweeney to do the nigger dance" and then she called Sweeney over to the table, saying to him, "Do that nigger wiggle dance" and Sweeney said, "I am tired of doing that fucking dance all night, but seeing it's you, kid, I will get my chicken and wiggle it" and then Sweeney stood up from our table and went over to a table on the opposite side of the hall and danced with another woman. . . .

Q. Describe what you saw Sweeney and that woman do at that time.

A. They started to dance.

Q. Dance what?

A. What is known as the nigger wiggle dance.

Q. Describe the nigger wiggle dance.

A. Sweeney placed his hands on her buttocks and she did the same to him and they started to move their abdomens against each other.

Q. And danced around the room?

A. Yes, sir. . . .

Q. At the time the defendant Sweeney was dancing the nigger wiggle with the woman, were there other people upon the floor at that time?

A. Yes, sir.

Q. What were they dancing?

A. The same thing. . . .

Q. And in the same way?

A. Not all of them.

Q. Some of them were?

A. Some of them; some had their hands placed the same as the defendant and more did not.

Q. How many were dancing the nigger wiggle at the time the defendant Sweeney was dancing it?

A. I should think 3 or 4 couples. . . .

Q. And what music was playing?

A. There was an electric piano there at the time.

Q. And what did Sweeney do after he danced the nigger wiggle?

A. He came over to our table where we were sitting and he said: "There was such a bunch of cunts dancing on the floor they pushed me all over the floor, but seeing it was you, kid, I obliged you, didn't I," and then he placed his arms around the neck of one of the girls that was sitting at our table.

Q. At the time the defendant and other parties were dancing the nigger wiggle on the floor, did you notice what the other people were doing?

A. They were drinking or smoking cigarettes.

Q. Did you see women smoking cigarettes?

A. Yes, sir.

Q. What else did you see the other women doing?

A. They had their clothes up as far as their knees and their limbs exposed. . . .

Q. What kind of a dance was it you saw on the floor after that?

A. The men and women were dancing with their hands on each other's buttocks, and moving their abdomens against each other.

Q. That continued for how long a time?

A. Three or four minutes.

Q. How many dances were carried on while you were in that place?

A. Probably eight or ten. . . .

Q. Some were dancing the nigger wiggle and others were dancing something else?

A. Yes, your Honor. . . .

Officer Walsh was then called to testify.

Q. [When] Sweeney came over what did he do, if anything?

A. The girl asked him to do the nigger wiggle dance, and Sweeney said he was "tired doing that fucking nigger dance all night" but as long as it was her that he would do it for her and he put his arms around her neck. Shortly afterwards he went over and while walking over he called a girl that was on the west side of the room, from a table, and she got up and the piano started playing and they did the nigger wiggle dance.

Q. Describe the dance.

A. The defendant Sweeney placed his hand upon the unknown girl's buttock and she placed her hands on his buttock and they commenced to move their abdomens towards each other.

Q. Did they stand still or go around the floor?

A. Went around the floor. . . .

Q. How long did that continue?

A. During the duration of the music furnished by an electric piano at the northwest corner of the room.

Q. How long a time did it take to dance it?

A. About three or four minutes. . . .

Q. What did [Sweeney] say when he came back?

A. He said there was "such a bum bunch of cunts dancing on the floor that I was pushed all over the floor." . . .

Q. What did you see the women do if anything while sitting at these tables?

A. While they were sitting at the tables they displayed their legs, some of them, almost up to the knee, so that the knee was visible, and when they got up to dance they lifted their skirts up so that you could see above their knees while they were dancing; the skirts were pulled tight and you could see the whole contour of the figure. . . .

Q. Were they [doing] the nigger wiggle or not?

A. Yes, sir.

Q. Describe the dance.

A. It was the ordinary half time Turkey Trot and Nigger Wiggle, they danced about the same as Mr. Sweeney did. . . .

Q. While you were seated at this table did you notice anything going on at any table adjoining you?

A. Yes, sir, on the table south of us Officer Gaffney called my attention to a man who had his right hand on the left breast of a women who wore a low-cut evening dress. The breasts were exposed so you could see the shape of the woman's two breasts; you couldn't see the nipple of her breast, and he had his hand over there and she said "Get away from here, you cocksucker. What do you think this is, free lunch?"

Q. Now while you were sitting at this table what conversation did you and the other officer have with the women who were sitting at this table?

A. After a while the girls asked us if we wished to dance. We said we didn't know how to dance and they got up and had a dance amongst themselves and came back and they had another drink, they were very thirsty. And they said "Don't you think it is time to get screwed, boys?" my girl said to me, and I heard the girl in company of Gaffney speaking to him; I don't know what she said; my girl said "Don't you think it is time to get screwed, it will cost you Five Dollars and I will guarantee you will have a good time." I said I didn't feel like having anything to-night. . . .

Near the end of the trial, the defense called Virgil J. Clifford.

Q. Where are you employed now? . . .
A. Tom Shanley's, 43rd and 44th Street and Broadway.
Q. In what capacity are you employed there?
A. Dancing.
Q. What do you mean by dancing?
A. Whirlwind dance, Turkey Trot and Bear Dance. . . .
Q. Were you employed at [Sweeney's]?
A. Yes sir. . . .
Q. And what was your occupation there?
A. Floor manager and dancing. . . .
Q. And you can testify what the different dances are?
A. Yes, Sir. . . .
Q. Will you demonstrate to the Court?
A. Yes, sir, I will demonstrate to the Court; I have my partner right here and will demonstrate it with any one. . . .

Clifford was then cross-examined by the deputy assistant district attorney.

Q. When did you become a dancer?
A. I have been dancing for the past fifteen years.
Q. Did you dance in the Berkeley Lyceum?
A. Yes, sir; teaching.
Q. When did you learn the Turkey Trot?
A. About 7 years ago.
Q. Where was it you learned the Turkey Trot?
A. San Francisco.
Q. When you were employed in Sweeney's what did you understand were to be your duties?
A. My duties [were] to take charge of the floor and the dancing. . . .
Q. What do you do in Sweeney's every morning [i.e., after closing time]?
A. Dancing.
Q. What dance do you give?
A. I give the Whirlwind Dance—
Q. And what other dance?
A. Turkey Trot.
Q. What other dance?
A. Bear Dance.

Q. You have seen the Nigger Wiggle being given in that place, have you not?

A. No sir. I don't know what it is. . . .

Q. What are the dances usually conducted?

A. I do the Whirlwind Dance; it is a combination between the Turkey Trot and the Grizzly Bear and the Whirl.

Q. You never heard of the Nigger Wiggle?

A. No, sir.

Q. Did you ever see it dance?

A. No sir.

Notwithstanding the best (and obviously dissembling) efforts of Clifford, Sweeney was convicted and sentenced to the penitentiary for six months. He appealed without success, whereupon he simply jumped bail. Apprehended in September 1912, he was by then reportedly suffering from advanced tuberculosis and not expected to live out his sentence. Perhaps it was a ploy to avoid jail time or perhaps he staged a miraculous recovery; in any case, Sweeney died in Chicago in 1939.[2]

NOTES

PREFACE

1 Noah Webster, *An American Dictionary of the English Language;...* (Springfield, MA: George and Charles Merriam, 1855), 347. *Black's Law Dictionary Free Online Legal Dictionary*, 2nd ed.; accessed at https://thelawdictionary.org/disorder/.

2 See George Chauncey, *Gay New York: Gender, Urban Culture, and the Making of the Gay Male World, 1890–1940* (New York: Basic Books, 1994), 14ff, for an analysis of terminology, history, and meanings.

3 Ruth Rosen, *The Lost Sisterhood: Prostitution in America, 1900–1918* (Baltimore: Johns Hopkins University Press, 1982), xvii. Quotes from Samuel Beckett, *The Unnamable* (London: Picador, 1976).

INTRODUCTION

1 Stephen Mitchell, *Gilgamesh: A New English Version* (New York: Free Press, 2004), 81.

2 Oral history interview with Peter Bocage, January 29, 1959, Hogan Jazz Archive, Tulane University; quoted in Gary Krist, *Empire of Sin: A Story of Sex, Jazz, Murder, and the Battle for Modern New Orleans* (New York: Crown, 2014), 80.

3 The full reference to Helen Campbell's account is Mrs. Helen Campbell, Col. Thomas W. Knox, and Supt. Thomas Byrnes, *Darkness and Daylight; or, Lights and Shadows of New York Life: A Pictorial Record of Personal Expe-*

riences by Day and Night in the Great Metropolis (Hartford, CT: Hartford Publishing Company, 1895), 237–38.

An historian of sexuality in New York also confronted my source problem and developed a parallel methodology, one in which she "read across the sources, interpreting them carefully and using them against each other to paint a larger portrait of working-class sexual behavior and morality." Elizabeth Alice Clement, *Love for Sale: Courting, Treating, and Prostitution in New York City, 1900–1945* (Chapel Hill: University of North Carolina Press, 2006), 10–11.

4 Members of the New York Press, *The Night Side of New York: A Picture of the Great Metropolis after Nightfall* (New York: J.C. Haney, 1866), 24. Jacob A. Riis, *How the Other Half Lives: Studies Among the Tenements of New York* (New York: Charles Scribner's, 1890).

CHAPTER ONE: LIBERTINES, BLACKFACE, MINSTRELS, AND THE SMALL-POTATOE HUMBUG

1 *Magdalen Report: First Annual Report of the Executive Committee of the N.Y. Magdalen Society, Instituted January 1, 1830* (New York: Printed and Sold for the Publisher, 1831), 8–9.

2 McDowall's numbers were likely exaggerated, although he claimed they were conservative. For instance, a grand jury convened to produce an analysis of prostitution could count only 1,438 prostitutes in the city. For background on prostitution during this period in New York, see Marilynn Wood Hill, *Their Sisters' Keepers: Prostitution in New York City, 1830–1870* (Berkeley: University of California Press, 1993), 39ff. Primary sources include *Charges Preferred Against the New-York Female Benevolent Society, and the Auditing Committee, in 1835 and 1836, by J.R. McDowall, in the Sun and Transcript, Answered and Refuted by Himself!! In His Own Journal!!! In the Year 1833* (New York: Osborn & Buckingham, 1836), 50ff and passim; and John R. McDowall, *Magdalen Facts* (New York: Printed for the Author, 1832), 66–72.

3 Melissa Hope Ditmore, ed., *Encyclopedia of Prostitution and Sex Work* (Westport, CT: Greenwood Press, 2006), 1: 293. Emily van der Meulen, "Moral Panic and the New York Magdalen Society: Nineteenth Century Prostitution and the Moral Reform Movement," *MP: An Online Feminist Journal* (July 2008). Paul Boyer, *Urban Masses and Moral Order in America, 1829–1920* (Cambridge: Harvard University Press, 1978), 18–20.

4 The indictment by the grand jury was reported in the *New York Courier and Enquirer*, March 15, 1834.

5 *Advocate of Moral Reform* 4/22 (November 15, 1838): 169–70. Ibid., 6/19 (October 1, 1840): 149.

6 *Polyanthos*, February 16, 1841.

7 Ibid. Restell's life and work is treated in Helen Lefkowitz Horowitz, *Rereading Sex: Battles over Sexual Knowledge and Suppression in Nineteenth-Century America* (New York: Alfred A. Knopf, 2002), 198ff.

8 *Polyanthos*, June 6, 1841. The "Palace of Love" article is reprinted in Patricia Cline Cohen, Timothy J. Gilfoyle, and Helen Lefkowitz Horowitz, *The Flash Press: Sporting Male Weeklies in 1840s New York* (Chicago: University of Chicago Press, 2008), 137–38.

9 Timothy J. Gilfoyle, *City of Eros: New York City, Prostitution, and the Commercialization of Sex, 1790–1920* (New York: W. W. Norton & Company, 1992), 58–59. *Flash*, October 31, 1841. *True Flash*, December 4, 1841. The lives of Dixon's cohort are covered in Cohen et al., *The Flash Press*, passim.

Short the subtleties inherent in satire and irony, the cohort developed the marks of a genre with a long reach. In 1845, one of this group, George Wilkes, edited the first issues of the *National Police Gazette*, which became enormously influential over the decades as a men's weekly specializing in the risqué, accompanied by engravings (later, photographs) of scantily clad women. It was central to American male fantasy life up to its demise in 1932, six years after the first issue of the *National Enquirer*.

10 On T. D. Rice and his Jim Crow, see the exemplary work by W. T. Lhamon Jr., both *Jump Jim Crow: Lost Plays, Lyrics, and Street Prose of the First Atlantic Popular Culture* (Cambridge: Harvard University Press, 2003) and *Jim Crow, American: Selected Songs and Plays (The John Harvard Library)* (Cambridge: Belknap Press, 2009).

11 On Dixon, Rice, and early blackface minstrelsy, see Dale Cockrell, *Demons of Disorder: Early Blackface Minstrels and Their World* (Cambridge: Cambridge University Press, 1997).

12 *The Autobiography of David Crockett* (New York: Charles Scribner's Sons, 1923), 158–59.

13 *Evening Tattler*, January 25, 1840. Anthony Street, on the Lower East Side, is now named Worth Street.

14 *New York Libertine*, June 15, 1842.

15 Ibid.

16 On Susan Bryant (alias, "The Little Belt"), see George Wilkes, *The Lives of Helen Jewett and Richard P. Robinson* (New York: n.p., ca. 1849), 25ff. Wilkes had been part of the Dixon cohort in the early 1840s and was in 1849 the editor of the *National Police Gazette*.

17 *Flash*, December 18, 1841. Phoebe Doty is generally portrayed in the sporting press as fat, old, and ugly; Dixon was thus ridiculed by the implied alliance.

18 New York Municipal Archives, Court of General Sessions, Minute Books, January 13, 1842, January 14, 1842, April 18, 1842, July 14, 1842, July 15, 1842, September 14, 1842, September 15, 1842, September 28, 1842, March 22, 1843. *Flash*, January 22, 1842. On the charges of bigamy, it turned out that Julia Warren, the prostitute, was already married, rendering her second "marriage" to Wooldridge null and void. See Cohen et al., *The Flash Press*, 41. A chronicle of Wooldridge's legal problems may be found in Horowitz, *Rereading Sex*, 181ff.

19 New York Municipal Archives, Court of General Sessions, Minute Books, January 13, 1842, April 13, 1842. *New York Herald*, February 7, 1842, February 9, 1842. *Weekly Rake*, November 12, 1842. *New York Sporting Whip*, March 4, 1843. *Baltimore Sun*, October 26, 1846. *Raleigh Register*, May 29, 1846. *Louisville Daily Courier*, July 30, 1846. *Baltimore Sun*, April 18, 1848. *New York Tribune*, August 6, 1846. *Baltimore Sun*, April 5, 1848. *Baltimore Sun*, August 30, 1849. *Brooklyn Daily Eagle*, May 18, 1848.

20 *Whip*, February 16, 1842, February 26, 1842.

21 *New York Sporting Whip*, January 28, 1843, February 4, 1843. *New York Herald*, February 6, 1843.

22 *New York Sporting Whip*, February 18, 1843, February 25, 1843, March 4, 1843.

23 *New York Herald*, March 16, 1843. Cohen et al., *The Flash Press*, 115.

24 His indictment for libeling Eliza Trust may be found in New York Municipal Archives, Court of General Sessions, Minute Books, March 22, 1843.

CHAPTER TWO: ASMODEUS, JUBA, AND BLOOD ON FIRE

1 Dating is suggested in *Whip and Satirist of New-York and Brooklyn*, March 12, 1842.

2 J. Frank Kernan, *Reminiscences of the Old Fire Laddies and Volunteer Fire Departments of New York and Brooklyn* . . . (New York: M. Crane, 1885), 42–44.

3 "Boz at the Five Points," *Whip and Satirist of New-York and Brooklyn*, March 12, 1842.

4 Ibid. The article is copied in Cohen et al., *The Flash Press*, 186–89.

5 Charles Dickens, *American Notes for General Circulation* (New York: Harper & Bros., 1842), 36.

6 On Lane, see James W. Cook, "Dancing Across the Color Line," *Common-Place: The Interactive Journal of Early American Life* 4/1 (October 2003);

online journal accessed at http://www.common-place-archives.org/vol -04/no-01/cook/index.shtml. *New York Evening Post*, September 1, 1841, September 17, 1841.

7 *New York Tattler*, February 13, 1840. *New York Daily Express*, September 14, 1840. New York Municipal Archives, New York City Police Office, September 13, 1840. Kernan, *Reminiscences*, 44.

8 *New York Tribune*, November 9, 1842. *New York Herald*, November 11, 1842. *New York Herald*, quoted in Cook, "Dancing Across the Color Line." Ned Buntline [Edward Zane Carroll Judson], *The Mysteries and Miseries of New York: A Story of Real Life* (Dublin: McGlashan, 1849), 71–72. *New York Daily Herald*, May 14, 1846.

9 On Foster's life and place in New York society and culture, see the "Introduction" by Stuart M. Blumin, in George G. Foster, *New York by Gas-Light and Other Urban Sketches* (Berkeley: University of California Press, 1856/1990).

10 George G. Foster, *New York in Slices: By An Experienced Carver*, rev., enlarged, and corrected (New York: W.F. Burgess, 1849), 4. *New York Times*, April 17, 1856.

11 Foster, *New York in Slices*, 23–25, 111.

12 *New York Times*, April 17, 1856. [Julie de Marguerittes], *The Match-Girl: or, Life Scenes as They Are* (Philadelphia: W.W. Smith, 1855), 108–9, 125.

13 G[eorge] G. Foster, *New York by Gaslight: With Here and There a Streak of Sunshine* (New York: Dewitt & Davenport, 1850), 54.

14 Ibid., 73–75.

15 *Philadelphia Evening Bulletin*, April 16, 1856. *Philadelphia Sunday Mercury*, April 20, 1856. Obituaries were cited in George Rogers Taylor, "Gaslight Foster: A New York 'Journeyman Journalist' at Mid-Century," *New York History* 58/3 (July 1977), 311–12.

16 Washington Irving, *Tales of the Alhambra* (London: Richard Bentley, 1835), 62. Edward Bulwer-Lytton, *Asmodeus at Large* (Philadelphia: Carey, Lea & Blanchard, 1833), 30, 189.

17 Alain René Le Sage, *Asmodeus; or, The Devil on Two Sticks* (London: Joseph Thomas, 1841). *New York Evening Post*, April 22, 1840, February 5, 1842. *Spirit of the Times*, April 12, 1840.

18 Harrison Gray Buchanan, *Asmodeus or, Legends of New York* . . . (New York: John D. Munson & Co., 1848), 5, passim. Tom Pepper [Charles Frederick Briggs], *Asmodeus; or, The Iniquities of New York being a Complete Exposé of the Crimes, Doings and Vices as Exhibited in the Haunts of Gamblers and Houses of Prostitution, Both in High and Low Life! Including a Sketch*

of the Life of a Model Artiste, and the Celebrated Report of Arthur Tappan, Esq. on the Magdalens of New York* (New York: C.G. Graham, 1848), 8, 84; Tappan was at that time the president of the Magdalen Society and a name sure to grab the attention of a reader in the 1840s, given his well-known and fiercely held abolitionist views.

19 Greenhorn [George Thompson], *New-York Life; or, The Mysteries of Upper-Tendom Revealed, by the Author of "Asmodeus," "Lady's Garter," &c.* (New York: Charles S. Attwood, ca. 1849), 5. This same book was also published, anonymously, under the title *Revelations of Asmodeus, or, Mysteries of Upper Ten-Dom: Being a Spirit Stirring, a Powerful and Felicitous Exposé of the Desolating Mystery, Blighting Miseries, Atrocious Vices and Paralyzing Tragedies, Perpetrated in the Fashionable Pandemoniums of the Great Empire City* (New York: C.G. Graham, 1849); to confuse matters yet more, the book is retitled again at the head of chapter 1 as *Asmodeus; Or the Mysteries of "Upper Ten-Dom" Revealed. Sharps and Flats; or the Perils of City Life; Being the Adventures of One Who Lived by His Wits* (Boston: W. Berry, 1850). *The Lame Devil* has either been lost or was never published. *Jenny Lind Mania* (Boston: n.p., 1850). See David S. Reynolds, *Beneath the American Renaissance: The Subversive Imagination in the Age of Emerson and Melville* (New York: Alfred A. Knopf, 1988), 385, 458–59, and elsewhere for a revealing analysis of Thompson and those of his ilk.

20 Greenhorn [Thompson], *New-York Life*, 7. The term "lower million" comes from George Lippard, *New York: Its Upper Ten and Lower Million* (Cincinnati, OH: E. Mendenhall, 1854). Lippard too visited the Five Points and wrote about the multiracial "orgie" he saw there, played out against the sound of a fiddle.

21 Cohen et al., *The Flash Press*, 110. "On Vice," *Brooklyn Daily Times*, June 20, 1857, copied in Walt Whitman, *The Uncollected Poetry and Prose of Walt Whitman*, Emory Holloway, ed. (Garden City, NY: Doubleday, Page & Co., 1921), 2: 5–8.

22 William W. Sanger, *The History of Prostitution: Its Extent, Causes, and Effects Throughout the World (Being an Official Report to the Board of Alms-House Governors of the City of New York)* (New York: Harper & Brothers, 1858), 212, 246.

23 Ibid., 550–54.

24 Ibid., 559–62.

25 Ibid., 563–64.

26 Ibid., 579, 600, 605–6, 613. Gilfoyle, *City of Eros*, 126. Sanger also conducted research on prostitution in other major American cities and from

that work calculated that there were 61,298 women working in the trade in 1858 America (614–15).

CHAPTER THREE: THE WICKEDEST MAN, THE PUGILIST, AND PRETTY WAITER GIRLS

1 Oliver Dyer, "The Wickedest Man in New York," *Packard's Monthly* 1/3 (July 1868): 37–39.

2 "The 'Wickedest Man' As He Is," *Harper's Weekly* 12/606 (August 8, 1868): 505–6.

3 "The 'Wickedest Man' As He Is," passim.

4 Oliver Dyer, "The Wickedest Man Summed Up," *Packard's Monthly* 1/4 (August 1868): 49–53. *New York Tribune*, August 31, 1868.

5 *New York Times*, September 19, 1868. *Brooklyn Daily Eagle*, October 23, 1868. Much of the story of Allen's dance hall can be found recounted in chapter thirty-six of James D. McCabe, *The Secrets of the Great City: A Work Descriptive of the Virtues and the Vices, the Mysteries, Miseries and Crimes of New York City* (Philadelphia: Jones Bros., 1868).

6 Junius Henri Browne, *The Great Metropolis: A Mirror of New York* (Hartford: American Publishing Company, 1869), 659–62.

7 Members, *Night Side*, 30, 31, 33, 61. Oliver Dyer, "The Magdalens of New York City: Shall They Have a Chance for Salvation?," *Packard's Monthly* 1/5 (September 1868): 65–69. Matthew Hale Smith, *Sunshine and Shadow in New York* (Hartford: J.B. Burr and Company, 1869), 208, 228, 632. Dyer, "Wickedest Man," 37.

8 On the development of the popular music concert, see Dale Cockrell, ed., *Excelsior: Journals of the Hutchinson Family Singer, 1842–1846* (Stuyvesant, NY: Pendragon Press, 1989), especially the Prologue.

9 *Brooklyn Evening Star*, March 15, 1849.

10 *New York Tribune*, September 24, 1856.

11 *New York Times*, June 14, 1858. *New York Clipper*, September 28, 1861. Part of the description given here is drawn from a report of an evening at the Brooklyn Melodeon, covered in a feature article titled "The Elephant in Brooklyn: An Hour at the Concert Saloons; A Story with a Moral," *Brooklyn Daily Eagle*, December 9, 1861. On variety, see Gillian M. Rodger, *Champagne Charlie and Pretty Jemima: Variety Theater in the Nineteenth Century* (Urbana: University of Illinois Press, 2010).

12 Smith, *Sunshine and Shadow*, 371. Browne, *The Great Metropolis*, 327. Don B. Wilmeth, "Foreword," in Brooks McNamara, *The New York Concert Saloon: The Devil's Own Nights* (Cambridge: Cambridge University Press,

2002), xi. George Ellington, *The Women of New York; or, The Under-World of the Great City, Illustrating the Life of Women of Fashion, Women of Pleasure, Actresses and Ballet Girls, Saloon Girls, Pickpockets and Shoplifters, Artists' Female Models, Women-of-the-Town, Etc., Etc., Etc.* (New York: New York Book Co., 1869), 459.

13 *New York Times*, August 11, 1860. *New York Tribune*, December 3, 1861.

14 *Brooklyn Daily Eagle*, December 9, 1861. Browne, *The Great Metropolis*, 327. *New York Times*, December 12, 1861. *The Rogues and Rogueries of New-York: A Full and Complete Exposure of all the Swindles and Rascalities Carried On or Originated in the Metropolis* (New York: J.C. Haney & Co., 1865), 61. Smith, *Sunshine and Shadow*, 424, 373. On prostitution in concert saloons, see Gilfoyle, *City of Eros*, 228.

15 *New York Times*, May 21, 1862.

16 Quotation from the *Demokrat* copied in the *New York Times*, May 2, 1862. Presumably, a "scrupler" is someone possessing scruples.

17 More on the effects of the Concert Saloon War may be found in William L. Slout, ed., *Broadway Below the Sidewalk: Concert Saloons of Old New York* (San Bernardino, CA: Borgo Press, 1994) and in Rodger, *Champagne Charlie*, 59–67.

18 McNamara, *The New York Concert Saloon*, 103.

19 *The Rogues and Rogueries of New-York*, 59–60. "The Tune the Old Cow Died On" did not appear in print until 1880; this reference might be the first citation of the song.

20 An Old Traveler [Henry Llewellyn Williams], *Gay Life in New York! or, Fast Men and Grass Widows* (New York: Robert De Witt, 1866), 91–94. James D. McCabe, *Lights and Shadows of New York Life; or, The Sights and Sensations of the Great City: A Work Descriptive of the City of New York in All Its Various Phases* (Philadelphia: National Publishing Co., 1872), 594.

21 *The Rogues and Rogueries of New-York*, 55. [Ferdinand Longchamp], *Asmodeus in New-York* (New York: Longchamp & Co., 1868), 240. Browne, *The Great Metropolis*, 329–30. Ellington, *The Women of New York*, 458, 471–73, 624.

22 *The Rogues and Rogueries of New-York*, 56.

23 [Gustav Lening], *The Dark Side of New York Life and Its Criminal Classes from Fifth Avenue Down to the Five Points: A Complete Narrative of the Mysteries of New York* (New York: Fred'k Gerhard, 1873), 90. From a "Return Check," Society for the Reformation of Juvenile Delinquents, Records, Shubert Archive, Box 10, Folder 12A.

24 *Brooklyn Daily Eagle*, September 2, 1863. *New York Sun*, September 8, 1868. *Brooklyn Daily Eagle*, September 12, 1868. A full account of Hill's

life and career can be found in Daniel Czitrom, *New York Exposed: The Gilded Age Police Scandal that Launched the Progressive Era* (New York: Oxford University Press, 2016), 184–92.

25 *New York Herald*, November 6, 1869.

26 Ellington, *The Women of New York*, 221. Smith, *Sunshine and Shadow*, 441. Edward Crapsey, *The Nether Side of New York; Or, The Vice, Crime and Poverty of the Great Metropolis* (New York: Sheldon & Company, 1872), 161–63.

27 Vera Brodsky Lawrence, *Strong on Music: The New York Music Scene in the Days of George Templeton Strong*; Vol. 2: *Reverberations, 1850–1856* (Chicago: University of Chicago Press, 1995), 714–15. *Putnam's Monthly Magazine of American Literature, Science, and Art* 3/17 (May 1854): 564; copied in Judith Tick, ed., *Music in the USA: A Documentary Companion* (New York: Oxford University Press, 2008), 163.

28 Ibid. McCabe, *Secrets of the Great City*, 332. Smith, *Sunshine and Shadow*, 227.

CHAPTER FOUR: THE BISHOP, COMSTOCK, AND JUVENILE DELINQUENTS

1 *New York Tribune*, January 17, 1866.

2 Gilfoyle, *City of Eros*, 58 and 343–44n4 makes the percentage estimate, based on an estimated female population aged fifteen to twenty-nine years. McCabe, *The Secrets of the Great City*, 284. *New York Times*, August 4, 1866.

3 Gilfoyle, *City of Eros*, 344n7.

4 *New York Times*, January 9, 1867.

5 *New York Tribune*, February 28, 1867.

6 Ibid., February 8, 1867.

7 *Brooklyn Daily Eagle*, March 7, 1867. *New York Times*, March 14, 1867.

8 *Brooklyn Daily Eagle*, March 13, 1867. *New York Times*, March 14, 1867. The particulars of the Starr bill may be seen in the *New York Tribune*, March 13, 1867.

9 *New York Times*, April 16, 1867.

10 Ibid., August 4, 1866. *Buffalo Commercial*, January 22, 1867. *New York Tribune*, February 5, 1867. Gilfoyle, *City of Eros*, 58. *New York Tribune*, August 12, 1867.

In response to the epidemic, a Society for the Suppression of Prostitution was organized but seems not to have been very effective. Ibid., March 2, 1868.

11 [Lening], *The Dark Side of New York Life*, 371–74, 387–88. Lening

described music in the concert saloons as "so-called" and condemned it for abusing the very notion of "concert."

12 *The Gentleman's Companion* (n.p.: n.p., 1870) may be accessed online.

13 *Brooklyn Daily Eagle*, July 3, 1868.

14 *New York Times*, April 4, 1867. *New York Tribune*, January 29, 1868. *New York Times*, March 7, 1868. *Buffalo Commercial*, April 25, 1868.

15 Heywood Broun and Margaret Leech, *Anthony Comstock: Roundsman of the Lord* (New York: Literary Guild of America, 1927), 81.

16 *New York Tribune*, November 2, 1874.

17 *New York Times*, March 15, 1873.

18 *Brooklyn Daily Eagle*, May 13, 1873. Broun, *Anthony Comstock*, 154.

19 Ibid., 165.

20 Ibid., 156.

21 *New York Evening World*, March 29, 1913. Broun, *Anthony Comstock*, 232. Heywood quoted in ibid., 193.

22 *Fifth Annual Report of the Managers of the Society for the Reformation of Juvenile Delinquents in the City and State of New-York* (New York: Mahlon Day, 1830), 41. Rodger, *Champagne Charlie*, 221n15.

23 *Thirty-Sixth Annual Report of the Managers of the Society for the Reformation of Juvenile Delinquents* (New York: Wynkoop, Hallenbeck & Thomas, 1861), 16. *Forty-Eighth Annual Report of the Managers of the Society for the Reformation of Juvenile Delinquents* (New York: Joseph Longking, 1873), 190.

24 A copy of the Act may be found in Appendix 1 of McNamara, *The New York Concert Saloon*, 124–26.

25 *Forty-Ninth Annual Report of the Managers of the Society for the Reformation of Juvenile Delinquents* (New York: Joseph Longking, 1874), 19. *Fifty-Fourth Annual Report of the Managers of the Society for the Reformation of Juvenile Delinquents* (New York: National Printing Company, 1879), 9. McNamara, *The New York Concert Saloon*, 23, 29; McNamara apparently based his number on figures he found in sources other than the *Annual Reports*. The "Treasurer's Report" from the *Fifty-Seventh Annual Report* (1881) shows that the "receipts of the past year" included $15,000 from "Theatre Licenses." It is not clear how to reconcile the difference in these figures, except through the powers of speculation.

26 Society for the Reformation of Juvenile Delinquents, Records, Box 1, Folder 16D.

27 McNamara, *The New York Concert Saloon*, 30–31.

28 Ibid.

29 Society for the Reformation of Juvenile Delinquents, Records, Box 12, Folder 5D.

30 See the list of entertainers in Appendix 3 of McNamara, *The New York Concert Saloon*, 130–31.

31 Ibid., 52–53. Like many musicians who appeared in New York from 1862–1875, some of Emerson's performances can be traced by searching the *Music in Gotham* website at https://www.musicingotham.org/.

32 See the full list of songs in Appendix 2; McNamara, *The New York Concert Saloon*, 127–29.

33 *The Night Side of New York*, 26.

34 *New York Clipper*, March 12, 1864.

35 Society for the Reformation of Juvenile Delinquents, Records, Box 7, Folder 12B.

CHAPTER FIVE: DIVES, CORNETS, AND THE CANCAN OUT-PARIS-ED IN NEW YORK

1 *Flash*, December 18, 1841. Like many saloons at the time, the Elssler was named pretentiously, in this case after the Austrian ballerina Fanny Elssler, then all the rage in New York for her lascivious interpretation of the cachucha dance. Or perhaps the naming was intended to be ironic.

2 See, for example, the *Boston Morning Post*, October 19, 1838, for another example of diving into a cellar. *Buffalo Daily Courier*, October 2, 1860. *Buffalo Commercial*, September 22, 1862. *Buffalo Evening Courier and Republic*, July 7, 1863. *Buffalo Daily Courier*, September 29, 1868, October 19, 1868. Doug's Dive is extensively described in ibid., May 21, 1875.

   The white man, whose name was Patrick Shields, was eventually convicted of manslaughter and fined forty dollars. With that inconvenience resolved, Shields got on with his modest performing career, using the stage name Johnny Somers. He performed as an Irish vocalist, banjoist, and member of the Campbell & Baker's Minstrel Show.

3 *New York Herald*, February 4, 1870, February 7, 1870. Laurens Street is now known as West Broadway. Leonard Street is in current-day Tribeca.

   On the "Kentuckian type," Chester P. Dewey described Abraham Lincoln at his first debate with Stephen Douglas as being of the "Kentucky type, . . . very tall, slender and angular, awkward even, in gait and attitude." *New York Evening Post*, August 28, 1858.

4 Lawlor and Thornton [Arthur Lloyd], "Upper Ten and Lower Five" (New York: Frank Harding, 1888). Percy Gaunt and Charles Hale Hoyt, "The Bowery" (New York: T.B. Harms & Co., 1892).

5 George W. Walling, *Recollections of a New York Chief of Police: An Official Record of Thirty-Eight Years as Patrolman, Detective, Captain, Inspector and Chief of the New York Police* (New York: Caxton Book Concern, 1887), 479–80.

6 William F. Howe, *Danger! A True History of a Great City's Wiles and Temptations: The Veil Lifted, and Light Thrown on Crime and Its Causes, and Criminals and Their Haunts; Facts and Disclosures* (Buffalo, NY: Courier Co., Printers, 1886), 50.

7 See Gilfoyle, *City of Eros*, 203, for documentation on the Clubber Williams claim.

8 Walling, *Recollections*, 480–82. *New York Times*, September 5, 1885.

9 *New York Sun*, December 29, 1885, April 6, 1886.

10 *New York Clipper*, June 14, 1862, August 22, 1863, August 25, 1877, May 11, 1878. Walling, *Recollections*, 482–84.

11 *New York Clipper*, August 7, 1886, and passim. Howe, *Danger!*, 51. Walling, *Recollections*, 484.

12 C. H. Graham and O. F. Lane, *Excise Law of the State of New York . . .* (Albany, NY: W.C. Little & Co., 1883), 73.

13 *New York Times*, October 10, 1885. *New York Sun*, October 10, 1885.

14 New York courts had decided and affirmed that "any liquor . . . whether fermented [i.e., beer and ale] or distilled, of which the human stomach can contain enough to produce intoxication" was covered under the statute. Graham, *Excise Law*, 37, 115. *New York Times*, May 4, 1887. *New York Sun*, May 4, 1887, May 8, 1887. *Brooklyn Daily Eagle*, May 8, 1887.

15 "I Tickled Her Under the Chin" (New York: G.P. Benjamin) was composed in 1876 by Harry Montague. The lyrics tell of a man-about-town who picked up a young woman on a Madison Avenue coach; she invited him in, they "spent a very pleasant evening together," and as he left her company he "tickled her under the chin." John J. Jennings, *Theatrical and Circus Life; Secrets of the Stage, Green-Room and Sawdust Arena* (St. Louis: Sun Publishing Co., 1882), 400, 403. Walling, *Recollections*, 485. Samuel A. MacKeever, *Glimpses of Gotham and City Characters* (New York: Richard K. Fox, 1880), 59–60.

16 *New York Times*, September 30, 1887, October 20, 1887.

17 Walling, *Recollections*, 488–89. *Cincinnati Enquirer*, July 15, 1891.

18 Walling, *Recollections*, 491. *Cincinnati Enquirer*, December 25, 1881. *Buffalo Evening News*, November 16, 1881, noted that McGlory was the cousin of Owney Geoghegan, another well-known dive owner in New York City.

19 Howe, *Danger!*, 119.

20 *New York Times*, February 9, 1868. *Brooklyn Daily Eagle*, February 10,

1868. *New York Tribune*, February 26, 1869. Ellington, *The Women of New York*, 200, 325. *Utica Daily Observer*, January 16, 1885, quoted in Gilfoyle, *City of Eros*, 230.

21 *Cincinnati Enquirer*, December 31, 1882. Howe, *Danger!*, 118.

22 Some have even suggested that the cancan encouraged some women to sew the drawers closed, giving rise to the prototype for the modern panty. See Jill Fields, "Erotic Modesty: (Ad)dressing Female Sexuality and Propriety in Open and Closed Drawers, USA, 1800–1930," *Gender & History* 14/3 (February 2003): 492–515. *Cincinnati Enquirer*, December 31, 1882. Howe, *Danger!*, 117. Edward Van Every, *Sins of New York: As "Exposed" by the Police Gazette* (New York: Benjamin Blom, Inc., 1972), 207.

23 James D. McCabe, *New York by Sunlight and Gaslight* . . . (Philadelphia: Douglass Brothers, 1882), 509.

24 Walling, *Recollections*, 494. MacKeever, *Glimpses of Gotham*, 38.

25 Victoria Woodhull quoted in Gilfoyle, *City of Eros*, 234. *New York Evening World*, February 28, 1888. Comstock quoted in Gilfoyle, *City of Eros*, 235.

26 Lyman Abbott, "Introduction," in Campbell, *Darkness and Daylight*, 38. *New York Sun*, September 5, 1886, estimated "only" four thousand unlicensed dives and saloons. Alfred Trumble, *The Mysteries of New York; A Sequel to Glimpses of Gotham and New York by Day and Night* (New York: Richard K. Fox, 1882), 36–37.

27 Jennings, *Theatrical and Circus Life*, 411–14. Trumble, *Mysteries of New York*, 37.

28 Jennings, *Theatrical and Circus Life*, 410. Howe, *Danger!*, 28.

29 Walling, *Recollections*, 485, put the Black-and-Tan at 153 Bleecker Street, but contemporaneous newspapers are consistent in the 151 Bleecker address. According to the *New York Times*, January 27, 1880, the "Bastile," a cigar store that ran a multiracial gambling and numbers racket den in the back, was at 153 Bleecker; other newspaper accounts show that illegal gambling was a longstanding tradition at that address. Stevenson (spelled "Stephenson" by Walling) apparently sold the Black-and-Tan in early 1886; *New York Sun*, September 5, 1886. The building and its previous usage are described in the *New York Times*, February 26, 1888. *New York Herald*, December 26, 1870, June 20, 1870. Campbell, *Darkness and Daylight*, 472–73. The extensive quoted passage, written by journalist Thomas W. Knox, located the Black-and-Tan on Baxter Street, which might mean that he was describing a dive other than the one at 151 Bleecker Street, or that he was mistaken about the address. Walling, *Recollections*, 485–87.

30 *Cincinnati Enquirer*, December 31, 1882.

31 The song's published title is "I've Only Been Down to the Club." McCabe, *New York by Sunlight*, 256.

32 Walling, *Recollections*, 486–87.

CHAPTER SIX: RAGTIME, SPIELING, AND LEAPFROGGING FOR THE REVEREND

1 Stephen Crane, *Maggie: A Girl of the Streets (A Story of New York)*, Thomas A. Gullason, ed. (New York: W. W. Norton & Company, 1893/1979), esp. chapters 7, 12, 14.

2 The definitive—and richly readable—study of Parkhurst, his crusades, and the subsequent Lexow Committee is Czitrom, *New York Exposed*.

3 *New York Times*, February 15, 1892, March 2, 1892. *New York Evening World*, February 15, 1892. *New York Sun*, February 24, 1892.

4 *New York Times*, March 14, 1892.

5 Charles W. Gardner, *The Doctor and the Devil, or, Midnight Adventures of Dr. Parkhurst* (New York: Gardner & Co., 1894), 6–20.

6 Ibid., 65–66.

7 Ibid., 66–67.

8 Richard Zacks, *Island of Vice: Theodore Roosevelt's Doomed Quest to Clean Up Sin-Loving New York* (New York: Doubleday, 2012), 53. Other potential witnesses fled as far as South Africa, where they set up "American-style" prostitution districts; see the surprising history of a global economy in prostitution during this time in Charles van Oncelen, *The Fox and the Flies: The Secret Life of a Grotesque Master Criminal* (New York: Walker and Company, 2007).

9 *Report and Proceedings of the Senate Committee Appointed to Investigate the Police Department of the City of New York* (Albany: James B. Lyon, 1895), 3118–21.

10 Ibid., 4579–80.

11 Ibid., 5214–16.

12 Ibid., 5591. *New York Evening World*, December 19, 1892. There are sporadic mentions of the Slide in New York newspapers at least as far back as 1890.

13 *New York Evening World*, January 4, 1892. For much greater detail on gay New York during the 1890s, see Chauncey, *Gay New York*, esp. chapter 1.

14 *New York Tribune*, October 17, 1891. *New York Evening World*, January 7, 1892, December 25, 1892. Gardner, *The Doctor and the Devil*, 58.

15 *New York Evening World*, March 11, 1893.

16 Ibid., June 9, 1894. *New York Sun*, October 23, 1890. That early singing

waiter, identified only as Phoebe, had worked earlier at the Slide, and might well have been the J. F. "Phoebe" Rankin who was shot in the leg by a policeman "suffering from spasms" in September 1890; *New York Tribune*, September 7, 1890.

17 Howe, *Danger!*, 222–24.

18 Czitrom, *New York Exposed*, 293.

19 On Roosevelt's tenure with the police commission, see Zacks, *Island of Vice*, passim. On the long and fascinating reach of the Lexow Committee into matters legal, political, social, and cultural, see Czitrom, *New York Exposed*, "Epilogue: The Lexow Effect."

20 *Elmira Star-Gazette*, November 10, 1898. *Brooklyn Daily Eagle*, March 29, 1899. *New York Sun*, March 30, 1899.

21 *Report of the Special Committee of the Assembly to Investigate the Public Offices and Departments of the City of New York and of the Counties Therein Included* (Albany: James B. Lyon, 1900).

22 Ibid., 1997–99. *New York Herald*, March 12, 1899. McGurk's reputation lasted for decades. Mae West even included a chapter on "Suicide Hall" in her 1932 novel *Diamond Lil*. The building that housed the dive survived until 2005, when it was razed for the construction of luxury apartments.

23 *Report of the Special Committee of the Assembly*, 174–76.

24 Ibid., 1429, 1431, 5125, 173. Little seems to be known about the "Ki-ki" from that time, nor is it known if there is any connection to the contemporary kiki dance scene associated with LGBTQ culture in today's New York.

25 *Brooklyn Daily Eagle*, October 27, 1898. *The Etude*, February 1899, 52.

26 "Will Marion Cook on Negro Music," *The New York Age*, September 21, 1918. An excellent overview of ragtime is Edward A. Berlin, "Ragtime," *Grove Music Online* at www.oxfordmusiconline.com.

27 The *Brooklyn Daily Eagle* notice listed Harney's surname mistakenly as "Harvey." The "brunette" from South Carolina was probably editorial code for "black woman"; Harney did indeed travel and perform with a "genuine southern plantation" black woman at this time. Antonín Dvořák in the early 1890s claimed that popular and African American music constituted the authentic American music; his *New World Symphony* (1893) is an expression of that idea.

28 From the *Baltimore Sun*, copied in *Rochester (New York) Democrat and Chronicle*, December 18, 1898. *New York Times*, November 2, 1898.

29 The term "tough dance" shows up in American newspapers in the 1880s,

but as descriptive of a type of dance event. By the late 1890s it was regularly applied to a dance style.

30 *New York Sun*, August 2, 1891. Julian Ralph, "Coney Island," *Scribner's* 20 (July 1896): 18. "My Pearl's a Bowery Girl" (New York: T.B. Harms and Co., 1894). *New York Sun*, April 12, 1891.

31 *New York World*, September 12, 1892.

32 The earliest reference to the turkey trot dance known to me is found (surprisingly) in the *Anaconda Standard* (Montana), April 10, 1893. See also the *Buffalo Enquirer*, March 29, 1898. These and other early references undermine the often-repeated conventional wisdom that the turkey trot came out of San Francisco in the 1910s.

CHAPTER SEVEN: TOUGH DANCING, WHITE SLAVERY, AND "JUST TELL THEM THAT YOU SAW ME"

1 Annie's story is told in Reita Childe Dorr, "The Prodigal Daughter," *Hampton's Magazine* 24/4 (April 1910): 530–34, and reprinted, with slight emendations, in *What Eight Million Women Want* (Boston: Small, Maynard & Company, 1910), 202–10. Annie's surname was changed by Dorr to protect her identity.

2 Mrs. Charles Henry Israels, "Percentage of Working Girls Going to Dance Halls," *The Playground* 4/2 (May 1910): 35. Hutchins Hapgood, *Types from City Streets* (New York: Funk & Wagnalls, 1910), 135. Ralph G. Giordano, *Satan in the Dance Hall: Rev. John Roach Straton, Social Dancing, and Morality in 1920s New York City* (Lanham, MD: Scarecrow Press, 2008), 6.

3 The film has been digitized by the Library of Congress and is available at https://www.loc.gov/item/00694157/. Kent's partner was advertised to be James T. Kelly, but it was surely James F. Kelly, with whom she partnered in a well-known vaudeville comedic duo.

4 "Lower Broadway" has been digitized by the Library of Congress and can be accessed at https://www.loc.gov/item/00694372/.

5 "A Tough Dance," also digitized by the Library of Congress, is at https://www.loc.gov/item/96520498/. Some dance historians have seen this performance as an imitation or parody of the French Apache dance, but the film predates the first media references to the Apache dance in New York by about six years. High-kicking and some modest tough dancing can also be seen in "A Night at the Haymarket" (1903).

6 For a nuanced analysis of tough dancing, see Kathy Peiss, *Cheap Amusements: Working Women and Leisure in Turn-of-the-Century New York* (Philadelphia: Temple University Press, 1986), 88–114.

7 Ibid., 93, 99.

8 *New York Sun*, June 19, 1906. Mrs. Charles Henry Israels, "The Dance Problem," *The Playground* 4/7 (October 1910): 246. Israels's study did lead to the changing of laws regarding dance academies; among new provisions, dance academies were no longer allowed to traffic in liquor. See also Elisabeth I. Perry, "'The General Motherhood of the Commonwealth': Dance Hall Reform in the Progressive Era," *American Quarterly* 37/5 (Winter, 1985): 722, and Peiss, *Cheap Amusements*, 88.

9 Israels, "The Dance Problem," 46. Giordano, *Satan in the Dance Hall*, 6. Belle Lindner Israels, "The Way of the Girl," *The Survey* 22 (July 3, 1909): 495. Peiss, *Cheap Amusements*, 95. Dorr, *What Eight Million Women Want*, 210. *New York Times*, January 4, 1912.

10 George B. H. Swayze, "The Social Evil," *The Medical Times: A Monthly Journal of Medicine, Surgery, and the Collateral Sciences* 34/7 (July 1906): 195. Dorr, *What Eight Million Women Want*, 208–9.

11 George J. Kneeland, *The Social Evil in New York City: A Study of Law Enforcement by the Research Committee of the Committee of Fourteen* (New York: Andrew H. Kellogg Co., 1910), 54,

12 Ibid., 38–39. See Gilfoyle, *City of Eros*, 243–48, for an overview of Raines Law hotels.

13 Ibid., 247.

14 Kneeland, *The Social Evil* (1910), 39.

15 October 24, 1906.

16 Conventional wisdom has it that Monroe Rosenfeld invented the term "tin pan alley" in a 1909 article he wrote in the *New York Herald*. The expression, however, was in print by 1903 and commonly appeared in New York newspapers by 1905. "Tin pan music" was a phrase frequently used to describe shivarees in the 1890s popular press; aural chaos was surely what people heard in "Tin Pan Alley."

17 Theodore Dreiser, "Whence the Song," *Harper's Weekly* 44/2294 (December 8, 1900): 1165–66a.

18 On Dresser, see the excellent Clayton W. Henderson, *On the Banks of the Wabash: The Life and Music of Paul Dresser* (Indianapolis: Indiana Historical Society Press, 2003).

19 Theodore Dreiser, *Dawn: A History of Myself* (New York: Horace Liveright, 1931), 154. On Dresser's relations with prostitutes, see Henderson, *On the Banks of the Wabash*, esp. chapter 8, "The Lady in Black."

20 Theodore Dreiser, "Concerning the Author of These Songs," in Paul Dresser, *The Songs of Paul Dresser* (New York: Boni & Liveright, 1927), vii.

21 Henderson, *On the Banks of the Wabash*, 75–80, questions some of Dreiser's assertions on Sal/Sallie's identity. *My Gal Sal* also serves as the title of the

biopic on Dresser's life, released in 1942 and starring Victor Mature and Rita Hayworth.

22 Jimmy Durante and Jack Kofoed, *Night Clubs* (New York: Alfred A. Knopf, 1931), 83.

23 Charles Hamm's *Irving Berlin, Songs from the Melting Pot: The Formative Years, 1907–1914* (New York: Oxford University Press, 1997) is the definitive study of Berlin's early years.

24 Ibid., 85–86.

25 *Ben Harney's Rag Time Instructor* (Chicago: Sol Bloom, 1897). Von Tilzer is quoted in Hamm, *Irving Berlin*, 90.

26 Ibid., 90, 92.

27 *New York Times*, December 29, 1900.

28 Ibid., November 17, 1900. A dated summary of events may be found in the *New York Tribune*, November 19, 1900.

29 Ibid., November 28, 1900. On the Committee of Fifteen, see Jennifer Fronc, *New York Undercover: Private Surveillance in the Progressive Era* (Chicago: University of Chicago Press, 2009), esp. chapter 2: "Public Raids, Undercover Investigators, and Native Informants."

30 Ibid., 48–49.

31 *The Social Evil: With Special Reference to Conditions Existing in the City of New York; A Report Prepared Under the Direction of the Committee of Fifteen* (New York: G.P. Putnam's Sons, 1902), 187.

32 Ibid., 183.

33 Kneeland, *The Social Evil* (1910), 60. *The Social Evil* (1902), 183–84.

34 *The Traffic in Girls: White Slavery as Now Practiced in America, Including Detailed Descriptions of the Customs and Manners of the White Women Slaves and Wives of Asia, Turkey, Egypt, Etc.* (Chicago: n.p., ca. 1900), [5]. James Marchant, *The Master Problem* (New York: Moffat, Yard and Company, 1917), 13–17. On white slavery, see Ruth Rosen, *The Lost Sisterhood: Prostitution in America, 1900–1918* (Baltimore: Johns Hopkins University Press, 1982), esp. chapter 7: "White Slavery: Myth or Reality?"

35 The "Famous Committee of Fifteen" did reassemble once more in January 1905, this time to eulogize its chair, William H. Baldwin Jr., who had died on January 4. *New York Times*, January 20, 1905.

CHAPTER EIGHT: C XIV, ALLEGED MUSIC, AND SUPERLATIVELY ROTTEN DANCES

1 Committee of Fourteen, Records, 1905–1932, Manuscripts, Archives, and Rare Books Division, New York Public Library [hereafter "C14"],

Box 28, Folder: 1912. Many of the folders have duplicate labels, and others have no labels at all, all of which makes reference to specific reports difficult.

2 Ibid.

3 C14, Box 28, Folder: Inv. Rep. 1905.

4 John P. Peters, *The Story of the Committee of Fourteen of New York* (New York: American Social Hygiene Association, 1918), 371.

5 Ibid., 367–68.

6 This abbreviated history of the Committee of Fourteen has been pieced together from the files of the C14; Kneeland, *The Social Evil* (1910); George J. Kneeland, *Commercialized Prostitution in New York City*, revised ed. (New York: Century, 1917); Gilfoyle, *City of Eros*; and Fronc, *New York Undercover*.

7 C14, Box 28, Folder: 1910 Grand Jury. Kneeland, *Commercialized Prostitution*, ix.

The Rockefeller "white slave" grand jury report was never distributed widely because the still-and-ever-vigilant Anthony Comstock declared it too salacious to be admitted to the postal service (Broun, *Anthony Comstock*, 249).

8 Fronc, *New York Undercover*, 73.

9 C14, Box 30, Folder: Police.

10 Investigators were charged primarily to report on prostitution activities and, secondarily, on violations of the laws governing alcohol consumption. Yet details and implications in their reports are always suspect, for it was in the best interest of job security to find disorderly behavior, as it was also in Whitin's best interest. And they were surely hypersensitive to anything smacking of the disorderly. Actual criminal behavior was one thing (and plenty of that was reported), but kissing, hugging, hands under clothing, bare flesh, lifting dresses to the knees (or above), swearing, women smoking cigarettes, and such, were also enthusiastically reported. Also fashion statements, for short dresses and low bodices signaled immoral behavior to the committee; one agent even had an eye for measurements and reported that one dress was hemmed an unladylike five inches above her shoe tops. Perhaps a prostitute signaled her availability through such things, but perhaps a young woman in question was just enjoying a night on the town and a mild taste of the risqué before heading back late to her parents' home.

11 Kneeland, *Commercialized Prostitution*, 3–21.

12 Ibid., 56.

13 Ibid., 67–68.

14 Ibid., 111.

15 C14, Box 28, Folder: 1910–1911; "Daisy" is identified by name as Jim Fielding. C14, Box 28, Folder: 1912. C14, Box 28, Folder: 1912.

16 C14, Box 28, Folder: 1906–07–09.

17 Israels, "The Way of the Girl," 494. C14; Box 31; Folder: [untitled].

18 C14, Box 28, Folder: Invest Rep 1912, but really throughout the C14 papers.

19 Ibid. Dance historian Danielle Robinson has surveyed the Committee of Fourteen investigative reports for evidence on social dance practices in New York; see her work in *Modern Moves: Dancing Race During the Ragtime and Jazz Eras* (New York: Oxford University Press, 2015).

20 C14, Box 28, Folder: 1912; Stockdale dated the report "25 day of April 1911," but surely meant 1912. C14, Box 28, Folder: 1910–1911.

21 C14, Box 28, Folder: 1912.

22 C14, Box 28, Folder: 1914–1915. C14, Box 28, Folder: 1910–1912.

23 C14, Box 28, Folder: 1912; more on "charity" later, but the term means "free" in this context.

24 C14, Box 28, Folder: 1910–1912. C14, Box 29, Folder: Brooklyn Inv Reports.

25 Hamm, *Irving Berlin*, 228, 246–47. C14, Box 28, Folder: 1912. Ibid. C14, Box 28, Folder: 1913.

26 Kneeland, *Commercialized Prostitution*, 56.

27 "P. Richards' Berlin Letter," *New York Clipper* (June 4, 1910), 410.

28 Julian Street, "'Oh, You Babylon!': A Taxi-cabaretta," *Everybody's Magazine* 27/2 (August 1912): 182–83. The article was reprinted in Julian Street, *Welcome to Our City* (New York: John Lane Co., 1913).

29 Ibid., 177.

30 C14, Box 31, Folder: [untitled]. C14, Box 32, Folder: [untitled].

31 C14, Box 28, Folder: 1912. C14, Box 31, Folder: 1916.

32 C14, Box 28, Folder: 1913. C14, Box 28, Folder: 1913 June July. On the "nigger" (or "nigger wiggle") and its disorderly potential, see Appendix 3: The People &c. Against Wallace W. Sweeney. C14, Box 29, Folder: [untitled]. C14, Box 29, Folder: Brooklyn/Queens—Investigator's Reports 1914.

33 C14, Box 32, Folder: [untitled]. C14, Box 31, Folder: [untitled].

34 See Appendix 1 for the list of songs by year.

35 C14, Box 29, Folder: Brooklyn Inv Reports.

36 C14, Box 28, Folder: 1914–1915. C14, Box 31, Folder: [untitled]. C14, Box 32, Folder: [untitled].

37 C14, Box 29, Folder: Brooklyn—Inv. Reports & Rel. Mats, 1914–15.

38 C14, Box 31, Folder: [untitled].

39 Ibid. C14, Box 31, Folder: Inv. Rep. on Cabarets.

40 Ibid.

41 C14, Box 30, Folder: [untitled]. C14, Box 32, Folder: [untitled]. C14, Box 31, Folder: 1916. C14, Box 29, Folder: Brooklyn Queens Inv. Reports & Related Mats, 1914–15.

42 C14, Box 32, Folder: [untitled]. Ibid. C14, Box 31, Folder: [untitled]. C14, Box 29, Folder: Brooklyn Queens Inv. Reports & Related Mats, 1914–15.

43 C14, Box 30, Folder: [untitled]. Ibid. Ibid.

   Feelings that moral vigilance committees were intolerant and unjust were deep, widespread, and national in scope. Filmmaker D. W. Griffith released his epic, three-and-a-half-hour *Intolerance* in 1916, and the middle-class, sanctimonious, moral-uplift "intolerant" institution that he featured prominently was based on a group much like the Committee of Fourteen.

44 C14, Box 29, Folder: Brooklyn—Inv. Reports & Rel. Mats, 1914–15. C14, Box 31, Folder: [untitled].

45 See Fronc, *New York Undercover*, 102, for a summary of civil rights legislation in New York.

46 C14, Box 28, Folder: 1906–07–09. C14, Box 31, Folder: 1916. C14, Box 28, Folder: 1910 1911.

47 C14, Box 28, Folder: 1910 1911. C14, Box 29, Folder: [untitled].

48 C14, Box 11, Folder: W. E. B. Du Bois Correspondence. See also Fronc, *New York Undercover*, 115–19, for more on the Marshall/Du Bois/Whitin exchanges. Also David Gilbert, *The Product of Our Souls: Ragtime, Race, and the Birth of the Manhattan Musical Marketplace* (Chapel Hill: University of North Carolina Press, 2015), passim.

49 C14, Box 29, Folder: Brooklyn, Staten Island, Manhattan—Inv. Reports & Rel. Material, 1914–15. C14, Box 29, Folder: Brooklyn—Inv. Reports & Rel. Mats, 1914–15. C14, Box 31, Folder: 1916. C14, Box 30, Folder: [untitled].

50 C14, Box 32, Folder: Coney Island, Queens, Staten Island Inv Reports, 1917–18.

51 C14, Box 30, Folder: [untitled]. Ibid. C14, Box 31, Folder: 1916.

52 C14, Box 29, Folder: [untitled].

53 C14, Box 32, Folder: [untitled]. C14, Box 31, Folder: [untitled].

54 The national census data for 1910 showed that about seventy-one percent of all male musicians/music teachers were professional musicians (and not music teachers). That percentage factored against the 5,757 male "musi-

cians and teachers of music" tabulated in Manhattan yields 4,088 male professional musicians. Although a guesstimate, this number gives some indication of population dimensions. In 1910 it is relatively unusual to find female professional musicians engaged full-time in places that actively supported the prostitution industry, hence the focus here on male musicians.

55 The 1910 census data are unusual in that professional musicians and music teachers are counted separately and not collected together as in most census years. That tabulation, however, is only available for the nation as a whole, and not broken down by state or city. It showed that thirty-nine percent of all musicians of both genders were professional, performing musicians and that sixty-one percent were music teachers. The percentage of professional musicians was likely higher in New York City, given its status as an entertainment center, but there are no census numbers to support that assumption.

EPILOGUE: REFLECTIONS

1 Paducah, Kentucky, *Report and Recommendations of the Paducah Vice Commission* (Paducah, KY: n.p., 1916), passim. To my knowledge, the only extant copy of the report is among the Lee Joseph Levinger papers at the University of Oregon. Levinger was, in 1916, the rabbi at Temple Israel in Paducah and an original member of the vice commission.

The "Sore Spots" map contained no streets or contextual reference points, lest some sporting man use it as a guide. In addition to the places of public prostitution, the map also marked sixty-seven saloons and twelve pool rooms.

For anecdotal comparison, as a teen-aged boy in 1960s Paducah, I tittered along with my buddies as we drove past 808 Washington Street, with its white picket fence and well-manicured lawn, and honked our car horns to disturb the alleged (and mysterious) goings-on in the house. So far as male teen-aged rumormongering had it, it was the only brothel in town.

2 *Report and Recommendations of the Paducah Vice Commission*, 8, passim.

3 On Marable, see William Howland Kenney, *Jazz on the River* (Chicago: University of Chicago Press, 2005), 38–42.

4 Marable's only published composition was "Barrel House Rag" (1916). Marable and I overlapped our lives on this planet for only six days.

5 Paul H. Haas, "Sin in Wisconsin: The Teasdale Vice Committee of 1913," *Wisconsin Magazine of History* 49/2 (Winter 1965–1966): 139. Howard B. Woolston, *Prostitution in the United States: Volume 1—Prior to the Entrance*

of the United States into the World War (New York: Century Co., 1921). On prostitution across the nation, see also Ruth Rosen, *The Lost Sisterhood: Prostitution in America, 1900–1918* (Baltimore: Johns Hopkins University Press, 1982).

6 In 1910 Chicago, there were about 275 dance halls, with at least two musicians in each; a bare minimum of 236 "disorderly" saloons and concert saloons, each of which employed on average at least one musician (likely more); and 192 brothels, with a minimum of one professor in each. That formulation yields a very conservative number of 978 professional, fully employed, well-paid musicians who have firsthand understanding of the relationship between music-making and sexuality, or about one of every 2,234 Chicagoans. Figures are taken from *The Social Evil in Chicago: A Study of Existing Conditions with Recommendations by the Vice Commission of Chicago* (Chicago: Gunthorp-Warren Printing Company, 1911), 71, 109, 185, passim. Since the vice commission investigations only canvassed 445 of the city's 7,152 saloons (and found 236 disorderly), the actual number of musicians employed in disorderly saloons was undoubtedly significantly higher than the report shows. My rough guess is a ratio of one musician to each two thousand in the general population.

The 1910 census also counted 15,694 female professional musicians. It was unusual (but not impossible) to find a female musician performing in a place that obviously supported prostitution at that time. There were many women musicians in variety, vaudeville, and the theater at large, and I expect that the bulk of the female census figures were employed there.

7 Joseph Mayer, *The Regulation of Commercialized Vice: An Analysis of the Transition from Segregation to Repression in the United States* (New York: Klebold Press, 1922), 9.

8 *The Descent of Man, and Selection in Relation to Sex* (New York: D. Appleton & Co., 1871), 880–81.

9 Darwin has not been alone in his myopia. Cognitive psychologist Steven Pinker famously expressed his suspicion that, in terms of evolution, music is just "auditory cheesecake." His analysis leading to this statement touched hardly at all on the role that rhythm plays in music expression or comprehension, and barely mentioned dance. His underlying assumption was that music is something to be listened to, not expressed actively, as in dance. Steven Pinker, *How the Mind Works* (New York: W. W. Norton & Company, 1997), 534, 537–38.

10 Geoffrey Miller, "Evolution of Human Music through Sexual Selection,"

in Nils L. Wallin, Björn Merker, and Steven Brown, eds., *The Origins of Music* (Cambridge: MIT Press, 2000), 348.

My special thanks to my colleague Gregory Barz for guiding me through the complex and problematic issues connected with the concept of *ngoma*. It is a difficult and fluid term, susceptible to multiple meanings, and with dense overlays of the political. See, for instance, Louise Meintjes, *Dust of the Zulu: Ngoma Aesthetics after Apartheid* (Durham, NC: Duke University Press, 2017).

11 Miller, "Evolution of Human Music through Sexual Selection," 356. Peter Lovatt, "Dance and Sexuality," *Psychology Today*, blog posted March 12, 2010. Bernhard Fink, Nadine Hugill, and Benjamin P. Lange, "Women's Body Movements Are a Potential Cue to Ovulation," *Personality and Individual Differences* 53/6 (October 2012): 759–63. Susanne Röder, Bettina Weege, Claus-Christian Carbon, Todd K. Shackelford, and Bernhard Fink, "Men's Perception of Women's Dance Movements Depends on Mating Context, but Not Men's Sociosexual Orientation," *Personality and Individual Differences* 86 (2015): 172–75.

12 C14, Box 28, Folder: 1914–1915. The date of the encounter was February 20, 1915.

APPENDIX 3: THE PEOPLE &C. AGAINST WALLACE W. SWEENEY

1 Court of Special Sessions, City of New York, First Division, Supreme Court of New York, Appellate Division, First Department, Minutes of Proceedings, January 29, 1912.

2 *New York Times*, September 24, 1912. Cook County Clerk, *Cook County Clerk Genealogy Records* (Chicago: Cook County Clerk, 2008); accessed through www.ancestry.com.

The *New York Times* gave the name of Sweeney's dive as "Independent Resperia of Young Manes Association," while the *New York Evening World* (September 23, 1912) identified it as the "Independent Order of Rummy Young Men."

BIBLIOGRAPHY

COLLECTIONS AND MANUSCRIPTS

New York City Municipal Archives and Records Center
Court of General Sessions, Minute Books.
Court of Special Sessions, First Division, Supreme Court of New York, Appellate Division.
New York City Police Office.

New York Public Library
Committee of Fourteen, Records, 1905–1932. Manuscripts, Archives, and Rare Books Division.

Shubert Archive
Society for the Reformation of Juvenile Delinquents, Records.

PRINTED MATERIALS

Abbott, Karen. *Sin in the Second City: Madams, Ministers, Playboys, and the Battle for America's Soul.* New York: Random House, 2007.
Alexiou, Alice Sparberg. *Devil's Mile: The Rich, Gritty History of the Bowery.* New York: St. Martin's Press, 2018.
Allen, Robert C. *Horrible Prettiness: Burlesque and American Culture.* Chapel Hill: University of North Carolina Press, 1991.
An Old Traveler [Henry Llewellyn Williams]. *Gay Life in New York! or, Fast Men and Grass Widows.* New York: Robert De Witt, 1866.

Aronovici, Carol. *The Social Survey*. Philadelphia: Harper Press, 1916.

Asbury, Herbert. *The Gangs of New York: An Informal History of the Underworld*. New York: Alfred A. Knopf, 1927.

Asmodeus [Thaddeus W. Meighan]. *The Jenny Lind Mania in Boston, or A Sequel to Barnum's Parnassus*. Boston: n.p., 1850.

Asmodeus. *Sharps and Flats; or the Perils of City Life; Being the Adventures of One Who Lived by His Wits*. Boston: W. Berry, 1850.

Baker, Benjamin Archibald. *A Glance at New York; A Local Drama, in Two Acts*. New York: Samuel French, 1848.

Beckett, Samuel. *The Unnamable*. London: John Calder, 1959.

Beer, Thomas. *The Mauve Decade; American Life at the End of the 19th Century*. New York: Alfred A. Knopf, 1926.

Bergman, Hans. *God in the Street: New York Writing from the Penny Press to Melville*. Philadelphia: Temple University Press, 1995.

Berlin, Edward A. *King of Ragtime: Scott Joplin and His Era*. New York: Oxford University Press, 1994.

———. "Ragtime," *Grove Music Online* at www.oxfordmusiconline.com.

———. *Ragtime: A Musical and Cultural History*. Berkeley: University of California Press, 1980.

Bocage, Peter. Oral History Interview, January 29, 1959. Hogan Jazz Archive, Tulane University.

Boyer, Paul. *Urban Masses and Moral Order in America, 1829–1920*. Cambridge: Harvard University Press, 1978.

Brace, Charles Loring. *The Dangerous Classes of New York and Twenty Years' Work Among Them*. 3rd ed. New York: Synkoop & Hallenbeck, 1880.

Brooks, Virginia. *Little Lost Sister*. New York: Macaulay Books, 1914.

Broun, Heywood, and Margaret Leech. *Anthony Comstock: Roundsman of the Lord*. New York: Literary Guild of America, 1927.

Browne, Junius Henri. *The Great Metropolis: A Mirror of New York*. Hartford: American Publishing Company, 1869.

Brownlow, Kevin. *Behind the Mask of Innocence*. New York: Alfred A. Knopf, 1990.

Buchanan, Harrison Gray. *Asmodeus or, Legends of New York: Being a Complete Exposé of the Mysteries, Vices and Doings, as Exhibited by the Fashionable Circles of New York*. New York: John D. Munson & Co., 1848.

Bullough, Vern, and Bonnie Bullough. *Prostitution: An Illustrated Social History*. New York: Crown Publishers, 1978.

Bulwer-Lytton, Edward. *Asmodeus at Large*. Philadelphia: Carey, Lea & Blanchard, 1833.

Buntline, Ned [Edward Zane Carroll Judson]. *The Mysteries and Miseries of New York: A Story of Real Life.* Dublin: McGlashan, 1849.

Burgess, William. *The World's Social Evil: A Historical Review and Study of the Problems Relating to the Subject.* Chicago: Saul Brothers, 1914.

Burrows, Edwin G., and Mike Wallace. *Gotham: A History of New York City to 1898.* New York: Oxford University Press, 1999.

Butsch, Richard. *The Making of American Audiences from Stage to Television, 1750–1990.* Cambridge: Cambridge University Press, 2000.

Calkins, Raymond. *Substitutes for the Saloon: An Investigation Originally Made for the Committee of Fifty.* 2nd ed. Boston: Houghton Mifflin, 1919.

Campbell, Mrs. Helen, Col. Thomas W. Knox, and Supt. Thomas Byrnes. *Darkness and Daylight; or, Lights and Shadows of New York Life: A Pictorial Record of Personal Experiences by Day and Night in the Great Metropolis.* Hartford, CT: Hartford Publishing Company, 1895.

Canby, Henry Seidel. *The Age of Confidence: Life in the Nineties.* New York: Farrar & Rinehart, 1934.

Charges Preferred Against the New-York Female Benevolent Society, and the Auditing Committee, in 1835 and 1836, by J.R. McDowall, in the Sun and Transcript, Answered and Refuted by Himself!! In His Own Journal!!! In the Year 1833. New York: Osborn & Buckingham, 1836.

Chauncey, George. *Gay New York: Gender, Urban Culture, and the Making of the Gay Male World, 1890–1940.* New York: Basic Books, 1994.

Clement, Elizabeth Alice. *Love for Sale: Courting, Treating, and Prostitution in New York City, 1900–1945.* Chapel Hill: University of North Carolina Press, 2006.

Cockrell, Dale. *Demons of Disorder: Early Blackface Minstrels and Their World.* Cambridge: Cambridge University Press, 1997.

———, ed. *Excelsior: Journals of the Hutchinson Family Singers, 1842–1846.* Stuyvesant, NY: Pendragon Press, 1989.

Cohen, Patricia Cline, Timothy J. Gilfoyle, and Helen Lefkowitz Horowitz. *The Flash Press: Sporting Male Weeklies in 1840s New York.* Chicago: University of Chicago Press, 2008.

Connelly, Mark Thomas. *The Response to Prostitution in the Progressive Era.* Chapel Hill: University of North Carolina Press, 1980.

Cook, James W. "Dancing Across the Color Line." *Common-Place: The Interactive Journal of Early American Life* 4/1 (October 2003): accessed at http://www.common-place-archives.org/vol-04/no-01/cook/index.shtml.

Crane, Stephen. *Maggie: A Girl of the Streets (A Story of New York).* Thomas A. Gullason, ed. New York: W. W. Norton & Company, 1893/1979.

Crapsey, Edward. *The Nether Side of New York; Or, The Vice, Crime and Poverty of the Great Metropolis.* New York: Sheldon & Company, 1872.

Cray, Ed. *The Erotic Muse: American Bawdy Songs.* 2nd ed. Urbana: University of Illinois Press, 1999.

Crockett, David. *The Autobiography of David Crockett.* New York: Charles Scribner's Sons, 1923.

Czitrom, Daniel. *New York Exposed: The Gilded Age Police Scandal that Launched the Progressive Era.* New York: Oxford University Press, 2016.

Darwin, Charles. *The Descent of Man, and Selection in Relation to Sex.* New York: D. Appleton & Co., 1871.

D'Emilio, John, and Estelle B. Freedman. *Intimate Matters: A History of Sexuality in America.* New York: Harper & Row, 1988.

Dickens, Charles. *American Notes for General Circulation.* New York: Harper & Bros., 1842.

Ditmore, Melissa Hope, ed. *Encyclopedia of Prostitution and Sex Work.* Westport, CT: Greenwood Press, 2006.

Döpp, Hans-Jürgen. *Music & Eros.* Niels Clegg, trans. New York: Parkstone International, 2012.

Dorr, Reita Childe. "The Prodigal Daughter." *Hampton's Magazine* 24/4 (April 1910): 526–38.

———. *What Eight Million Women Want.* Boston: Small, Maynard & Company, 1910.

Dreiser, Theodore. *Dawn: A History of Myself.* New York: Horace Liveright, 1931.

———. "Whence the Song." *Harper's Weekly* 44/2294 (December 8, 1900): 1165–66a.

Dresser, Paul. *The Songs of Paul Dresser.* New York: Boni & Liveright, 1927.

Duis, Perry R. *The Saloon: Public Drinking in Chicago and Boston 1880–1920.* Urbana: University of Illinois Press, 1983.

Durante, Jimmy, and Jack Kofoed. *Night Clubs.* New York: Alfred A. Knopf, 1931.

Dyer, Oliver. "The Magdalens of New York City: Shall They Have a Chance for Salvation?" *Packard's Monthly* 1/5 (September 1868): 65–69.

———. "The Wickedest Man in New York." *Packard's Monthly* 1/3 (July 1868): 37–39.

———. "The Wickedest Man Summed Up." *Packard's Monthly* 1/4 (August 1868): 49–53.

Earle, Marcelle, with Arthur Homme Jr. *Midnight Frolic: A Ziegfeld Girl's True Story.* Basking Ridge, NJ: Twin Oaks Publishing Co., 1999.

Edwards, Richard Henry. *Popular Amusements.* New York: Associate Press, 1915.

Ellington, George. *The Women of New York; or, The Under-World of the Great City, Illustrating the Life of Women of Fashion, Women of Pleasure, Actresses and Ballet Girls, Saloon Girls, Pickpockets and Shoplifters, Artists' Female Models, Women-of-the-Town, Etc., Etc., Etc.* New York: New York Book Co., 1869.

Erenberg, Lewis A. *Steppin' Out: New York Nightlife and the Transformation of American Culture, 1890–1930.* Westport, CT: Greenwood Press, 1981.

Faulkner, Thomas A. *From the Ball-Room to Hell.* Chicago: The Henry Publishing Co., 1892.

———. *The Lure of the Dance.* Los Angeles: T.A. Faulkner, 1916.

Fields, Jill. "Erotic Modesty: (Ad)dressing Female Sexuality and Propriety in Open and Closed Drawers, USA, 1800–1930." *Gender & History* 14/3 (February 2003): 492–515.

Fink, Bernard, Nadine Hugill, and Benjamin P. Lange. "Women's Body Movements Are a Potential Cue to Ovulation." *Personality and Individual Differences* 53/6 (October 2012): 759–63.

Fishbein, Leslie. "Harlot or Heroine?: Changing Views of Prostitution, 1870–1920." *The Historian* 43/1 (November 1980): 23–35.

Foster, George G. *New York by Gas-Light and Other Urban Sketches.* Stuart M. Blumin, ed. Berkeley: University of California Press, 1856/1990.

———. *New York by Gaslight: With Here and There a Streak of Sunshine.* New York: Dewitt & Davenport, 1850.

———. *New York in Slices: By an Experienced Carver.* Revised, enlarged, and corrected. New York: W.F. Burgess, 1849.

———. *New York Naked.* New York: De Witt & Davenport, 1850.

Fronc, Jennifer. *New York Undercover: Private Surveillance in the Progressive Era.* Chicago: University of Chicago Press, 2009.

Gardner, Charles W. *The Doctor and the Devil, or, Midnight Adventures of Dr. Parkhurst.* New York: Gardner & Co., 1894.

The Gentleman's Companion. N.p.: n.p., 1870.

Gilbert, David. *The Product of Our Souls: Ragtime, Race, and the Birth of the Manhattan Musical Marketplace.* Chapel Hill: University of North Carolina Press, 2015.

Gilfoyle, Timothy J. *City of Eros: New York City, Prostitution, and the Commercialization of Sex, 1790–1920.* New York: W. W. Norton & Company, 1992.

———. *A Pickpocket's Tale: The Underworld of Nineteenth-Century New York.* New York: W. W. Norton & Company, 2006.

Giordano, Ralph G. *Satan in the Dance Hall: Rev. John Roach Straton, Social Dancing, and Morality in 1920s New York City.* Lanham, MD: Scarecrow Press, 2008.

Graham, C. H., and O. F. Lane. *Excise Law of the State of New York . . .* Albany, NY: W.C. Little & Co., 1883.

Greenhorn [George Thompson]. *New-York Life; or, The Mysteries of Upper-Tendom Revealed, by the Author of "Asmodeus," "Lady's Garter," &c.* New York: Charles S. Attwood, ca. 1849.

Gushee, Lawrence. "The Nineteenth-Century Origins of Jazz." *Black Music Research Journal* 14/1 (Spring 1994): 1–24.

———. *Pioneers of Jazz: The Story of the Creole Band.* New York: Oxford University Press, 2005.

Haas, Paul H. "Sin in Wisconsin: The Teasdale Vice Committee of 1913." *Wisconsin Magazine of History* 49/2 (Winter 1965–1966): 138–51.

Ham, Mordecai Fowler. *The Modern Dance: A Historical and Analytical Treatment of the Subject; Religious, Social, Hygienic, Industrial Aspects as Viewed by the Pulpit, the Press, Medical Authorities, Municipal Authorities, Social Workers, Etc.* San Antonio, TX: San Antonio Printing Co., 1916.

Hamm, Charles. *Irving Berlin, Songs from the Melting Pot: The Formative Years, 1907–1914.* New York: Oxford University Press, 1997.

Hapgood, Hutchins. *Types from City Streets.* New York: Funk & Wagnalls, 1910.

Harney, Ben. *Ben Harney's Rag Time Instructor.* Chicago: Sol Bloom, 1897.

Heap, Chad. *Slumming: Sexual and Racial Encounters in American Nightlife, 1885–1940.* Chicago: University of Chicago Press, 2009.

Henderson, Clayton W. *On the Banks of the Wabash: The Life and Music of Paul Dresser.* Indianapolis: Indiana Historical Society Press, 2003.

Hill, Marilynn Wood. *Their Sisters' Keepers: Prostitution in New York City, 1830–1870.* Berkeley: University of California Press, 1993.

Horowitz, Helen Lefkowitz. *Rereading Sex: Battles over Sexual Knowledge and Suppression in Nineteenth-Century America.* New York: Alfred A. Knopf, 2002.

Howe, William F. *Danger!: A True History of a Great City's Wiles and Temptations; The Veil Lifted, and Light Thrown on Crime and Its Causes, and Criminals and Their Haunts: Facts and Disclosure.* Buffalo: Courier Co., 1886.

Ingersoll, Ernst. *A Week in New York.* New York: Rand, McNally, and Co., 1891.

Inglis, William. "Is Modern Dancing Indecent?" *Harper's Weekly* 57 (May 17, 1913): 11–12.

Irving, Washington. *Tales of the Alhambra.* London: Richard Bentley, 1835.

Israels, Belle Lindner. "Regulation of Public Amusements." *Proceedings of the Academy of Political Science* 2/4 (1912): 123–26.

———. "The Way of the Girl." *The Survey* 22 (July 3, 1909): 486–97.

——— [Mrs. Charles Henry Israels]. "The Dance Problem." *The Playground* 4/7 (October 1910): 241–50.

——— [Mrs. Charles Henry Israels]. "Percentage of Working Girls Going to Dance Halls." *The Playground* 4/2 (May 1910): 35.

Jennings, John J. *Theatrical and Circus Life; Secrets of the Stage, Green-Room and Sawdust Arena.* St. Louis: Sun Publishing Co., 1882.

Johnson, Claudia D. "That Guilty Third Tier: Prostitution in Nineteenth-Century American Theaters." *American Quarterly* 27/5 (1975): 575–84.

Keire, Mara L. "The Committee of Fourteen and Saloon Reform in New York City, 1905–1920." *Business and Economic History* 26/2 (Winter 1997): 573–83.

———. *For Business & Pleasure: Red-Light Districts and the Regulation of Vice in the United States, 1890–1933.* Baltimore: Johns Hopkins University Press, 2010.

Kenney, William Howland. *Jazz on the River.* Chicago: University of Chicago Press, 2005.

Kernan, J. Frank. *Reminiscences of the Old Fire Laddies and Volunteer Fire Departments of New York and Brooklyn . . .* New York: M. Crane, 1885.

Kibler, M. Alison. *Rank Ladies: Gender and Cultural Hierarchy in American Vaudeville.* Chapel Hill: University of North Carolina Press, 1999.

King, Moses. *King's Handbook of New York City: An Outline History and Description of the American Metropolis . . .* Boston: Moses King, 1892.

Kneeland, George J., *Commercialized Prostitution in New York City.* Revised ed. New York: Century Co., 1917.

———. *The Social Evil in New York City: A Study of Law Enforcement by the Research Committee of the Committee of Fourteen.* New York: A.H. Kellogg Co., 1910.

Krist, Gary. *Empire of Sin: A Story of Sex, Jazz, Murder, and the Battle for Modern New Orleans.* New York: Crown, 2014.

Langum, David J. *Crossing over the Line: Legislating Morality and the Mann Act.* Chicago: University of Chicago Press, 1994.

Lawrence, Vera Brodsky. *Strong on Music: The New York Music Scene in the Days of George Templeton Strong.* Vol. 2: *Reverberations, 1850–1856.* Chicago: University of Chicago Press, 1995.

[Lening, Gustav]. *The Dark Side of New York Life and Its Criminal Classes from Fifth Avenue Down to the Five Points: A Complete Narrative of the Mysteries of New York.* New York: Fred'k Gerhard, 1873.

Le Sage, Alain René. *Asmodeus; or, The Devil on Two Sticks.* London: Joseph Thomas, 1841.

Levitin, Daniel J. *This Is Your Brain on Music: The Science of a Human Obsession.* New York: Plume, 2006.

Lewis, Alfred Henry. *The Apaches of New York.* Chicago: M.A. Donohue & Co., 1912.

Lhamon, W. T., Jr. *Jim Crow, American: Selected Songs and Plays (The John Harvard Library).* Cambridge: Belknap Press, 2009.

———. *Jump Jim Crow: Lost Plays, Lyrics, and Street Prose of the First Atlantic Popular Culture.* Cambridge: Harvard University Press, 2003.

The Life and Death of Fanny White, Being a Complete and Interesting History of the Career of that Notorious Lady. New York: n.p., 1860.

Lippard, George. *The Empire City; or, New York by Night and Day; Its Aristocracy and Its Dollars.* Philadelphia: T.B. Peterson & Brothers, 1864.

———. *New York: Its Upper Ten and Lower Million.* Cincinnati: E. Mendenhall, 1854.

Lippmann, Walter. *A Preface to Politics.* New York: Mitchell Kennerley, 1913.

[Longchamp, Ferdinand]. *Asmodeus in New-York.* New York: Longchamp & Co., 1868.

Lovatt, Peter. "Dance and Sexuality." *Psychology Today*: online blog posted March 12, 2010.

MacKeever, Samuel Anderson. *Glimpses of Gotham and City Characters.* New York: Richard K. Fox, 1880.

Mackey, Thomas C. *Pursuing Johns: Criminal Law Reform, Defending Character, and New York City's Committee of Fourteen, 1920–1930.* Columbus: Ohio University Press, 2005.

———. *Red Lights Out: A Legal History of Prostitution, Disorderly Houses, and Vice Districts, 1870–1917.* New York: Garland, 1987.

Magdalen Report: First Annual Report of the Executive Committee of the N.Y. Magdalen Society, Instituted January 1, 1830. New York: Printed and Sold for the Publisher, 1831.

Marchant, James. *The Master Problem.* New York: Moffat, Yard, and Company, 1917.

[Marguerittes, Julie de]. *The Match-Girl: or, Life Scenes as They Are.* Philadelphia: W.W. Smith, 1855.

Marks, Edward B., as told to Abbott J. Liebling. *They All Sang: From Tony Pastor to Rudy Vallée.* New York: Viking Press, 1934.

Mayer, Joseph. "The Passing of the Red Light District—Vice Investigations and Results." *Journal of Social Hygiene* 4 (April 1918): 197–209.

———. *The Regulation of Commercialized Vice: An Analysis of the Transition from Segregation to Repression in the United States.* New York: Klebold Press, 1922.

McBee, Randy D. *Dance Hall Days: Intimacy and Leisure among Working-Class Immigrants in the United States.* New York: New York University Press, 2000.

McCabe, James D. *Lights and Shadows of New York Life; or, The Sights and Sensations of the Great City: A Work Descriptive of the City of New York in All Its Various Phases . . .* Philadelphia: National Publishing Co., 1872.

———. *New York by Sunlight and Gaslight: Its High and Low Life; Its Splendors and Miseries; Its Virtues and Vices; Its Gorgeous Palaces and Dark Homes of Poverty and Crime; Its Public Men, Politicians, Adventures; Its Charities, Frauds, Mysteries, Etc. Etc.* Philadelphia: Douglass Brothers, 1882.

———. *The Secrets of the Great City: A Work Descriptive of the Virtues and the Vices, the Mysteries, Miseries and Crimes of New York City.* Philadelphia: Jones Bros., 1868. Also published as Edward Winslow [pseud]. *A Work Descriptive of the Virtues and the Vices, the Mysteries, Miseries and Crimes of New York City.* Philadelphia: n.p., 1868.

McDowall, John R. *Magdalen Facts.* New York: Printed for the Author, 1832.

McNamara, Brooks. *The New York Concert Saloon: The Devil's Own Nights.* Cambridge: Cambridge University Press, 2002.

Meinties, Louise. *Dust of the Zulu: Ngoma Aesthetics after Apartheid.* Durham: Duke University Press, 2017.

Members of the New York Press. *The Night Side of New York: A Picture of the Great Metropolis After Nightfall.* New York: J.C. Haney, 1866.

Miller, Geoffrey. "Evolution of Human Music through Sexual Selection." In Nils L. Wallin, Björn Merker, and Steven Brown, eds, *The Origins of Music.* Cambridge: MIT Press, 2000.

Millett, Kate. *The Prostitution Papers.* New York: Ballantine, 1976.

Miner, Maude. *The Slavery of Prostitution.* New York: Macmillan, 1916.

Mitchell, Stephen. *Gilgamesh: A New English Version.* New York: Free Press, 2004.

Mithen, Steven. *The Singing Neanderthals: The Origins of Music, Language, Mind, and Body.* Cambridge: Harvard University Press, 2006.

Moss, Frank. *The American Metropolis: From Knickerbocker Days to the Present Time; New York City Life in All Its Various Phases: An Historiograph of New York.* New York: P.F. Collier, 1897.

Mumford, Kevin J. *Interzones: Black/White Sex Districts in Chicago and New York in the Early Twentieth Century.* New York: Columbia University Press, 1997.

Music in Gotham. Online database: accessed at https://www.musicingotham.org/.

Nasaw, David. *Going Out: The Rise and Fall of Public Amusement.* New York: Harvard University Press, 1993.

"New Reflections on the Dancing Mania." *Current Opinion* 55/4 (October 1913): 262–64.

Ogren, Kathy J. *The Jazz Revolution: Twenties America & the Meaning of Jazz.* New York: Oxford University Press, 1989.

Paducah, Kentucky. *Report and Recommendations of the Paducah Vice Commission.* Paducah, KY: n.p., 1916.

Parkhurst, Rev. Charles H. *My Forty Years in New York.* New York: Macmillan Company, 1923.

Peiss, Kathy. "'Charity Girls' and City Pleasures: Historical Notes on Working-Class Sexuality, 1880–1920." In Ann Snitow, Christine Stansell, and Sharon Thompson, eds. *Powers of Desire: The Politics of Sexuality.* New York: Monthly Review Press, 1983.

———. *Cheap Amusements: Working Women and Leisure in Turn-of-the-Century New York.* Philadelphia: Temple University Press, 1986.

"The People &c. Against Wallace W. Sweeney." Court of Special Sessions, City of New York, First Division, Supreme Court of New York, Appellate Division, First Department, Minutes of Proceedings, January 29, 1912.

Pepper, Tom [Charles Frederick Briggs]. *Asmodeus; or, The Iniquities of New York being a Complete Exposé of the Crimes, Doings and Vices as Exhibited in the Haunts of Gamblers and Houses of Prostitution, both in High and Low Life! Including a Sketch of the Model Artiste, and the Celebrated Report of Arthur Tappan, Esq. on the Magdalens of New York.* New York: C.G. Graham & Co., 1849.

Perry, Elisabeth I. "'The General Motherhood of the Commonwealth': Dance Hall Reform in the Progressive Era." *American Quarterly* 37/5 (Winter 1985): 719–33.

Peters, John P. *The Story of the Committee of Fourteen of New York.* New York: American Social Hygiene Association, 1918.

Pinker, Steven. *How the Mind Works.* New York: W. W. Norton & Company, 1997.

Prime, Samuel Irenaeus. *Life in New York.* New York: Robert Carter, 1847.

Report and Proceedings of the Senate Committee Appointed to Investigate the Police Department of the City of New York. Albany: James B. Lyon, 1895.

Report of the Special Committee of the Assembly Appointed to Investigate the Public Offices and Departments of the City of New York and of the Counties Therein Included. Albany: J.B. Lyon, 1900.

Reynolds, David S. *Beneath the American Renaissance: The Subversive Imagination in the Age of Emerson and Melville.* New York: Alfred A. Knopf, 1988.

Riis, Jacob A. *How the Other Half Lives: Studies Among the Tenements of New York*. New York: Charles Scribner's, 1890.

Robinson, Danielle. *Modern Moves: Dancing Race During the Ragtime and Jazz Eras*. New York: Oxford University Press, 2015.

Robinson, Solon. *Hot Corn: Life Scenes in New York Illustrated; Including the Story of Little Katy, Madalina, the Rag-Picker's Daughter, Wild Maggie, &c, with Original Designs*. New York: De Witt and Davenport, 1854.

Röder, Susanne, Bettina Weege, Claus-Christian Carbon, Todd K. Shackelford, and Bernhard Fink. "Men's Perception of Women's Dance Movements Depends on Mating Context, but Not Men's Sociosexual Orientation." *Personality and Individual Differences* 86 (2015): 172–75.

Rodger, Gillian M. *Champagne Charlie and Pretty Jemima: Variety Theater in the Nineteenth Century*. Urbana: University of Illinois Press, 2010.

———. "Legislating Amusements: Class Politics and Theater Law in New York City." *American Music* 20/4 (Winter 2002): 381–98.

Roe, Clifford G. *The Great War on White Slavery, or Fighting for the Protection of Our Girls*. Philadelphia: International Bible House, 1911.

The Rogues and Rogueries of New-York: A Full and Complete Exposure of all the Swindles and Rascalities Carried On or Originated in the Metropolis. New York: J.C. Haney & Co., 1865.

Rose, Al. *Storyville, New Orleans: Being an Authentic, Illustrated Account of the Notorious Red-Light District*. Tuscaloosa: University of Alabama Press, 1974.

Rosen, Ruth. *The Lost Sisterhood: Prostitution in America, 1900–1918*. Baltimore: Johns Hopkins University Press, 1982.

Rosenberg, Charles, and Carroll Smith-Rosenberg, eds. *The Prostitute and the Social Reformer*. New York: Arno, 1974.

Rugoff, Milton. *Prudery and Passion*. New York: G.P. Putnam's Sons, 1971.

Sanger, William W. *The History of Prostitution: Its Extent, Causes and Effects Throughout the World (Being an Official Report to the Board of Alms-House Governors of the City of New York)*. New York: Harper & Brothers, 1858.

Sante, Luc. *Low Life: Lures and Snares of Old New York*. New York: Farrar, Straus & Giroux, 1991.

Schuller, Gunther. *Early Jazz: Its Roots and Musical Development*. New York: Oxford University Press, 1968.

Segel, Harold B. *Turn-of-the-Century Cabaret*. New York: Columbia University Press, 1987.

"Sex o'Clock in America." *Current Opinion* 55/2 (August 1913): 113–14.

Slout, William L., ed. *Broadway Below the Sidewalk: Concert Saloons of Old New York*. San Bernardino, CA: Borgo Press, 1994.

Smith, Christopher J. *The Creolization of American Culture: William Sidney Mount and the Roots of Blackface Minstrelsy.* Urbana: University of Illinois Press, 2013.

Smith, Matthew Hale. *Sunshine and Shadow in New York.* Hartford, CT: J.B. Burr and Company, 1869.

Smith, Willie the Lion, with George Hoefer. *Music on My Mind: The Memoirs of an American Pianist.* New York: Da Capo, 1964/R1978.

Snyder, Robert W. *The Voice of the City: Vaudeville and Popular Culture in New York.* New York: Oxford University Press, 1989.

The Social Evil: With Special Reference to Conditions Existing in the City of New York; A Report Prepared under the Direction of the Committee of Fifteen. New York: G.P. Putnam's Sons, 1902.

The Social Evil in Chicago: A Study of Existing Conditions with Recommendations by the Vice Commission of Chicago. Chicago: Gunthorp-Warren Printing Company, 1911.

Society for the Reformation of Juvenile Delinquents, Annual Reports. Accessed online at various locations.

Stead, William Thomas. *Satan's Invisible World Displayed; or, Despairing Democracy.* Toronto: Theo W. Gregory, 1897.

Stearns, Marshall, and Jean Stearns. *Jazz Dance: The Story of American Vernacular Dance.* New York: Macmillan Company, 1968.

Street, Julian. "'Oh, You Babylon!': A Taxi-cabaretta." *Everybody's Magazine* 27/2 (August 1912): 171–83.

———. *Welcome to Our City.* New York: John Lane Company, 1913.

Swayze, George B. H. "The Social Evil." *The Medical Times: A Monthly Journal of Medicine, Surgery, and the Collateral Sciences* 34/7 (July 1906): 193–98.

Symanski, Richard. *The Immoral Landscape: Female Prostitution in Western Societies.* Toronto: Butterworths, 1981.

Taylor, George Rogers. "Gaslight Foster: A New York 'Journeyman Journalist' at Mid-Century." *New York History* 58/3 (July 1977): 297–312.

Thompson, George. *City Crimes, or, Life in New York and Boston: A Volume for Everybody; Being a Mirror of Fashion, a Picture of Poverty, and a Startling Revelation of the Secret Crimes of Great Cities.* Boston: W. Berry, 1849.

———. *The Gay Girls of New-York, or, Life on Broadway: Being a Mirror of the Fashion, Follies and Crimes of a Great City.* New York: n.p., 1853.

Tick, Judith, ed. *Music in the USA: A Documentary Companion.* New York: Oxford University Press, 2008.

The Traffic in Girls: White Slavery as Now Practiced in America, Including Detailed

Descriptions of the Customs and Manners of the White Women Slaves and Wives of Asia, Turkey, Egypt, Etc. Chicago: n.p., ca. 1900.

Trumble, Alfred. *The Man-Traps of New York: What They Are and How They Are Worked.* New York: Richard K. Fox, 1881.

———. *The Mysteries of New York; A Sequel to Glimpses of Gotham and New York by Day and Night.* New York: Richard K. Fox, 1882.

United States. Census Bureau. *Census Reports* [various years].

Van der Meulen, Emily. "Moral Panic and the New York Magdalen Society: Nineteenth Century Prostitution and the Moral Reform Movement." *MP: An Online Feminist Journal* (July 2008).

Van Every, Edward. *Sins of New York: As "Exposed" by the Police Gazette.* New York: Benjamin Blom, 1972.

Van Oncelen, Charles. *The Fox and the Flies: The Secret Life of a Grotesque Master Criminal.* New York: Walker and Company, 2007.

Vices of a Big City; An Exposé of Existing Menaces to Church and Home in New York City. New York: J.E. Clark, 1890.

Vogel, Shane. *The Scene of Harlem Cabaret: Race, Sexuality, Performance.* Chicago: University of Chicago Press, 2009.

Wagner, Ann. *Adversaries of Dance: From the Puritans to the Present.* Urbana: University of Illinois Press, 1997.

Walkowitz, Judith R. *Prostitution and Victorian Society: Women, Class, and the State.* Cambridge: Cambridge University Press, 1980.

Wallace, Mike. *Greater Gotham: A History of New York City from 1898 to 1919.* New York: Oxford University Press, 2017.

Wallin, Nils L., Björn Merker, and Steven Brown, eds. *The Origins of Music.* Cambridge: MIT Press, 2000.

Walling, George W. *Recollections of a New York Chief of Police: An Official Record of Thirty-Eight Years as Patrolman, Detective, Captain, Inspector and Chief of the New York Police.* New York: Caxton Book Concern, 1887.

Waterman, Willoughby Cyrus. *Prostitution and Its Repression in New York City, 1900–1931.* New York: Columbia University Press, 1932.

Webster, Noah. *An American Dictionary of the English Language;* . . . Springfield, MA: George and Charles Merriam, 1855.

Werther, Ralph [Earl Lind]. *Autobiography of an Androgyne.* New York: Medico-Legal Journal, 1918.

———. *The Female-Impersonators; a Sequel to the Autobiography of An Androgyne and An Account of Some of the Author's Experiences during His Six Years' Career as Instinctive Female-Impersonator in New York's Underworld* . . . New York: Medico-Legal Journal, 1922.

Whiteaker, Larry. *Seduction, Prostitution, and Moral Reform in New York, 1830–1860*. New York: Garland Publishing, 1997.

Whitman, Walt. *The Uncollected Poetry and Prose of Walt Whitman*. Emory Holloway, ed. Garden City, NY: Doubleday, Page & Co., 1921.

"The 'Wickedest Man' As He Is." *Harper's Weekly* 12/606 (August 8, 1868): 505–6.

Wilkes, George. *The Lives of Helen Jewett and Richard P. Robinson*. New York: n.p., ca. 1849.

Willemse, Cornelius W., George J. Lemmer, and Jack Kofoed. *Behind the Green Lights*. New York: Alfred A. Knopf, 1931.

Winick, Charles, and Paul M. Kinsie. *The Lively Commerce: Prostitution in the United States*. Chicago: Quadrangle Books, 1971.

Woolston, Howard B. *Prostitution in the United States*. Vol. 1: *Prior to the Entrance of the United States into the World War*. New York: Century Co., 1921.

Zacks, Richard. *Island of Vice: Theodore Roosevelt's Doomed Quest to Clean Up Sin-Loving New York*. New York: Doubleday, 2012.

INDEX

Page numbers in *italics* refer to illustrations.